'In my line of business, if you aren't working with Jonathan Coad, you aren't doing it right.'

Max Dundas, Founder, Dundas Communications

'A confident Coadification of the many perils and pitfalls of trying to bring the modern media to heel, this book should be on the shelves of all those who work in the reputation business. It contains a well-reasoned invective thread regarding what drives the conduct of print, online and broadcast media. Coad's advice and experience lies at the intersection of the law and PR.'

Jon McLeod, Partner at DRD Partnership, previously Partner at Brunswick and Chairman at Weber Shandwick

'Jonathan Coad is a giant amongst lawyers with a vast array of experience working for the great and the good from all walks of life as well as many powerful media institutions. This book is a fascinating insight and clear description of how the media and the law works in regard to reputation. It is a must-read for anyone who wants to protect their brand in today's information age.'

Paul McKenna, hypnotist and author

'It's revealing when in his introduction, when discussing the British media, Coad states that *"there is virtually no democratic restraint over these companies and individuals who are therefore substantially free to mislead us for reasons either of financial expediency and/or in pursuit of an agenda. The only limits to this power come from a modest array of regulations and laws by which the media is supposed to abide, but in the case of the press, frequently ignores."*

'But make no mistake, this is *not* the perspective of an unhinged conspiracy theorist, this is the view of one of the UK's top media lawyers. A man who for the last 25 years has been *in the room* in those crucial hours before numerous high-profile media stories have been published.

'*Reputation Matters* is a fascinating, sometimes worrying but always informative read into a pretty grubby and little known world at the centre of the British establishment.'

Ben Smith, founder, PRmoment

'With integrity, huge skill and high-level knowledge Jonathan Coad guides you successfully through the ethical, legal and personal dilemmas of interacting with the media. A powerful and important book.'

Robin Dyer, Head of Ampleforth College

'Jonathan's vast experience and expertise shines through on every page, as does his warm story-telling prowess. A must-read for anyone responsible for the reputation of others.'

Mark Southern, Director, Polygon PR

'This is a must-read book for anyone working in legal PR and corporate communications or media management. The cases are well selected, hugely insightful, and very relevant to our modern-day global and digital era.'

Yuliya Matvyeyeva, PR and Communication Professional, Ukraine

'Buckets of sage advice from one of the very best media lawyers. Read it and save yourself millions in lawyers' fees and settlements.'

Nick Bastin, *Senior Consultant*

'Compelling and impressive. Coad's book is a must for anyone potentially affected by unwanted press attention. This means it should be read by everyone, so they are ready to respond effectively. For, as *Reputation Matters* confirms, it is a myth that the press is interested only in exposing the crooked and corrupt.'

Professor Paul Wragg, *Professor of Media Law, University of Leeds and Director, Hacked Off*

'With the rapidly evolving information landscape, companies have never been more in the spotlight. As a crisis management expert, Jonathan Coad provides in *Reputation Matters* a highly accessible tool for business leaders, communications professionals and individuals to understand the most effective strategies to mitigate reputational damage.'

Angela Gray, *Senior Associate Partner, Consilium Strategic Communications*

'This book is a must read for anyone or any "thing" – e.g. a business or brand – in the public eye. And those advising them. Whether you're a celebrity, politician, academic or Coca Cola, understanding the art and science of reputation management within the current legal framework is essential. Jonathan's intelligent, practical and sage advice shines through in this brilliant book. He's your man; in the boardroom and, if needs must, the court room.'

Angie Moxham, *PR practitioner and founder of 3 Monkeys Communications and The Fourth Angel*

'*Reputation Matters* is a detailed, yet thoroughly engaging guide to navigating media hostility, informed by both technical expertise and professional experience. In the harrowing, true stories of press misconduct it describes, it is also a powerful expose of the practices which persist in parts of Fleet Street. It promises to be an essential resource both for individuals personally affected by press abuse, and for those of us campaigning for improvement to press behaviour.'

Nathan Sparkes, *Chief Executive of the Hacked Off Campaign*

Reputation Matters

How to Protect Your Professional Reputation

Jonathan Coad

BLOOMSBURY BUSINESS
LONDON · OXFORD · NEW YORK · NEW DELHI · SYDNEY

BLOOMSBURY BUSINESS
Bloomsbury Publishing Plc
50 Bedford Square, London, WC1B 3DP, UK
29 Earlsfort Terrace, Dublin 2, Ireland

BLOOMSBURY, BLOOMSBURY BUSINESS and the Diana logo are
trademarks of Bloomsbury Publishing Plc

First published in Great Britain 2022

A catalogue record for this book is available from the British Library

Library of Congress Cataloguing-in-Publication data has been applied for

ISBN: HB: 978-1-4729-9443-1; eBook: 978-1-4729-9442-4

2 4 6 8 10 9 7 5 3 1

Typeset by Deanta Global Publishing Services, Chennai, India
Printed and bound in Great Britain by CPI Group (UK) Ltd, Croydon CR0 4YY

To find out more about our authors and books visit www.bloomsbury.com and
sign up for our newsletters

Warren Buffett, who knows a bit about making a profit, says this: '*It takes 20 years to build a reputation and five minutes to ruin it. If you think about that, you'll do things differently.*' He also said, '*Lose money and I will forgive you. But lose even a shred of reputation and I will be ruthless.*' Corporate reputation really matters because the World Economic Forum has declared it to be the most important measure of success and it represents more than 40 per cent of a company's market value. I could not find a suitable dictionary definition of reputation for the purpose of this book, so here is mine: '*quality or character as perceived by others*'. The purpose of this book is to empower you to protect your reputation.

This book is gratefully dedicated to all the clients who have entrusted their reputation and privacy to me; and to Charlotte, Emily and Benjy, whom I love dearly.

Acknowledgements

I am immensely grateful to Bloomsbury for affording me the opportunity to write this book. Thank you to Matt James for commissioning the book; and to him, Allie Collins and Jane Donovan for their expert advice which improved it immensely. Thank you to all my colleagues over the years who have so helped me in my work; especially to the wonderful Shelley Vincent and Stephanie Brunton. Thank you also to the brilliant Hannah Ready of 11 Kings Bench Walk for checking and correcting my law.

Contents

1

Introduction

Apart from the microscopic scope of our first-hand knowledge, we are almost entirely reliant on the media for our insight into the events that impact both our lives and society as a whole. Very few of us know how the media operates, or the characters and values of that small coterie of individuals who decide what we are told and what we are *not* told about what goes on in the world around us.

That is despite the fact that the power that these individuals and companies wield as arbiters of what information we are permitted to glean, and the extent to which that information is true, is immense. There is virtually no democratic restraint over these companies and individuals who are therefore substantially free to mislead us for reasons either of financial expediency and/or in pursuit of an agenda. The only limits to this power come from a modest array of regulations and laws by which the media is supposed to abide, but in the case of the press, frequently ignores.

In the UK most of the major media outlets are governed by some form of code of practice; the broadcast media being regulated with a degree of efficacy by Ofcom (Office of Communications), and most of the big beasts of the print media being tamely and inadequately 'regulated' by the Independent Press Standards Organisation (IPSO). Some major corporate news providers, including three of the Fleet Street titles and business news providers such as Bloomberg, have elected to be subject to no form of even token regulation.

The slight restrictions on the media imposed by the democratic state come primarily from the laws of defamation, privacy and copyright, which apply to all media content. However, these restrictions only impact if invoked – either prior to the article/ programme at issue, or subsequently – by an individual or company who is either threatened by or has been subjected to some form of media abuse.

In practice this is done all too rarely, and since both reputation and privacy matter to all of us – reputation in particular so we can distinguish between the good and the bad – all society suffers the consequences. The PR industry has failed both its clients and society by not, as a matter of course, deploying the means whereby fake or misleading news about their clients can be curtailed. That needs to change.

Even when the media at least starts out by doing its job properly and is faithfully reporting events that genuinely engage public interest, its pervasive proclivity – particularly the press – is both to awfulize and ascribe blame indiscriminately. This ill-serves us all.

This book proceeds on the basis that the first priority of crisis PR is to prevent, or at least minimize the emission of damaging material by the media which threatens reputation when – as is usually the case – it contains at least some errant elements. The second priority is to minimize the adverse impact that the media can have by astute use of all the available regulatory means; and by communicating to customers, stakeholders and the public as a whole.

The book provides the key knowledge and tools that allow you to restrain the media from damaging commercial reputation for profit by deploying the full array of regulatory and legal tools available. It starts out as a guide to the media and how it works, and goes on to explain what methodologies are available to delimit its destructive power.

I concentrate in this book on the risks posed by the commercial media because in addition to what I have learned in my own practice, all that I have read since its inception convinces me that on matters of importance to commercial enterprise the social media does not wield the influence sometimes attributed to it. It is normally only when its content is uploaded to the commercial media that real damage is done. Only a tiny proportion of the instructions that come to me concern the social media, which I nonetheless address during the course of this book.

This book is based on a crisis management seminar which I have delivered for over 25 years to audiences ranging from supermarket chains, PR agencies, charities, multinationals, elite sports teams, business continuity conferences and the cast of Eastenders. You can read crisis PR updates by following me on LinkedIn.

THE 'DARK SIDE' OF THE MEDIA

Most people associate the dark side of the British media – primarily the press, though in its attempt to compete the broadcast media is catching up – with blatant criminality such as the phone hacking.

A PR professional must however factor into their work that the abuse by the media of its privileges – the prime culprits being the denizens of Fleet Street – is endemic. It goes on daily and frequently concerns issues of immense importance. It therefore impacts us all and can have seismic consequences; one being our departure from the European Union (EU).

In March 2016 in the run-up to the Brexit referendum, the *Sun* newspaper daubed 'QUEEN BACKS BREXIT' in huge capital letters all over its front page; a headline which was seen by tens of millions of people on news apps, newsstands, held up to TV cameras and heard when read out by radio stations.

The proprietor of the paper, Rupert Murdoch (a Europhobe republican), is reported to have complained that whereas he is influential in Downing Street, he is ignored in Europe. Since against nearly every expectation the wafer-thin majority was 52 per cent to leave against 48 per cent to stay, the *Sun's* headline would only have to have swayed a small proportion of the 33 per cent of the then undecided voters for the paper's disgraceful abuse of its Article 10 (free speech) right to have had the desired effect. If you add to this the refusal by the bogus press regulator that is

IPSO, which Fleet Street unilaterally foisted on us, to order a front-page correction – which meant that 99 per cent of those who saw the headline would not see the retraction, then this illegitimate flexing of editorial muscle may have had immense and long-term ramifications for the UK.

There is much that is commendable in the media, which I have been privileged to serve throughout my career as an editorial lawyer. At its best, it plays a vital role in our democracy and informs us faithfully about issues of which we need to be aware. At its worst, it wields its immense power to inflict terrible damage both on society and on individuals within it.

The broadcast media is regulated by Ofcom with a degree of efficacy and generally serves us well. However, the grim revelations about the web of deceit spun by British BBC journalist Martin Bashir to secure his now infamous interview with Princess Diana, and the BBC's failure properly to investigate him, shows that even that august and precious institution has feet of clay. The hypocrisy of Fleet Street in tearing into the BBC because of its governance failures when it invests vast sums of money covering up its own wrongdoing is, however, breath-taking.

The press's lack of effective regulation and consequent lack of accountability means not only is it free to administer poison into the psychological and spiritual bloodstream of society by its predilection for damning awfulization, it can have a devastating direct impact on individuals and enterprises alike; as I have seen repeatedly in my practice.

How I became a media lawyer

I was born in Cambridge where my parents lived just a few hundred yards from Jesus College in the University of Cambridge. Neither had a university education. Mum was a dispatch-rider during World War II and dad chased black marketeers around occupied Berlin in the RAF Police. Mum later told me he looked down into my cradle and decreed that I would read law at that beautiful ancient college and, 18 years later, that's what I did.

After securing my degree, I turned from the straight and narrow to become a professional musician, at which I was so successful that I went on to train as a solicitor at a city firm.

I AM TRAINED BY TOP MEDIA LAWYERS

I chose one with a media practice in an attempt to make some sense of my scrambled CV. My first of three 'seats' (training placements with a senior lawyer) was with a TV business affairs specialist and the third one was with Susan Aslan, a leading media lawyer who also specialized in TV work. While working for Susan I was exposed to the wonderful world of defamation, which I decided would be the future direction of my career.

On qualification two years later, I managed to blag my way into Schillings (one of the two market-leading firms of reputation and privacy lawyers, the other being Carter-Ruck), where I was hired as Keith Schilling's assistant, despite his wanting someone two or three years qualified. Apparently I got the job because when he took me on during the interview I stood my ground. Although it was the professional equivalent of white-water rafting, my learning curve was vertical.

When I walked into Schillings' offices on my first day I found two files on my desk. To my immense good fortune, which shaped the whole of my career, one was for a claimant and the other was for a defendant. Both were – in their different ways – wonderful pieces of work.

The claimant file

This started out as a defamation action against a glamour magazine for a young woman who was called a Page 3 Girl because she appeared topless on page three of the *Sun*. The claim was based on the commentary to nude photographs of her and another female model published in the magazine, which suggested they were having an affair. The difficulty was that even back in 1991 an allegation of homosexuality was probably not defamatory – especially of a glamour model.

The claim subsequently became a breach of confidence action when my enterprising boss Keith Schilling noticed that the model release form signed by the client for the photo shoot was executed before she was 18.

Think of the excellent court scene in the fantasy comedy film *Liar Liar* where Jim Carrey wins the day at a trial when he realizes that his errant client was too young to sign a pre-nuptial agreement and so would secure a vast sum in her divorce. Our client could not as a matter of law consent to the publication of the photographs, which therefore comprised a breach of confidence in those areas of her body not previously in the public domain. Yes, I really am serious!

A few days later I had the surreal experience of sitting with a barrister – for obvious reasons I selected female counsel – where we went through a number of other glamour magazines to ascertain how much more of our client's frame was visible in the magazine that we were suing as compared to other publications that she had graced. I was working with the brilliant Adrienne Page, who was then a junior barrister at the leading media set, 5 Raymond Buildings, and is now a distinguished QC.

The defendant file

The other file was a key factor in enabling me both to do my job as a PR lawyer well and to write this book. Despite Schillings being a claimant firm, it had been asked for a second opinion by a broadcaster which was being sued by a local councillor whom it had accused of corruptly manipulating the planning process to make large sums of money. Its panel firm had advised that the claimant be offered substantial damages.

The feisty in-house lawyer at the broadcaster was not happy with this advice and asked Schillings to review the file. To my immense good fortune it arrived the week before I started work there and so I had first look. I was also fortunate that whereas I had spent two-thirds of my time as a trainee doing media work, the other third had been spent in the planning department, so I was able to understand the planning documents in the file. I was also blessed that all my defamation experience as a trainee was defendant work for broadcasters.

The allegation against this local councillor was that he was buying up local land on the cheap where there was not the slightest prospect of securing planning permission; using his masonic contacts to secure planning permission, and then selling the land at an immense profit. He had sued for libel using a large city firm which was pursuing the claim aggressively.

After reading the file I had no doubt that this individual was justly accused. I dictated a note of advice to that effect to Keith Schilling, which then formed the basis of the advice to the broadcaster, and we were duly instructed in place of their panel solicitors. Despite my lack of experience, Keith had sufficient confidence in me to let me run the file. I loved it.

Within a couple of weeks we had to tackle an application to strike out the not-very-convincing defence which had been served by our predecessors, a leading firm of defendant solicitors and a less-than-expert QC whom I had sacked.

The hearing turned out to be a farce. The judge walked into the courtroom and made two announcements. The first was that he knew nothing about the law of defamation and the second was that he had not read the papers. As to the former, that now does not happen as we have a Media and Telecommunications List with specialist judges. As to the latter, they are all of high quality.

What both legal teams should have done was to have stepped outside the courtroom, flipped a coin to decide the outcome of the application, and then gone out and spent the morning drinking coffee and eating cake. As it was, most of the hearing was taken up by both barristers trying to teach the judge, who looked like he had enjoyed an evening of excess prior to the day of the hearing, the basics of the law of defamation; and in particular those principles relevant to the application.

It was evident that this was not working, which became abundantly clear when in his judgment the judge wrongly identified the issue before him, misapplied the principles he had been taught during the course of the hearing and decided a point which was never before him to determine – and managed even to do that wrongly. The effect, however, was that the defence was struck out and so we were back to square one.

As it turned out, this was the best thing that could have happened. At the time there was a long queue for the Court of Appeal, where, given the hopelessly inept judgment, we were seeking a remedy. This meant that we had at least a year to go back to the drawing board and construct a new defence.

I took on the job of thoroughly investigating the facts. One summer's day I drove out in my scruffy but much-loved convertible to the constituency where the claimant was a councillor and surveyed the various pieces of land that were the subject of the planning applications at issue. This came to an abrupt end when I was chased off by a guard dog!

My favourite moment was when I arranged a meeting with the Leader of the Council and his lawyer, where I confronted him with these two options. Either he provided me with the documentation which he was withholding and that I needed to prove that this councillor was corrupt, or I would take the whole local masonic lodge down, and him with it, since I had no doubt that he too was part of the local masonic fraternity.

It was a complete bluff. There was no way that I could have done it, but by his reddened face and perspiring forehead I knew that I had convinced him that I could. The documents I needed arrived a couple of days later and proved beyond doubt that my man was a crook.

I was fortunate to be working again with the excellent Adrienne Page who was my 'go to' junior barrister. Armed with the extensive evidence I had managed to gather against this individual, she produced a stunning defence running to over a dozen pages, which not only asserted that we could prove all the allegations made against him in the programme but also several more. We served this defence in draft on our opponents and then applied to a judge to amend it formally.

At that point the case took a surreal turn. Out of the blue I received a phone call from a senior local police officer who offered to act as a mediator between me and the councillor to resolve the defamation claim. I can only conclude that he was part of the same masonic lodge as the claimant and was trying to protect one of his own. It was a remarkable gesture since it was an utterly inappropriate offer for a police officer to make, and I can only wonder at his sense of invulnerability in making the call. I declined his offer and told him that the right course was for the councillor to abandon his claim.

Our application was to be heard on a Friday and the trial was listed for the following Monday. The unfortunate representative from the insurer had not fully appreciated the potentially catastrophic state of affairs until the morning of the hearing. All that was left of our defence was a paragraph admitting publication. We were about to go into a jury trial with serious allegations of corruption against a local councillor for which we had no defence unless that day's application succeeded. If not, the only issue at the trial would have been how much the councillor would have been awarded in damages, which would have been substantial; at which point we would have had to pay an even larger sum in costs. The poor insurer looked like he was about to walk the Green Mile.

I had spent days drafting a detailed witness statement in support of the application, which set out all that I had learned about the activities of this individual, exhibiting planning applications, maps, etc. I was much assisted in this by Adrienne whose gutsy defence drawn from that statement pulled no punches. All this was before the judge and it was clear that he had read it carefully.

A leading defamation QC, Tom Shields, representing this individual, realized that there was no prospect of keeping out the new defence unless he could persuade the judge of at least the possibility that his client was innocent of the array of grave allegations set out in my witness statement and much more elegantly in Adrienne's defence.

Tom opened his submissions to resist the amendments we were seeking by extolling the virtues of local democracy; how local councillors did an important job for their constituents, and should be protected from unwarranted attacks on their integrity by the media.

Before he had finished, the judge in a rare gesture raised his hand to bring his oration to a halt. I can hear his next words as clearly now as I did then: 'Mr Shields, I entirely accept from you that there are many local MPs and councillors who do a good job and are true public servants. However, you must accept that there are some who abuse their positions for their own personal gain'; i.e. 'Your client is obviously a rank crook so don't waste my time in trying to persuade me otherwise.' At that point we knew we had won.

The judge allowed in our amended defence in full, including a section which Adrienne and I were not sure we would get in because it concerned events which were damning of the councillor but also somewhat peripheral to the issues in the case. It was a triumph and the trial was duly postponed to give the local councillor an opportunity to put in a reply to the defence, which is imaginatively called a 'Reply'.

In fact no such document was ever served and a few days later his lawyers served a formal Notice of Discontinuance (a document of whose existence I had not previously known). Its effect was not only to abandon the claim but to concede that the councillor had to pay our costs.

This was such a novel event for the broadcaster that it had to create a new accounting process to allow the money that had been expended in legal fees to be paid back. It was this hard-fought win that established my credentials as a defendant lawyer, which in turn founded the defendant practice which has taught me so much about reputation management.

A PERSPECTIVE FROM BOTH SIDES

As any PR professional will tell you, for all your study and training the only way to become an effective practitioner is to do the job for many years while making sure that you learn as much as you can as you go along from friend and foe alike. This is especially true of managing media crises, which come in every shape and size because there are so many variables. My experience is that you learn something new from dealing with most of them and it has been my privilege to work a great deal with many top PR individuals and agencies from whom I have learned much via osmosis.

I have also had the most unusual privilege of not only being a media poacher (a PR lawyer), but also a media gamekeeper (editorial lawyer). In my capacity as an editorial lawyer I have had 30-plus years of gleaning invaluable intel and experience from my content work for publishers and broadcasters about how editorial decisions are made. I have also learned what crisis PR works and what does not work.

My work as an editorial lawyer

I have undertaken pre-publication clearance and/or post-publication contentious editorial work for clients such as ITV, Sky, *Huffington Post*, MTV, Viacom, Voice Group, Haymarket Media Group, Capital Radio and *Newsweek*, during which time I have in effect made many editorial decisions in potential and/or active crisis PR situations. I have also trained journalists, delivered lectures and written for professional publications in media law.

I have legalled out live current affairs programmes, hard-hitting documentaries and controversial satire such as *South Park*, magazines, newsprint and literature such as non-fiction, fiction, autobiographies and a major non-governmental organization (NGO) report on pollution – all immensely rewarding work. At the risk of being regarded as a shameless name-dropper, one of the autobiographies I legalled was by the British national treasure that is Basil Brush. You would not believe what that fox gets up to off-camera!

The job of an editorial lawyer should be to get out a true story that serves the public interest in a way that minimizes the regulatory and legal risks. I explain this in greater detail later in this book (*see also* Chapter 3). It is a great feeling to work on a legitimate and well-evidenced public interest story, which may in its raw form be too risky to broadcast or publish, and hone it to a point where all the key points are made but you have de-risked it to the greatest possible degree. This requires not only acute legal skills, but also a deft hand at writing. If you are acting for properly regulated entities which also operate from an ethical perspective, then this an exercise that you can undertake with a clear conscience. I have learned an immense amount about crisis PR from doing this work.

If you are acting for the numerous Fleet Street titles who will neither submit themselves to any form of independent or effective regulation, and for whom the truth is often an unwanted impediment to pursuing editorial and financial agendas, then for at least a proportion of your time you are facilitating the serial infringement of the human rights both of the subjects and the readers of the resulting copy.

MY WORK AS A PR LAWYER FOR COMPANIES

I have acted for a host of corporate clients such as Amazon, Procter & Gamble, Hitachi, Jaguar Land Rover, TalkTalk, Gucci, GlaxoSmithKline and Cambridge University. I have normally done this work in tandem with top PR agencies which have called on my services, one of which went on to become a client.

MY WORK AS A PR LAWYER FOR INDIVIDUALS

I have also acted for numerous high-profile business moguls, senior politicians, music, TV, film and sports stars and members of the Royal Family, both to protect their reputation and/or secure their privacy. My celebrity clients have included Lady Gaga, the Beckhams (for whom I secured their first published apology), Holly Willoughby, Ant and Dec, and Ginger Spice as she was then (now Geri Horner), for whom I secured what I believe to be the only apology and correction to take up the entire front page of a national newspaper.

Some of that work for clients such as the Duchess of York and Tulisa Contostavlos has been undertaken in the full glare of the media. While acting for the former I was interviewed by a young Michael Gove when he was still a journalist at *The Times*.

Learning on the job

The starting point for anyone who wants to deal effectively with the media is to gain the best possible understanding of its diverse nature and how it works. You can learn a great deal from careful observation, as you can from dealing with it professionally by seeking to influence it from the outside. But you only gain a comprehensive understanding of the media if you have also observed it from the inside.

I have tried to squeeze most of what I have learned doing the fascinating work of a content and PR lawyer for 30-plus years into the most practical and readable book that I can. This book also has a subsidiary purpose of serving as a grateful memoir of some of the toe-to-toe battles that I have had on behalf of my clients – both to right wrongs visited on them by the media, principally the print press, as well as to protect the work of high-quality journalists who genuinely want to fulfil their role as public servants. These anecdotes however serve an important role as a window into how the media works.

Whichever side I have found myself on, while always trying to hold fast to my Christian faith principles, I have fought my client's corner as hard as I can. One leading legal directory was kind enough to describe me as an 'indestructible warrior for [my] clients'.

The vital lessons that this book teaches

Drawing on what I have learned both as an editorial and PR lawyer, I have delivered crisis PR seminars to a plethora of audiences ranging from supermarket chains, PR agencies, charities, multinationals and elite sports teams. This has taught me that even among PR professionals there is a lack of knowledge of both how the British media works and how it is regulated (to the limited extent that it is). Only when armed with that knowledge can PR professionals effectively influence editorial decisions that pose a threat to them or their clients.

Although the print media in particular has for many decades exploited its counter-democratic power over our elected representatives to ensure that its liberty to mislead and abuse is subject to minimal restraint or sanction, that has been possible partly because so few people know how to deploy such restraints as there are, effectively. As this book explains, there are various means whereby the damage that it can inflict on companies, brands and individuals can be reduced (see Chapter 7 for prevention and Chapter 8 for cure).

The challenge for everyone from chief executives to junior communications folk is both how to learn about those techniques and how to access the means of deploying them, all of which can be found in this book. This knowledge is essential if you are to have any prospect of either, as is the best outcome, preventing a media crisis altogether; or at least attenuating it so that its adverse impact is substantially reduced.

The orthodox way of approaching 'crisis communications' is merely to try to feed positive material into the poisonous PR mix as some form of antidote, where you are effectively competing for influence with international news websites like the *Mail Online* with its millions of subscribers; something of a finger-in-the-dyke exercise.

So far as I know, the techniques described here, which are based on the astute deployment of the regulations and law created for this very purpose, are neither deployed by PR practitioners, nor taught by PR academics or courses. I have never fully understood why this is the case, although there appears to be some element of PR professionals protecting their turf from encroachment by media lawyers.

My research for this book tells me that you will not find this content in any crisis PR section of PR agency websites, nor in anything other than a footnote to a 'crisis communications' book; and then it may be suggested that there is no effective way to stem a media crisis, which is 100 per cent wrong. It is high time that changed, because just trying to mitigate the damage by means of 'crisis communications' is by no means as effective. It also leaves a permanent reputation stain in the internet ether which is very hard to shift.

'Fake news' – agenda-driven false stories – does no good for anyone except those that promulgate it. The UK media has much to say on fake news, which according to them is spun out by pretty well everyone except themselves. The most dangerous fake news comes from powerful media companies who disseminate it convincingly to millions via their various means of distribution, including social media, and thereby does immense societal damage on issues to do with health, business, politics and the environment – the press being far more at fault than the broadcast media because of its lack of effective regulation.

The most valuable service that a PR professional can render to a client is to prevent a media crisis from happening at all, which should be the first aim of crisis PR. This book is written to help you prevent yourself or your organization from becoming the victim of fake news, which is most effectively done by the astute deployment of the regulations and laws that are out there for the very purpose of protecting you. Where you are suffering damage from legitimate news coverage, at least initially, there is much that can still be done via the same methodology to decrease the damage that a media crisis can cause.

One of the defining differences between this book and all the other literature that I have read about 'crisis communications' is that it tackles the problem at source. All the others that I have read appear to give up on stopping a media crisis from breaking, or at least reduce the quantity and virulence of the publication/ broadcast which whips up the media storm. The purpose of this book however is not to stymie the work of good journalism, which it has been my privilege to support throughout my career, but to prevent bad journalism inflicting unwarranted damage on companies, organizations and individuals, as well as misleading the public into believing things which are not true. This is the essence of crisis PR.

THE BOOK'S APPROACH AND STRUCTURE

Approach

My intention is that this book will educate, stimulate and entertain. I have included a host of anecdotes from my own practice with the aim of doing all three. I also intend the book to be immensely practical, though fully to grasp its methodology some degree of understanding of the relevant regulation and law is essential, which is why I have included those elements. I have also done so because I believe that in some cases such is the significance to society of these provisions that they should be more widely known.

One reason for this is that the British media, especially its print element, pumps out propaganda claiming both that it labours under oppressive laws of privacy and defamation, and is subject to robust and effective regulation. At least as far as the print media is concerned, these are myths which need to be exploded. There are a number of other ways in which we are serially misled by the media – especially its print element, which I also address. This is especially true when the interests of the media are engaged.

There is another important recurring theme in this book. Some of the methodologies it teaches can be deployed by those who are not schooled in the relevant regulatory and legal principles; some cannot. The media employs an army of highly trained crack experts in such regulations and law that – assuming they are effectively deployed – do inhibit the extent to which it is free to inflict unwarranted damage to businesses and the livelihoods and private lives of individuals. Some editorial lawyers conduct themselves ethically; some do not. Either way, dealing with them – as you must if you tackle a media crisis at its source – without an equivalent skill set is unlikely to go well.

Where the media is doing its job properly and reporting legitimately on failings on the part of businesses and individuals, then the best approach is almost always to accept that mistakes have been made, apologize and pledge to learn from them. Trying to mislead the media almost always ends badly. Your stakeholders and customers do not expect perfection and will generally forgive trespasses to which you have owned up and for which you have apologized. Then you are engaging in communications aimed at damage limitation, but vigilance still needs to be maintained to parry the media's corrosive proclivity for embellishment and awfulization.

Structure

After the introduction I explain why reputation matters, which it does in two respects. It matters much to the company or individual to whom it belongs. Its preservation from unwarranted assault is no less important to society as a whole. We need to know who are the 'good guys' and those who are not. When a reputation is wrongly wrecked because of the often-indiscriminate assaults mounted by the press in particular, we all lose out.

I summarize the key regulatory provisions with which we have been furnished for the very purpose of protecting reputation and privacy either by government or the media industry itself. Despite this, I have yet to find even reference to them on any crisis PR website or in any crisis PR book; an astonishing omission.

While one of the primary aims of this book is to enable you and/ or your client to avert a media crisis, that is not always possible. Running your business ethically and treating those with whom you interact well is the best place to start, but that does not guarantee you immunity from the lash of the media. There are however many preparations that can be made to place you in the best possible position to deal with one should one come, which are set out in the next chapter (*see also* Chapter 6).

The best possible outcome when a media crisis looms is to take effective steps to nip it in the bud, which should always be the primary aim of crisis PR. In the next chapter I go into detail about how to deploy the tools out there to do just that.

Even where a media crisis cannot be fully averted, there is a great deal that can be done to reduce its size, impact and longevity – as there are lessons to be learned from it, which is the subject of the next chapter.

Chapter 9 is devoted to litigation PR, a practice area where litigators are a mysterious rarity. In addition to acute media savvy, to do this work well you need both a good working knowledge of how litigation works and the mindset of lawyers and judges.

Just before the conclusion to the book, I look forward to the future, which I divide into the elements we can change and those we cannot. I regard the former as by far the more important of the two. The conclusion is something of a *crie de coeur* for change to the currently chaotic, anachronistic and inadequate system of media regulation.

MY TWIN AIMS IN WRITING THIS BOOK

Aim One: Crisis PR that works

There is no other source of intelligence you need for crisis PR. The primary aim of this book is to provide in a comprehensive form the intelligence without which effective reputation and privacy management is impossible. The press is not going to tell you how best to tame its excesses. Rather, it will – as journalist Piers Morgan once did in a very shouty call with me – set out to mislead you on this issue for obvious self-interested reasons.

I have found no reference to any of these vital professional tools in the reading that I have undertaken about crisis PR as part of my research for this book, or in anything that I have read about crisis PR to date, including perusing the crisis comms pages of many PR agency websites. Some of what I have read about crisis PR is plain wrong – which I know primarily on the basis of my work as an editorial lawyer. I often encounter the phrase 'crisis communications', but this is only necessary when a PR crisis, which may have been prevented altogether, is permitted to run its course and you are reduced to trying to mitigate the damage.

Avoiding the need for 'crisis communications'

The starting point for all crisis PR should be to obviate the need for any 'crisis communications' at all: save to say to a newspaper or broadcaster that this story is wrong and for these regulatory and legal reasons you should not publish it. I use the word 'publish' in this book because it is the legal term for the dissemination of material either via print, sound or moving images. 'Crisis communications' should therefore only be necessary if a PR crisis cannot be averted. Once a negative story is online, there are only two really effective ways to deal with it: persuade the publisher to retract or delete it, or at least include qualifications under threat of a regulatory and/or legal penalty; or pay substantial sums of money to try and push it down on a search, which in my experience is rarely efficacious.

Vital intelligence not taught by PR agencies

I have learned from delivering crisis PR seminars that much of my content comes new, even to audiences drawn from major PR companies. Speaking as both a PR and editorial lawyer, I cannot conceive of how you can undertake effective crisis PR without at the very least knowing the provisions of the primary press code as administered by the IPSO and the Broadcasting Code as administered by Ofcom.

I would not expect any hard-pressed general counsel to be familiar with such information, or board members or senior management. But in considering both how to prepare for and deal with PR crises, anyone tasked with reputation management should have at least a working knowledge of the key provisions of these codes and how to deploy them.

Observations from my work inside the media

So far as I know, I am the only leading crisis PR practitioner who does their work with the benefit of 30-plus years' experience both as an editorial and a PR lawyer. That experience from both sides of the equation has taught me what does and does not work in terms of crisis PR. It has also taught me that some things which pass as crisis PR can actually make matters worse. One of those is the indiscriminate use of statements, which as I explain may have the effect of making what is still merely a potential PR crisis one that is more likely to break.

Bridging the gap between the two species of PR professionals

I also wanted to break down the false divide that exists between the practice of crisis PR in the context of a PR agency and the work of PR lawyers. There appears to be a mindset among some PR agencies and practitioners that a PR lawyer should only be called in after everything else has been tried and failed. However, by that time it may well be too late.

When a media crisis looms, the PR practitioner most likely to stave it off is a PR lawyer. Ideally, they will work closely with the PR agency to decide such things as whether, when and how the company's stakeholders should be pre-warned of the impending bad news; that is assuming that the conclusion of the PR lawyer – who is in the best position to judge – is that it will not be possible to prevent its publication.

A key purpose of this book is to empower its readers better to protect themselves and those whom they represent from the media when it unjustly threatens hard-earned corporate reputations, causes damage to carefully honed brands, or for individuals jeopardizes their fundamental human rights to privacy and reputation. This is not only in the best interests of those individuals and companies, but also society as a whole.

Even where there are media crises deriving from truly-reported facts, there is still much that can be done to navigate the company or individual safely through the storm. If prevention is not possible, then, using the same methodology, the second aim should be to reduce its initial impact by prevailing on the publisher/broadcaster to reduce the volume and severity of the threatened allegations. Not only will this minimize the impact of the original story, it will also reduce the likelihood of it being picked up by other elements of the media and via the social media; i.e. reducing the severity and/or quantity of the secondary iterations of the adverse story by other elements of the media. This book sets out the various means whereby this can be achieved.

Aim Two: To improve the quality of the news media
The second and overlapping purpose of this book is bold in its ambition. It is to improve the quality of the news media.

First, by teaching people the reality about our diverse media and the widely divergent range of quality that we get from it, and how they can play their part in stemming the abuse of which elements of it are guilty. Second, by enabling people – especially PR professionals – to reduce the amount of errant news being peddled.

This would mean a reduction of the risk to all of bad journalism, and not only on consumer issues, which are important. But as I make clear during the course of this book, we are so dependent on the media's depiction of major issues such as politics, the environment, health issues, etc., that it should be all of our business to try to improve the quality of the news we consume and which inevitably shapes us.

The two aims of the book complement each other because, through empowering individuals and corporations to protect themselves from bad press and reduce the media's ability to breach their regulatory and legal obligations, a better news media will be the inevitable consequence, and the amount of misinformation disseminated will decrease. Another consequence will be the stifling of unjust criticism with its corrosive consequences for consumers and subjects alike and a more level playing field for businesses and entrepreneurs vis-à-vis the media.

So just how bad is it?

Back in 2011, the Leveson Inquiry opened the Pandora's box of the worst practices and ethics of the British print media, though it failed to fix them because of the obstinate refusal of the press to accept its recommendations and the craven failure of the government to force the issue – a pattern that goes back some 70 years. That substantial box of horrors has therefore by no means been cleaned out. Its lid has just been partially closed, but most of its malign content remains – though it generally manifests itself more subtly.

In this book you will find many examples taken from my professional experience of the appalling way that some titles and individuals that work for them – especially lawyers – conduct themselves as a matter of routine, and of the dreadful consequences of those actions on their victims and their families, friends and colleagues who become collateral victims of that wrongdoing.

The stark lack of genuine contrition on the part of the newspapers – contrary to what they say to judges – is evident from my experience and of others acting for phone-hacking victims. It is manifested (inter alia) by the papers' determination to fight every inch of the way against compensation claims and their preference to spend money on lawyers rather than compensating victims.

The victims of abuse of press freedom are much wider than those who are directly impacted – though that is good enough reason to try to end it. When a newspaper publishes something untrue, we are all victims. The spreading of misinformation is at last being recognized as a threat both to our democracy and to the very fabric of society.

There are those who recognized this long ago. William Wilberforce, the great nineteenth-century Christian campaigner against slavery and for social justice, spoke of his concern at the media of the day misreporting the business of Parliament. The press's misleading of voters on political issues in pursuit of a political agenda poses more of a threat to our democracy now than it did 200 years ago because its reach has so increased via modern technology.

In my practice I have seen much which purports to be journalism, but is in fact little different from the agenda-driven propaganda which the British media attacks when it criticizes the media of countries which do not pretend to have a free press.

Just as the state media of countries such as China and North Korea will not breathe a word of criticism of the ruling elite, so the vast majority of Fleet Street will scarcely ever tell you about its own wrongdoing – unlike the BBC, which appears to relish doing so. By contrast, Fleet Street invests vast sums in time and money – primarily on lawyers – to ensure that we are kept in ignorance of its own wrongdoing. Fleet Street is a serial human rights abuser, both of the Article 8 right of individuals to their reputation and privacy and the Article 10 right of society to be told the truth, and wields its immense political power to ensure that it remains free to be so.

THE VICE OF AWFULIZATION

A corrosive media vice, which is far worse in Fleet Street than in the broadcast media, is that of awfulization, which I define as reporting events in the most negative and alarming manner and casting blame excessively and indiscriminately. For every time I have had to take a broadcaster to task for unwarranted attacks on a brand or individual, I have had to do so at least 50 times with newspapers. The broadcast media in the UK is bound by the Ofcom Code, which requires (inter alia) both fairness and impartiality and so tempers its output. But the DNA of the broadcast media is also different (*see also* page 82).

Fleet Street paints a picture of society which is much darker than the truth – while whitewashing its own conduct. It now has the direct financial incentive of creating 'clickbait' headlines, ones that are sensationalized to lure the reader into reading them, which will then sometimes be contradicted in whole or in part by the article itself. There is now a specific regulatory code provision about such headlines, which I deal with in the next chapter (*see also* pages 53–4). It also illustrates why arming yourself to prevent publication of negative stories at all, a key purpose of this book, is so important.

This also appears to be a British characteristic. A recent study[1] shows that UK and the Netherlands are the most depressing countries when it comes to news coverage. However, at least the Netherlands counters this negativity by also being the place that has the most positive news stories.

The research, conducted in six countries, showed that negative or neutral news stories made up 85 per cent of output. Negative news was covered 32 per cent of the time, neutral 53 per cent and positive 15 per cent of the time. Examining the international data, news on TV was the most positive in tone, ahead of the print media.

[1] https://www.prmoment.com/pr-research/uk-tops-the-charts-for-negative-news-stories

Awfulization in practice – Great Britain Snow Sports attacked by *Daily Mail*

As I was writing this book I was instructed by Great Britain Snow Sports, whose senior management was the subject of a vicious and wholly unjustified attack by the *Daily Mail*.

Had the newspaper done its research properly it would have learned that *all* the current members of the team were happy with the way it was being run. But there were disgruntled individuals with past associations with the sport who had destructive axes to grind, and the *Daily Mail* became their witting accomplice.

Despite it having been made 100 per cent clear to the journalist that none of these allegations was true, he wrote a story claiming that some of the athletes (the implication was that it was many) had to pay up to £33,500 to compete in the team, that there had been a major failure by the directors to raise sponsorship money and that vast sums were paid to 'administrators' rather than on sporting excellence.

The two articles also claimed that the members of the team were supportive of the claims made by the paper, which was not true. This was the statement from the whole team which I sent along with an IPSO complaint on the following day: 'Our Governing Body has dramatically improved everything we do, increased the funding across the board, turned the organisation into a professional and well-managed set up and given us what we need. We don't recognise any of the characterisation in the articles and don't support any of the comments and opinions in the article which seem to relate only to athletes from decades ago.'

The team's passionate chief executive was plainly heartbroken as she instructed me, fearing the articles would wreck the negotiations underway with a major supermarket chain to be the main sponsor and a planned crowdfunding campaign, which in turn would undermine her efforts – especially vis-à-vis funding – and all those Olympians and Paralympians in the team.

THE IMPACT OF AWFULIZATION ON MENTAL HEALTH

The long-term impact on the psyche of the consumers of the UK print media is both to convince them that their lot is worse than it is, engendering angst and discontent; and that they cannot safely put their trust in anyone or anything, with the same effect. The damage that this does to us as a society is incalculable.

In a 2018 *Guardian* article,[2] Steven Pinker stated:

> 'The consequences of negative news are themselves negative. Far from being better informed, heavy news watchers can become mis-calibrated. They worry more about crime, even when rates are falling, and sometimes they part company with reality altogether: a 2016 poll found that a large majority of Americans follow news about Isis closely, and 77 per cent agreed that "Islamic militants operating in Syria and Iraq pose a serious threat to the existence or survival of the United States," a belief that is nothing short of delusional.
>
> 'Consumers of negative news, not surprisingly, become glum: a recent literature review cited "misperception of risk, anxiety, lower mood levels, learned helplessness, contempt and hostility towards others, desensitization, and in some cases, complete avoidance of the news."'

This is a recurring theme in my work. In my PR practice, time and again an accusatory story is sent over from a newspaper, where a selective set of facts is presented for which there is no context or balance; and which therefore comprise a tail of unmitigated wickedness and woe, making us all victims who are goaded into being angry, resentful and fearful. We are bombarded with such stories on a 24/7 basis. How can this do other than poison our mental health?

We know that trolling and bullying has this effect. The UK is routinely both trolled and bullied by Fleet Street, and because of the power that the press wields over them, our politicians do

[2] https://www.theguardian.com/commentisfree/2018/feb/17/steven-pinker-media-negative-news

nothing to protect us. In fact, in passing the 2013 Defamation Act, Parliament extended the media's licence to mislead.

Several of my overseas clients have asked me, 'But how can they do that?' Even some politician clients make similar observations, to which I reply that the fault lies with them for not ensuring that our press is properly regulated. One promptly sacked me when I did so.

THE TRAGIC SUICIDE OF CAROLINE FLACK

In the case of one of my clients, TV presenter Caroline Flack, the brutality of the tabloid press towards her was such that in February 2020 she committed suicide. This was the coroner's finding: 'I find the reason for her taking her life was she now knew she was being prosecuted for certainty, and she knew she would face the media, press, publicity – it would all come down upon her.' Her death was the direct result of sense of impunity enjoyed by the tabloid press, for which IPSO bears much of the responsibility.

The chief culprit in her death was the *Sun*. You will look in vain for any reference to 'press' or 'media' in the *Sun*'s coverage of the inquest. That title was careful to apportion all blame on the police, who in turn doubtless felt under pressure from that very tabloid to make an example of Caroline. Its readers were therefore denied their Article 10 right to know that their paper was held responsible in part for her death.

THE BROADSHEETS MISLEAD US ON WEIGHTIER ISSUES

I have also seen many things asserted by broadsheet titles which are an affront to the obligation imposed on them by the Article 10 free speech right, that with that privilege comes responsibilities. Their transgressions also tend to be on more weighty issues and therefore potentially more dangerous.

I was instructed by an MEP who had been accused by *The Sunday Times* of speaking about 'fracking' at the European Parliament without having declared an interest from the fact that he had a minor role at a fracking company. I asked him to send over all the relevant documents, from which it was 100 per cent clear that the allegation was false.

I made a complaint to the then press regulator, the Press Complaints Commission (PCC), in which I was able to show that virtually every factual assertion in *The Sunday Times* article was inaccurate and/or misleading, contrary to the stipulations of the PCC Code. Despite this, in an adjudication replete with intellectual dishonesty, the PCC refused to uphold the complaint against one of its creators and primary funders (News UK, as it now is).

The result was that the newspaper had trashed the reputation of the MEP, the livelihood of a good politician was placed at risk, as was that of his family, and the democratic rights of the voters in the constituency were violated because they were fed fake news about their representative in the European Parliament. All of this was then cemented by a corrupt regulator which the press had set up to ensure that it would not be held accountable for its actions – as it has with the PCC's successor (IPSO). Former UK prime minister Tony Blair was right when he described the UK press as 'feral'.

The unprincipled bully Piers Morgan

The work of a PR lawyer will also occasionally bring down the wrath of those who object to their hegemony over public opinion being challenged. Piers Morgan epitomizes the value system of a tabloid editor and has brought all that is spiteful and ugly from the tabloids on to our TV screens. He is also a vicious, self-righteous, hypercritical and hyperbolic columnist for the *Sun*.

As I wrote this book, the debate raged about Piers Morgan's relentless abuse of Meghan Markle – cheered on by the baying popular press. Nobody seemed to have observed that he was simultaneously asserting his right to free speech while brutally attacking the Duchess of Sussex for exercising the same right; just as her much-revered mother-in-law Princess Diana had done 25 years previously, provoking a very different media response. He was also attacking a woman who had opened up about her mental health problems just over a year after the suicide of my client Caroline Flack, who was driven to it in part by such media abuse.

Some months later, Morgan tore into Japanese professional Naomi Osaka for having pulled out of the French Open rather than risk her mental health by face a hostile media which Morgan epitomizes; this from a man who stomped out of a TV studio when subjected to mild criticism on-air from a BAME colleague over his abuse of Meghan Markle.

Morgan has torn into Prince Harry for what he perceives of as attacks on the Queen, conveniently forgetting that when he edited the *Mirror* he grossly invaded her privacy by sending a reporter to take photographs of her private chambers, which were then published in an article[3] which concluded thus: 'I soon realised life as a footman is not my cup of tea. With long hours and pitiful pay, no wonder the novelty of working for the Queen soon wears thin.'

I know from my dealings with this man that he is an unprincipled bully. While he was editor of the *News of the World*, it published a highly inaccurate and defamatory article about a celebrity author client of mine. In response to my claim letter, Morgan himself sent a letter settling the claim on the basis of a follow-up article about my client, over which he had copy approval, doubtless after being told by his lawyers that there was no defence to my threatened libel action.

When the draft article came in over the fax machine at my client's home where I was awaiting it, it was even worse than the original and riddled with typos. When in a phone call I politely invited him to abide by the agreement that he had made, I was subjected to a tirade of abuse and invective, after which he hung up on me. He then told my client that if he heard from me again, 'I will fucking destroy you.'

---

[3] https://www.google.co.uk/amp/s/www.mirror.co.uk/news/real-life-stories/buckingham -palace-queen-tupperware-philip-13663437.amp

Five myths about the media and the law that I explode in this book

In my crisis PR seminar, among the practical advice that I give from my experience as both a crisis PR and editorial lawyer, I explode five myths which I have at various times encountered either being espoused by the media (primarily the print press) and/or which have been imbibed by PR folk or their clients.

The print/broadcast divide

My crisis comms seminar at the conference was followed by a joint presentation by a BBC current affairs editor and the managing editor of a national newspaper, who were asked to comment on my presentation. Their contrasting responses were testament to the profound ethical divide which, despite a recent degree of convergence, still exists between the broadcast and print media.

The BBC editor told the delegates that the BBC did indeed take note of communications by respected media lawyers in making editorial decisions, some of which were changed as a result. As a long-time programme lawyer, I know that to be true. The managing editor, an ex-journo and dyed-in-the-wool newspaper hack, said that no account was taken of such communications and that all that was achieved by them was to convince the newspaper that the individual or company had something to hide. He was lying – as I know from my extensive work as an editorial lawyer for a wide variety of publishers and from friends of mine who work in Fleet Street.

I can also illustrate the mendacity of that individual by my experience of visiting the legal offices of Associated Newspapers for a settlement meeting. There was a large noticeboard on which there was nothing but a letter from the firm where I was then a partner (Schillings), which concerned four high-profile celebrities who had formed something of a love square. A large red arrow pointed at the letter and underneath was a note from the head of legal stating that no copy was to go out about those individuals without his permission.

Myth One: If you threaten regulatory action and/or legal proceedings, you will be perceived as being defensive.

There are some journalists who think this, but it is mere self-serving cynicism. In fact, if you are perceived as having a robust policy of investing in the protection of your reputation or brand, that is beneficial because the media will be more circumspect before they set out to trash you.

Myth Two: If you stand up against the media they will make things worse for you.

The reverse is true. As an editorial lawyer I can tell you that material is legalled out via a two-stage process. Is there a regulatory legal issue? In other words, is it an infringement of reputation or privacy and/ or a code breach? If the answer is 'yes', how likely are they hold us to account? The answer to the second question should be 'very likely'.

Myth Three: There is no effective means of defending yourself in the face of adverse reporting.

Nonsense! There are the regulatory codes (IPSO and Ofcom) and a variety of legal provisions that can effectively be deployed (all of which are set out in this book); as I have done successfully numerous times in my capacity as a PR lawyer.

Myth Four: If you threaten regulatory or legal proceedings, it will increase circulation of the story.

This is obverse of the truth. The role of an editorial lawyer is to assess and mitigate against risk. A PR lawyer injects risk by his mere instruction via the signal that is sent, that this company takes the protection of its reputation seriously.

Myth Five: You will get a fair response from the media without the assistance of a PR lawyer.

Alas, no. Hubris, editorial agendas and the pursuit of profit are all powerful motivations which can generally only be parried by the prospect of a sanction for infringing the rights of others and/or breaching regulatory codes.

2

Why Reputation Matters

You do not have to be a crisis PR expert to know no one wants to buy a bad product or service, and they would also prefer to avoid buying even a good product or service from what they perceive to be crooks and shysters. But the reputation of a corporation not only matters to the company. It also matters to the consumer who cannot make informed choices when purchasing products and services if there is no reliable information out there on which to base their choices. Prospective employees are increasingly looking to work for organizations whose values extend beyond just making a profit, so your reputation is also going to impact on the quality of your team.

The value of corporate reputation is also measured in financial terms. Here are some authoritative quotations to make the point:

- Corporate reputation is 'the most important measure of success' (*World Economic Forum*).
- 'The World Economic Forum Survey found Corporate brand and reputation represents more than 40 per cent of Company's market value' (*Business Ethics* magazine).
- 'Many savvy Companies are starting to realise that a good name can be the most important asset, and actually boost the stock price' (*Bloomberg*).

For the purposes of this book, the most important quotation comes from American business magnate Warren Buffett, who knows a bit about turning a profit: 'It takes 20 years to build a reputation and five minutes to ruin it. If you think about that, you will do things differently.' He also said somewhat ominously: 'Lose money and I will forgive you. But lose even a shred of reputation and I will be ruthless.'

However, I cannot leave this section without adding a wonderful observation by Napoleon Bonaparte: 'Four hostile newspapers are more to be feared than 1,000 bayonets.' How extraordinary that some 200 years ago, reputation management was apparently already a necessary adjunct to an immensely powerful European military dictator, who was apparently more afraid of the French press than of Wellington's muskets.

THE PUBLIC INTEREST IN KILLING OFF FAKE NEWS

In addition to the obvious PR benefits, there is an important public interest in preventing the publication of false and damaging stories of any kind; including those which concern a company's services, products or practices. At last there is beginning to be a realization in society as a whole of the profound damage that can be caused by 'fake news', though the commercial media is naturally not keen for its own propensity to peddle it to be restrained.

I am not sure that this has yet found its way into the thinking of the PR community. The importance of the public not being misled is however recognized in the IPSO, IMPRESS (Independent Monitor for the Press), NUJ (National Union of Journalists) and Ofcom codes. The US Society of Professional Journalists (SPJ) also publishes a code which makes this clear. However intense lobbying by Fleet Street has succeeded in undermining the right of a company or individual to secure vindication via the law as it has undermined the right of the public to learn that it has been misled on a matter of public interest.

This is a serious loss to us all.

THE EUROPEAN CONVENTION ON HUMAN RIGHTS RECOGNIZES THE IMPORTANCE OF REPUTATION

The starting point for any discussion of the importance of reputation (and the related right to privacy) must be the key articles of the European Convention on Human Rights – Article 8, which protects both privacy and reputation, and Article 10, which protects free speech.

Article 8
This is the wording of Article 8:

1. Everyone has the right to respect for his private and family life, his home and his correspondence.
2. There shall be no interference by a public authority with the exercise of this right except such as in accordance with the law and is necessary in a democratic society ... or for the protection of the rights and freedoms of others.

Unlike in the US where the First Amendment of the Constitution overwhelmingly prioritizes free speech over any equivalent Article 8 right, in the European forum we have – I believe rightly – chosen to balance these two rights, and it has been said by the highest judicial authority in the UK that neither takes priority over the other.

The European Court of Human Rights has said this about the importance of reputation: 'the right to protection of one's reputation is one of the rights guaranteed by Article 8 of the Convention, as one element of the right to respect for private life.'

The necessary rights of companies
Although it is now well established in European jurisprudence that the protection afforded by Article 8 covers not only privacy, but also the right of an individual to protect their reputation from

unwarranted attacks on it, Article 8 does not apply to companies. However, it is also well established in the UK that companies have a right to reputation which the courts will at least to some extent protect.

Common sense dictates that they must do so because society needs to be protected against fake news about companies at least as much as any other sort of fake news; otherwise, how can consumers make informed choices?

A company's reputation also has a substantial monetary value in which it should invest. For reasons that I have never fully understood, there is a diffidence on the part of some corporates to engage the protections which our democratic system has provided for them, their businesses, their employees, stakeholders, etc. I fear that this is at least in part the result of having been badly advised by their PR folk. There is no benefit to the general public in being fed misinformation. In fact, the law goes further than that – i.e. that the dissemination of misinformation contravenes the public interest.

Article 10
This is the wording of Article 10:

1. Everyone has the right to freedom of expression. This right shall include freedom to hold opinions and *to receive* and impart *information* and ideas without interference by public authority and regardless of frontiers ...
2. The exercise of these freedoms, since it *carries with it duties and responsibilities*, may be subject to such formalities, conditions, restrictions or penalties as are prescribed by law and are necessary in a democratic society ... for the protection of the reputation or rights of others, for preventing the disclosure of information received in confidence, ... [my emphasis]

There are three features of this precious human right which are often overlooked by advocates for unrestricted 'free expression' for the media. The first part of the right of free speech is the right of the individual to *receive* information. The second is that the right requires that 'information' should be freely imparted; information being 'facts provided or learned about something or someone'. I take that to mean that 'information' that is in fact false is not information at all and therefore falls outside the Article 10 right. The third is that the right carries with it 'duties and responsibilities', and so there should be effective regulation to ensure those 'duties and responsibilities' are observed.

These key features of the Article 10 right are recognized in the IMPRESS, IPSO and the NUJ codes, all of which stress the need for care to be taken not to disseminate false 'information', and where that happens for the falsity to be corrected. The codes recognize that the dissemination of untruths has no place in genuine free speech, and that those who have been misled have the right to receive information in the form of a correction of the false information that they have received.

THE HIGHEST COURT WARNS OF THE DANGERS POSED TO SOCIETY BY FAKE NEWS, ONLY THEN TO FACILITATE IT

The abandonment by the law of the fundamental importance of truth in reporting public affairs was initially the fault of the then House of Lords in a pivotal 1999 libel action concerning a *Sunday Times* story about the then Irish Taoiseach Albert Reynolds.

The dangerous and errant principles established in that case – the most serious effect of which is that, at the unilateral election of a newspaper, a false and damaging story that it has published about a matter of public interest will go uncorrected – then found their way into the 2013 Defamation Act in the form of the Section 4 'publication on a matter of public interest' defence. This is despite what Lord Hobhouse said in his speech in the Reynolds case about why the sanctity of reputation is so crucial to the public as a whole:

The liberty to communicate (and receive) information has a similar place in a free society but it is important always to remember that it is the communication of information not misinformation which is the subject of this liberty. There is no human right to disseminate information that is not true. No public interest is served by publishing or communicating misinformation. The working of a democratic society depends on the members of that society being informed not misinformed. Misleading people and the purveying as facts statements which are not true is destructive of the democratic society and should form no part of such a society. There is no duty to publish what is not true: there is no interest in being misinformed. These are general propositions going far beyond the mere protection of reputations.

As the Law Lord makes clear, you ill-serve your customers, stakeholders, business partners and the general public as a whole if you do not take every precaution possible to prevent them being misled by fake news about you, your products and services. I am therefore mystified by the absence of a policy of prevention in the crisis PR material that I have read.

If the public are misled by the media, then their ability to make informed choices about the products and services they use is undermined. Even more serious is the situation where their democratic rights are undermined when – as is usually the case – they are misled by a newspaper. By contrast, as someone much greater than the Law Lord rightly said, '[It is] the truth [that] will set you free.'[1]

---

[1] Jesus Christ (Gospel of John 8:32)

3

Key Regulations and Laws

In PR circles you hear the expression 'going legal', which is generally used to describe some form of last-resort nuclear option after a publication or broadcast has taken place. First, the time to consider whether this is a moment for 'going legal' is as soon as the PR threat arises. Second, for most corporate reputation situations, it would be more apt to 'go regulatory'.

This is my definition of crisis PR on which this book is based: 'restraining the media from damaging reputation or invading privacy by the deployment of the full array of regulatory and legal tools available'. So, what are those 'regulatory and legal tools'?

THE REGULATORY LANDSCAPE FOR CRISIS PR AND THE NATIONAL SCANDAL THAT IS IPSO

Most of the press is regulated by the IPSO. All the linear broadcast media is regulated by Ofcom. These are two very different animals, as I will now explain.

Fleet Street and the IPSO Code
IPSO was foisted on us in 2014 by Fleet Street, which because of its hubris and lack of regard for the truth has refused flatly to be independently regulated according the moderate and reasonable recommendations of Lord Leveson made in his report at the conclusion of his inquiry, which report was a devastating indictment

of the British press and the regulator it had created (PCC). Fleet Street, which constantly demands full accountability from others, refuses point-blank to be held accountable itself.

For most newspapers there is the Editors' Code as composed and administered by IPSO, by which those titles both set and mark their own homework. The IPSO regime also covers many local newspapers and magazines, which are owned by such major publishing conglomerates as Associated Newspapers and Reach. The full list of the publications regulated by IPSO can be accessed on its website:[1]

This is what IPSO mendaciously says of itself:

> IPSO is the independent regulator for the newspaper and magazine industry in the UK. We hold newspapers and magazines to account for their actions, protect individual rights, uphold high standards of journalism and help to maintain freedom of expression for the press.

On the first page of IPSO's website, under a heading, What We Do, it makes this further entirely false claim: 'We make sure that member newspapers follow the Editors' Code.' It does nothing of the sort. The truth is that IPSO is neither independent, nor does it in any real sense impose standards on the publications that it regulates. It will not step in to prevent lies being told, privacy being invaded (with very limited non-mandatory exceptions) or even to protect vulnerable children from press abuse. It merely publishes a code of practice and rather than truly holding the press 'to account', inadequately, selectively and sluggishly sanctions breaches of that code.

IPSO's true primary function is to ensure that the publications that it oversees remain free to mislead the public and trash human rights with the minimum possible interference, while at the same maintaining the pretence of being properly regulated.

[1] https://www.ipso.co.uk/complain/who-ipso-regulates/

KEY ISSUE AFTER LEVESON WAS PRESS REGULATION

After the Leveson Inquiry of 2011–12, the only issue of real importance was what would replace the disgraced PCC, which was finally laid to rest after 21 undistinguished years after its failings were finally exposed to such an extent by the Leveson Inquiry that even the combined power of Fleet Street could not save it. Would it be a reincarnation of the failed PCC, or something genuinely independent and effective?

When setting out his recommendations for a body to replace the PCC, Lord Justice Leveson was not working in isolation. He was informed by a team of six assessors appointed from a variety of backgrounds, including journalism. Leveson's report records that:

> 'All the relevant Assessors have clearly advised that the
> system I am recommending, organised by the industry to
> objective standards, delivers the independent regulation
> which is essential; it safeguards press freedoms, will not chill
> investigative journalism that is in the public interest, and can
> command public confidence. It is their unanimous advice that
> it is in the interests of both the industry and the Government
> to accept and implement the recommendations to that end.'

The government, despite the personal promise of then Prime Minister David Cameron to phone-hacking victims, under intense pressure from Fleet Street, refused to do what was required to implement the Leveson recommendations. So it is that an entire county was let down by its political leaders and a once-in-a-lifetime opportunity to improve press standards substantially was spurned. Instead Fleet Street foisted IPSO on us. A re-badged PCC that had been rightly slated by Lord Leveson, IPSO even opened in the same offices and hired many of the PCC personnel. IPSO is the fourth incarnation of press self-regulation. All three predecessors failed, as was the intention of the press in creating them, as it was when creating IPSO.

IPSO is neither independent, nor does it in any real sense regulate the press. It has the power both to launch investigations and to fine papers up to £1 million, though it was set up in a way that effectively ruled out any such sanction being imposed. So far it has neither undertaken a single investigation nor issued a single fine, even when overwhelming evidence of serial press abuse is presented to it. I suggest no one holds their breath.

I GET THROWN OUT OF THE OFFICE OF THE CHAIRMAN OF IPSO

IPSO's first chairman Sir Alan Moses – a former appeal court judge – dragooned me out of his office during a meeting with him and Matt Tee, IPSO's chief executive, when I had the temerity to challenge IPSO's disgraceful policy on the prominence of corrections, which are invariably a small fraction of the offending material. He explained to me that IPSO had the benefit of having senior newspaper people on its committee when it was adjudicating complaints. I responded that their problem was how to explain why it is that, according to their editorial judgement, a story should enjoy a certain prominence at the point of publication, but for some reason when that story required correction, a much lesser prominence was appropriate.

When Matt Tee interjected that the IPSO committee was not interested in my views, I responded with polite surprise since I thought I had been invited by IPSO to its offices for the very purpose of airing them. At this point I was told by Sir Alan Moses that I had been rude to Mr Tee and that I should leave his office immediately. Mr Tee then frogmarched me off the premises in front of all the IPSO staff. So much for free speech at IPSO! I wrote a full account of that entertaining and enlightening encounter for the excellent *INFORRM* magazine.[2]

---

[2] https://inforrm.org/2015/04/29/ipso-the-inconvenient-truth-part-one-jonathan-coad/

IPSO IS FAR BETTER THAN HAVING NO REGULATOR

IPSO is however far better than no regulator at all. It rightly and robustly called out the *Telegraph* and its journalist Toby Young for spreading fake news about COVID-19.[3] IPSO deemed the article to be 'significantly misleading' when it said catching a cold could protect people from coronavirus and claimed that London was approaching herd immunity.

The comment piece had this headline: 'WHEN WE HAVE HERD IMMUNITY BORIS WILL FACE A RECKONING ON THIS POINTLESS AND DAMAGING LOCKDOWN'. It also claimed that some people 'will have a natural immunity because they've already successfully fought off other coronaviruses, such as the common cold' and that 'people in [this] category will be immune'.

IPSO concluded that the *Telegraph* was unable to support its position and that it had 'failed to take care not to publish inaccurate and misleading information'. 'The statement was significantly misleading,' it said, noting that the *Telegraph* had not offered to run a correction. 'It misrepresented the nature of immunity and implied that people previously exposed to some common colds might be automatically immune to suffering symptoms and passing on COVID-19 to others.' IPSO ordered the *Telegraph* to publish a correction.[4]

A WORD OF WARNING

I have already said that I cannot understand how you can undertake effective crisis PR without deploying the very tools that were created to do the job – though it appears that many PR professionals try to do just that. At my crisis PR seminars, I warn that this may one day result in a negligence claim against them.

---

[3] https://www.ipso.co.uk/rulings-and-resolution-statements/ruling/?id=11845-20
[4] https://www.theguardian.com/media/2021/jan/14/daily-telegraph-rebuked-over-toby-youngs-herd-immunity-covid-column

I was asked by a blue-chip school to advise on a possible negligence claim against its PR agency which had failed to deal with a media problem concerning two pupils. This was because they had not deployed the relevant section of the IPSO Code against the errant title, without which (in that case as in many others) no effective crisis PR was possible, nor was any affective action to protect the pupils.

THE IPSO EDITORS' CODE

The IPSO Code is a moderately updated and, in some respects, weakened version of the old PCC Code, which was written entirely by newspaper editors. The Code Committee now comprises 14 individuals, including two senior IPSO officers. Ten of the Committee represent the press. There are three token 'independent lay members'. One is a compliance lawyer and another chairs oversight boards for such as healthcare regulators. Doubtless they were appointed by IPSO because they apparently have no significant professional media experience and will therefore present no challenge to the press's hegemony over the Code Committee and the content of the Code.

Despite this the IPSO Code is generally a good document. It is occasionally cited in court judgments; normally against papers which ignore its provisions. Its two major defects are the 'due prominence' provision for corrections, which permits IPSO invariably to authorize ones which are a tiny fraction of the size of the offending material. The other is inadequate protection for children.

If IPSO were a truly independent body which enforced the Code robustly and conscientiously, then the quality of our press would both improve massively and start to regain the confidence of the public. The problem is that IPSO does not do so.

The effectiveness of the Code in ensuring that the papers that purport to adhere to it is primarily determined by the extent to which it is invoked by those seeking its protection. It is of zero value either to a PR professional or society unless invoked expertly, promptly and robustly.

THE KEY PROVISIONS OF THE IPSO CODE

These are the primary provisions of the IPSO Code and the ones which I most commonly use in my reputation management work. I explain how you make complaints to IPSO next.

Accuracy
Section 1 deals with accuracy and reads as follows:

i) The Press must take care not to publish inaccurate, misleading or distorted information or images, including headlines not supported by the text.

ii) A significant inaccuracy, misleading statement or distortion must be corrected, promptly and with due prominence, and – where appropriate – an apology published. In cases involving IPSO, due prominence should be as required by the regulator.

iii) A fair opportunity to reply to significant inaccuracies should be given, when reasonably called for.

iv) The Press, while free to editorialise and campaign, must distinguish clearly between comment, conjecture and fact.

v) A publication must report fairly and accurately the outcome of an action for defamation to which it has been a party, unless an agreed settlement states otherwise, or an agreed statement is published.

'Queen backs Brexit' (not)

Sub-section (i) of this provision was used successfully by HM The Queen in her IPSO complaint over the outrageous 'QUEEN BACKS BREXIT' front-page *Sun* headline published in the run-up to the Brexit referendum of 2016. It is a favourite trick of tabloid editors especially to draw attention (i.e. 'clickbait') in a disingenuous headline to an article which then has something rather different to say.

After a complaint by the Queen, the headline was found to breach Section 1(i) of the Code because it was not 'supported by the text'. The correction stipulated by IPSO was however not required to be on the front page and the *Sun*'s editor defiantly continued to justify his paper's publication of the headline even after the adjudication.

Making a false story out of true facts

Another popular ruse favoured particularly by the press in pursuit of an editorial agenda is to cobble together a series of broadly accurate facts in a way which creates a net impression to the reader which is 'misleading' and/or 'distorted'. This provision can be deployed to remedy such situations.

However, Paragraph 1 of the IPSO Code is of use primarily in situations where advance notice is given by a newspaper subject to the IPSO Code that it intends to publish a story which contravenes it. Newspapers will almost invariably give such notice to place them in a stronger position should they be subject to any regulatory or legal complaint. If the story which the paper is threatening to publish is to any substantial degree inaccurate or misleading, then the paper should be robustly and promptly told so.

The sole IPSO remedy

IPSO has eschewed the power to award damages or costs and will never impose a fine. Its sole remedy for breaches of subsection 1(i) of the Code is for newspapers to publish corrections 'promptly' and 'with due prominence', both of which are honoured primarily in the breach. The extent to which a publication will pay any attention to this provision is determined primarily by the vigour and expertise of the subject of the Code breach in pressing for the remedy to be activated.

The right of reply provision at subsection 3 was amended as the Code journeyed from being the PCC Code to the IPSO Code. Originally, it was for 'inaccuracies'. Now (like subsection (ii)), it applies only to 'significant inaccuracies'. It is invariably a second best to achieving a correction, although a newspaper will sometimes offer it as a softer alternative for the press, for whom admitting error appears to be near impossible.

Privacy

Section 2 of the IPSO Code effectively incorporates into the Code Article 8 of the European Convention on Human Rights:

i) Everyone is entitled to respect for his or her private and family life, home, health and correspondence, including digital communications.

ii) Editors will be expected to justify intrusions into any individual's private life without consent. In considering an individual's reasonable expectation of privacy, account will be taken of the complainant's own public disclosures of information and the extent to which the material complained about is already in the public domain or will become so.

iii) It is unacceptable to photograph individuals, without their consent, in public or private places where there is a reasonable expectation of privacy.

Since the popular press earns a significant proportion of its income by infringing the Article 8 rights of individuals, this is not a provision which IPSO is particularly keen to enforce. However, as I set out below, it can in limited circumstances be persuaded to do so by means of an IPSO 'private advisory'; though as the terms suggests these are advisory only.

Harassment

Section 3 of the IPSO Code prohibits harassment:

i) Journalists must not engage in intimidation, harassment or persistent pursuit.

ii) They must not persist in questioning, telephoning, pursuing or photographing individuals once asked to desist; nor remain on property when asked to leave and must not follow them. If requested, they must identify themselves and whom they represent.

iii) Editors must ensure these principles are observed by those working for them and take care not to use non-compliant material from other sources.

This section can also be the subject of a 'private advisory', especially where relatives of a celebrity are being approached for comment on some life event, or where victims of a tragedy seek to be left alone by the press.

Children

There is some protection, albeit inadequate, for children at Section 6 of the IPSO Code:

i) All pupils should be free to complete their time at school without unnecessary intrusion.

ii) They must not be approached or photographed at school without permission of the school authorities.

iii) Children under 16 must not be interviewed or photographed on issues involving their own or another child's welfare unless a custodial parent or similarly responsible adult consents.

iv) Children under 16 must not be paid for material involving their welfare, nor parents or guardians for material about their children or wards, unless it is clearly in the child's interest.

v) Editors must not use the fame, notoriety or position of a parent or guardian as sole justification for publishing details of a child's private life.

This provision has been most useful when I have been instructed by high-profile schools where a crisis has arisen over a pupil issue and the press has set out to make a difficult situation for the staff even more difficult.

Public interest

Sections 2, 3 and 6 are subject to what the IPSO Code describes as a 'public interest' exception. This is what is said on the issue of public interest:

1. The public interest includes, but is not confined to:

   - Detecting or exposing crime, or the threat of crime, or serious impropriety.
   - Protecting public health or safety.
   - Protecting the public from being misled by an action or statement of an individual or organisation.
   - Disclosing a person or organisation's failure or likely failure to comply with any obligation to which they are subject.
   - Disclosing a miscarriage of justice.
   - Raising or contributing to a matter of public debate, including serious cases of impropriety, unethical conduct or incompetence concerning the public.
   - Disclosing concealment, or likely concealment, of any of the above.

2. There is a public interest in freedom of expression itself.
3. The regulator will consider the extent to which material is already in the public domain or will become so.
4. Editors invoking the public interest will need to demonstrate that they reasonably believed publication – or journalistic activity taken with a view to publication – would both serve, and be proportionate to, the public interest and explain how they reached that decision at the time.

With the exception of Section 3, these provisions broadly reflect the UK law of privacy/breach of confidence, which I summarize later in this chapter. It is appropriate then that the IPSO Code includes these exceptions. It is also important to note that there is no public interest exception to Section 1 of the Code, which bizarrely represents a departure from the law, as I also explain below. On this occasion the IPSO Code is right and the law is wrong.

IPSO's double standards

IPSO does not accept that these exceptions should apply to its own activities. I was threatened with a professional conduct complaint by IPSO's lawyers when I stated my intention to bring some of its correspondence into the public domain to illustrate its 'failure to comply with [the] obligation[s] to which they are subject', 'Disclosing a miscarriage of justice [and] Raising or contributing to a matter of public debate, including serious cases of impropriety, unethical conduct or incompetence concerning the public'.

The ironic element of the Code

There is a bitter irony in the public interest section proclaiming that 'There is a public interest in freedom of expression itself', which must be an allusion to Article 10, which also stresses the right of individuals to receive information.

This right is routinely denied the general public by IPSO by virtue of its policy on 'due prominence' for corrections, which ensures that most people who are misled by the newspapers that it regulates never find out about it. The lack of reference in the Code to the public interest in Article 8 is conspicuous by its absence.

The Editors' Codebook[5]

IPSO publishes what it calls the *Editors' Codebook*, which is primarily a window-dressing exercise. It has two nauseating self-congratulatory introductory pieces. The first is by the chairman of the Editors' Code Committee, which includes this: '… at a time when accountability is perhaps slipping out of fashion, by signing up to the Code and the self-regulatory regime for when the press sends a clear signal that it is prepared to be held fully accountable for its actions …' As the writer must know, the very existence of IPSO rather than a

[5] https://editorscode.org.uk/downloads/codebook/Codebook-2020.pdf

Leveson-compliant regulator is proof indeed that the press has no intention of being 'held fully accountable for its actions'.

The Codebook's guidance is generally ignored by the papers that it regulates
The *Codebook* observes, 'More than 55 per cent of the complaints considered by IPSO involve clause 1.' It also sets out a number of 'key questions an editor should ask about a story' prior to publication, which can sometimes be effectively deployed in dealing with a paper prior to publication, either to eliminate or at least attenuate a looming media crisis:

- Can I demonstrate that the story is accurate?
- Can I demonstrate that we have taken care? For example, do we have notes to support the story?
- Have we put the key points of the story to the people mentioned in it? Do we need to? If we have, have we given proper consideration to how or whether the story should reflect what they have told us?
- Is the headline supported by the text of the story?
- Are the pictures misleading?

All of these provisions requiring a story to be properly substantiated prior to publication are then ignored by IPSO in its conduct of the complaints process, which allows newspapers ample time to try and scrape together a post-publication justification for a story. How much better would our press be if IPSO insisted on adherence to these stipulations.

This section of the *Codebook* includes this provision, 'IPSO may insist on seeing evidence that a publication has taken care, particularly when the subject of the story is also the source and it is told in his or her own words.' There is no way that during the course of an investigation IPSO is going to do that without robust insistence on the part of the complainant.

On the issue of headlines, the *Codebook* says this: 'Eye-catching headlines won't necessarily summarize everything in the story beneath, but Clause 1(i) requires any claim made in the headline to be supported by the text of the article.'

So far as corrections are concerned this is an important provision of the *Codebook*: 'Readers now access stories through a variety of channels, so it is best practice for corrections to be carried on all the media platforms that carried the story originally.' Again, this will only be done by a newspaper if you insist on it.

IPSO AND 'DUE PROMINENCE'

There is no more conclusive proof of IPSO's complete lack of independence than its policy on prominence, i.e. what constitutes 'due prominence'. Contrast the independent monitor for the IMPRESS Code, which states: 'Publishers must correct any significant inaccuracy with due prominence, *which should normally be equal prominence*, at the earliest opportunity' (emphasis added).

IPSO neither permits an appeal against its adjudications, nor does it allow anyone (other than the parties to the complaint) to see the evidence on which those adjudications are based. The fact that more often than not IPSO finds 'no breach' rather than an even spread of decisions is not absolute proof of IPSO's corrupt nature. Its policy on prominence is.

The Interested Parties
On the issue of the prominence accorded to corrections there are three interested parties:

- The newspaper;
- The complainant;
- The general public.

IPSO INVARIABLY FAVOURS THE NEWSPAPER

It only serves the interests of the newspaper that corrections enjoy a small fraction of the prominence of the offending article, or the proportion of it that breaches the IPSO Code. The interests both of the complainant and the general public require at least equal prominence.

Despite this, IPSO invariably orders that the prominence of the correction should be a small fraction of the offending article, which means that only a small fraction of those deceived by the newspaper learn of the fact. Apart from the failure that this constitutes to bring to the attention of readers that they have been misled, it also means that IPSO's sole sanction is administered with pathetic leniency.

IPSO IS FULLY AWARE THAT THIS POLICY IS UNTENABLE

Leaving aside the fact that such decisions on the prominence of corrections being a faction of that of the offending article (or its errant part) constitute a volte-face from the original editorial decision on the importance of the initial story, there is another monstrous element of dishonesty on the part of the print press.

In selling its advertising, a newspaper applies the clearest measure of prominence by means of its rate cards. Can you imagine an employee of Associated Newspapers trying to explain to an advertiser that the same number of people will read an advertisement that is 10cm in area as one which is 100cm? Yet that is what IPSO is asking complainants and the public to accept, corrections almost invariably being substantially less than 10 per cent of the area of the original.

When you want to advertise with a newspaper you are accorded the prominence that you pay for based on a well-established measurement in the form of a rate card. So according to this measurement, whereupon a story that takes up a page is comprehensively wrong, that page is accorded a monetary value by the paper. So, it should be that the monetary value of the correction in terms of prominence should be no less.

THE UNIQUE IMPACT OF THE FRONT PAGE

Unlike any other page of a newspaper, the front page (and especially its headlines) is viewed by a substantial proportion of the population in the following non-exhaustive ways:

- In hardcopy form; via newspaper stands at railway stations, tube stations, petrol stations, newsagents, supermarkets, being read by fellow passengers on trains, buses, tubes, in cafés, canteens, restaurants, etc.; and in the waiting area of the IPSO offices;
- Held up to television cameras on late evening and early morning news and magazine programmes;
- Read out by radio presenters, both on evening and morning programmes;
- On news apps;
- Disseminated via social media.

It follows then that a banner headline such as the *Sun*'s iniquitous QUEEN BACKS BREXIT will have been read by tens of millions of individuals, the vast majority of whom would not dream of either buying the *Sun* or visiting its website. Not one of these individuals would see a small strip at the foot of a front page published weeks later referring to an adverse IPSO adjudication which will not be visible to anyone other than a sharp-eyed purchaser of the paper or visitor to its website; still less would they read that adjudication on any inside page.

The remedy ordered by IPSO on this vital constitutional issue was therefore virtually useless because the other 99 per cent of those who saw the headline would not have seen the correction.

THE FACTORS APPLIED BY IPSO ON THE ISSUE OF PROMINENCE

On the issue of prominence, the factors which IPSO have set out in its Codebook are as follows:

- The seriousness and consequences of the breach of the Code.

- The position, the prominence and the extent of the breach of the Code.
- The public interest in remedying the breach of the Code.
- Any action taken by the publisher to address the breach of the Code.

These are all reasonable provisions. But just as the Code is a good document which IPSO elects not to enforce, in reality these factors are deployed by IPSO solely to diminish the prominence of the correction or apology.

THE FAILURE OF THE LAY MEMBERS OF IPSO's COMPLAINTS COMMITTEE TO DO THEIR JOB

There are lay members on IPSO's Complaints Committee. The impression that I have when reading adjudications is that they either do not turn up, or spend their time fast asleep – particularly when the issue of prominence arises.

How can any truly independent person possibly believe that a front page which in letters you can see from a couple of hundred yards away tells rank lies to the general public, a correction on page two is sufficient, which will mean that it is seen by only a minute fraction of those who have been misled by the front page, can possibly constitute 'due prominence'?

Imagine the care that newspaper editors would apply to get their stories right if 'due prominence' were interpreted according to the plain meaning of the words; how many errant front-page stories would be published if they had to be corrected on the front page? The lay members of the IPSO committee which determines prominence issues should hang their heads in shame for being party to a policy which leads to the misleading of so many people on a daily basis. Here they are:

Miranda Winram is chair of the IPSO Readers' Panel and former Head of Strategy and Insight and board member of Forest Enterprise. She was a non-executive

member of the Nursing and Midwifery Council's Fitness
to Practice Committee and is currently a public appointee
to the Lord Chancellor's Advisory Committee for the
North East.

Asmita Naik is an independent consultant on international
development and human rights following a career at the
United Nations in Geneva in the 1990s. She serves as a
magistrate and on various professional regulatory bodies. She
co-authored a 2002 landmark report which put the issue of
sexual exploitation by aid workers on the global agenda and has
been involved in measures to strengthen oversight of the aid
sector since then.

Helyn Mensah is a barrister specializing in intellectual
property law at 33 Bedford Row chambers. She has experience
in a broad range of intellectual property matters and has
advised a number of well-known domestic and international
clients. In addition to her practice, Helyn sits as a member
of the Strategic Governance Panel to the new English
non-household water retail market and chairs its General Data
Protection Regulation Committee.

David Hutton spent 22 years as a senior leader in secondary
schools, initially as deputy head and then as head. He
represented fellow headteachers on Suffolk's Schools Forum,
chaired the governing body of a special school and was a
founder member of the Ipswich Opportunity Area board. He is
also a qualified Ofsted inspector.

Andy Brennan was a deputy director in the National Crime
Agency and, prior to this, a senior police officer in the West
Yorkshire Police, where he held positions as the Head of the
Homicide and Major Enquiry Team and Head of Professional
Standards and Counter Corruption Unit. He was awarded the
Queen's Police Medal for services to policing and the public
in 2012.

Nazir Afzal was chief crown prosecutor for the North
West of England and has prosecuted some of the UK's most

high-profile cases, including child sex abuse in Rochdale in 2012. More recently, he has worked as an international expert on extremism and radicalization and is a member of the Manchester Mayor's Commission for Cohesion. Nazir was awarded an OBE for his work with the Crown Prosecution Service and involvement with local communities.

These people do one of the most important jobs in the country; one at which they fail dismally. The whole nation loses out as a consequence.

Giving evidence to the Culture, Media and Sport Committee

Shortly before the Leveson Inquiry I appeared before the Culture, Media and Sport Committee which was taking evidence on the future of media regulation. I had recently acted for Peaches Geldof (sadly, one of three young female clients who have passed away through the course of my career, the others being Caroline Flack and Amy Winehouse – all three of which were relentlessly hounded by the tabloid press). A tabloid newspaper had covered its front page with the headline: 'PEACHES GELDOF – SPEND THE NIGHT WITH ME FOR £5,000'. You do not have to be of a particularly toxic mindset to gain the impression that it was not her services as a DJ that she was offering for this sum.

I complained to the then PCC which accepted the headline was misleading and upheld the complaint. However, it permitted the newspaper to publish a correction the size of a large postage stamp on its page two – an utterly absurd interpretation of the same 'due prominence' stipulation which was in the old PCC Code as it is in the current IPSO Code.

When my turn came to give evidence I first held up the front page of the offending newspaper and all the members of the committee – who were a few yards away from me – could read it with ease. I then held up the front page of the newspaper in which the correction had been published and was told that none of them could see the correction. I explained that was because it was not on the front page. It was clear by the reaction of the committee that some scales were beginning to fall from their eyes.

I then held up the inside page of the newspaper on which the publication had carried the correction. Again, I was told by the committee that they could not see it and I had to point it out with my finger. Needless to say, they still could not read it. I explained that the public could read the offending front page at petrol stations, tube stations, mainline stations, newsagents or on news apps, held up to camera during evening news programmes, reviewed and held up to cameras at morning news programmes, read out on radio stations, etc.; the vast majority of whom will never have purchased the newspaper, not even a substantial proportion of the readers will have picked up the correction when it was eventually published as it was in a small box on the inside page.

To my delight, in *Private Eye*'s coverage of the meeting I was branded a 'smug git', from which excellent invective I took that that fine publication had no reasoned arguments to rebut mine.

DESPITE ALL THIS, IPSO HAS ITS USES

Nonetheless, as I explain later in this book, the IPSO processes, imperfect though they are, are still capable of producing a reasonably worthwhile and inexpensive remedy in a media crisis if you know how to deploy them (*see also* pages 237–41). As I also explain, an IPSO complaint may carry a tactical value in an ongoing media crisis. The press will be cautious about re-running a story which is the subject of an ongoing complaint.

IPSO's 'PRIVATE ADVISORIES'

The *Editors' Code of Practice* explains the process whereby IPSO will send a note to those titles that it regulates at the request of someone who is the subject of harassment:

> 'IPSO staff will either advise complainants what they should say to journalists who they believe are harassing them, or alert editors directly to the fact that a complaint has been received. In some cases IPSO will contact individual publications or groups of publications to make them aware of people's concerns that the Editors' Code is being breached or may be breached, via a 'private advisory' notice. The informal alerts issued by IPSO are advisory only and are not binding. The press makes its own judgments according to the circumstances. But an editor who ignored a desist request would – in the event of a complaint – need to be able to demonstrate to IPSO a sound public interest reason for doing so. Desist notices have proved effective in dealing with scrums caused by particularly intense media interest in a major story. The widely distributed advisory notices serve to alert all media organizations – even those not regulated by IPSO – about concerns over a story and are usually heeded by press and broadcasters alike.'

How 'PRIVATE ADVISORIES' WORK
IN PRACTICE

The Section 2 privacy provision obviously has primary importance pre-publication because, once lost, privacy is impossible to recover. This is one of the sections where occasionally and in a narrow set of circumstances IPSO can be persuaded to send out an 'advisory' – i.e. a notice which will impact publications that are part of the IPSO regime.

The only circumstance where I have managed to do that is where a celebrity has a baby which they do not want photographed. They are always however asked for an assurance that they themselves will not subject the child to publicity – such as for a *Hello!* article. The harassment provision at Section 3 is another one which IPSO can sometimes be persuaded to act upon with a degree of promptness. The legal equivalent of this provision is the Protection from Harassment Act 1997.

My experience both of PCC and IPSO 'private advisories' is that they are nearly always adhered to. The one occasion on which a magazine stepped out of line concerned paparazzi pictures of a celebrity client's newborn. But it turned out that this was due to an administrative error, which meant the magazine in question had not received the notice. When I brought the notice to the attention of the magazine it ceased any further violations. If IPSO were the regulator that it claims to be, then it would not just issue 'advisories', it would issue stipulations that its Code be obeyed.

IPSO refuses to step in to protect vulnerable children

On one extraordinary occasion I sought IPSO's help in the form of a 'private advisory' when I was acting for the very concerned parents of two distressed and traumatized children, who were afraid that an article, which was being threatened by a national title about a serious incident in which one was a victim, would cause them to suffer further trauma and psychological injury. IPSO flatly refused to intervene to protect these children, suggesting – as an alternative – that if the article was published and damage was caused, I could then make a complaint to IPSO! Fortunately, in that case I was able to persuade the newspaper to drop the story by sending them direct pleas from the parents themselves. That should however not have been necessary.

THE NATIONAL NEWSPAPERS THAT ARE NOT PART OF THE IPSO REGIME

The national titles which have shunned the IPSO regime are the *Guardian*, the *Financial Times* and the *Independent*, which have their different reasons for not signing up to IPSO. They have also shunned the Leveson-compliant IMPRESS, despite the fact Lord Leveson made his recommendations after an extensive inquiry where there was an army of QCs, barristers and solicitors representing the press; and one junior barrister and a couple of solicitors representing victims of press abuse.

I approached the *Guardian* with a request for it to tell me where it stood, both on IPSO and IMPRESS. This is what it told me:

'While GNM [*Guardian News & Media*] believes that IPSO is an improvement on the PCC, it did not and still does not believe that it demonstrates sufficient independence from its members, so we continue to remain outside it. Given that, our primary concern has been to ensure that readers can get access to swift redress through an efficient complaints process. As you know, we seek to ensure this through the longstanding and successful readers' editor system, which has been strengthened further with the establishment of an independent review panel, which mirrors the role of the PCC/IPSO in allowing a review of decisions made by the readers' editor against the GNM Editorial Code.'

Apparently the *Guardian* thinks that by appointing its own complaints adjudicator that 'demonstrates sufficient independence from' the *Guardian*. This is what it says about IMPRESS: 'while we have welcomed it in terms of providing an alternate form of protection for small publishers and micro-blogs, we didn't like the way it arrived on the stage via the Royal Charter and the Press Recognition Panel'; not a very convincing reason for its refusal to be regulated by a Leveson-regulated body and electing rather to be regulated in a way which it would severely criticize were it the judge rather than the defendant in this issue. Though the paper does not entirely mark its own homework as it has appointed its own invigilator, it would be quick to point out the lack of credibility of its complaints process were the boot on the other foot.

I asked the *Independent* for a comment on these issues, but my request was declined. My best guess is that the primary reason for the *Independent* titles to stay out of the IPSO system is the cost, funding being a serious issue there as I learned when I co-defended a defamation claim for them – I was acting for the *Huffington Post* (*see also* Chapter 9).

All the Fleet Street titles have in common their flat refusal to be regulated according to the Leveson principles, which enjoyed the near-unanimous approval both of Parliament and the UK. Either they have taken refuge in IPSO, which has no democratic, independent or regulatory legitimacy; or they have set up forms of in-house regulation which are even less credible than IPSO. This is a sad indictment of the print press, and one that cannot be ignored in undertaking crisis management.

THE *GUARDIAN*

A Google search will take you to a page entitled 'Editorial Guidelines, *Guardian* News & Media Editorial Code'. At the time of writing these pages have not been updated since 2011 and, accordingly, rather than the IPSO Code, they cite the now-obsolete PCC Code.

Despite the fact that the *Guardian* does not apparently care enough about its self-regulatory processes to keep them up to date, there is an encouraging opening to this section: 'A newspaper's primary office is the gathering of news. At the peril of its soul, it must see that the supply is not tainted. Our most important currency is trust. This is as true today as when C P Scott marked the centenary of the founding of the *Guardian* with his famous essay on journalism in 1921.'[6]

---

[6] https://www.theguardian.com/news/audio/2021/may/05/from-the-archive-special-cp-scotts-centenary-essay-podcast.

There then follows a section entitled 'Professional practice'. To its credit, the Editorial Guidelines include this provision: 'Copyright: journalists should not use content from non-authorised third-party sources – whether pictures, text or other media, without obtaining the necessary permission.' There are a number of less reputable titles which routinely infringe copyright – especially in photographs – while at the same time fiercely enforcing their own intellectual property rights.

It says this about errors: 'It is the policy of GNM to correct significant errors as soon as possible.' Again (so far as I am aware) uniquely in Fleet Street, it includes a 'fairness' provision: 'The voice of opponents no less than of friends has a right to be heard ... It is well to be frank; it is even better to be fair (C P Scott, 1921).'

Here is another worthy provision from the *Guardian* Editorial Values pages: 'Verification – Trust in the authenticity and reliability of our sources is essential.' This provision also resonates with the relevant law in the form of defences to defamation claims.

One of the appendices for the Editorial Guidelines is the old PCC Code which in most respects does not differ substantially from the IPSO Code. C P Scott's 1921 essay is also one of the appendices in which he says 'Comment is free, but facts are sacred', which is also both a cardinal free speech principle and a good summary of the law which treats the two differently – as does the IPSO Code.

My experience of the *Guardian* is that of all the Fleet Street titles it conducts itself the most ethically. It strays sometimes driven by its overt political agenda, but its courage in holding its peers to account is much to its credit.

THE *FINANCIAL TIMES*

The *FT* has its own Editorial Code and page to set out its provisions. Unsurprisingly, there are plenty of provisions concerning financial journalism. At its commencement is this commitment on the part of the *FT*: 'It is fundamental to the integrity and success for the *Financial Times* that we uphold the highest possible standards of ethical and professional journalism, and that we are seen to do so.'

We are told that employees of the *FT* are obliged by means of their contracts of employment to comply with its Code and we are told that the IPSO Code is the one to which they are contractually obliged to comply. However, complaints go not to IPSO but to the '*FT* Complaints Commissioner'.

Another unique aspect of their Code is set out at Paragraph 5, which states that except in exceptional cases: 'Telephone conversations should not be recorded unless all parties to the conversation give consent.' Departures are permitted in legitimate public interest situations: 'Employees must not do so without first having obtained clearance from *FT* in-house legal counsel and either the Editor or the Deputy Editor or the relevant *FT* title.' A stark contrast with the approach at News UK and Mirror Group Newspapers.

Section 6 of the *FT* Code could usefully find its place in those of other less reputable newspapers, which begins at 6.1 with this provision: 'It goes without saying that no *FT* employee or contributor should commit any criminal offence in relation to journalism or any other matter.' Again, News UK and Mirror Group Newspapers, please note.

There are various specific legal provisions then cited. Unlike the *Guardian*, the *FT* Editorial Guide was updated in 2020 and uses the current edition of the IPSO Code rather than the old PCC Code. The *FT*'s 'Editorial Complaints Commissioner' is Christina Michalos QC from the leading media set 5RB. She describes it as an 'appellate regulatory role'. Time will tell how independent she is of the newspaper, which will emerge from her willingness to uphold complaints against the title.

The principal practical provision in the *FT*'s Code is headed 'Accuracy', which says this: 'It is our primary endeavour to publish information that is accurate and will not mislead readers. You must take care not to distort information either by disingenuous phrasing or by omission. If you think that material has been published or broadcast that is wrong, you should notify your line manager and the managing editor's office. It may be necessary to take corrective action, but you should not generally proceed without discussion.'

THE *INDEPENDENT*

The *Independent*'s Code is generally consistent with the IPSO Code, but in a number of ways it is stronger. In particular, its banning of material which is 'disingenuous' would be a most welcome addition to the IPSO Code since this form of abuse is endemic at certain Fleet Street titles, as it is sadly on the part of their lawyers.

On the subject of 'Corrections', the *Independent*'s Code says, 'If we publish information that turns out to be inaccurate, it is important that the position be corrected. Sometimes an online amendment may be suitable, at other times it may be appropriate to publish a correction or apology in print or broadcast a statement.'

There is no complaints officer or equivalent at the *Independent*, presumably for the same financial reasons, so you will probably – as I have – find yourself dealing with the Head of Legal at the paper.

BLOOMBERG

Though not a Fleet Street title, Bloomberg gets a dishonourable mention because, during the time of writing this book, it published something about a business client which was manifestly wrong; partly because it had not bothered to contact the client prior to publication. It then flatly refused to correct it via correspondence, which was replete with intellectual dishonesty. On that basis, and its refusal to submit to any form of independent regulation, its claim to be a premium source of business information looks dubious.

IMPRESS

There is a press regulator which is compliant with the moderate and reasonable stipulations made by Lord Leveson at the conclusion of his inquiry. This is the body to which all of Fleet Street should sign up, but which it flatly rejects. IMPRESS says of itself on its website:

> 'IMPRESS is at the vanguard of a new, positive future for news publishers, ensuring quality independent journalism flourishes in a digital age. We help to build understanding and trust between journalists and the public – and provide the public with trusted sources of news.
>
> We are a regulator designed for the future of media, building on the core principles of the past, protecting journalism, while innovating to deal with the challenges of a digital age.
>
> What we do:
>
> - Award a "Trust in Journalism" mark to publishers that meet our standards for membership.
> - Maintain a progressive Standards Code, and assess any breaches of this code by our members.
> - Provide an arbitration scheme which is free to all parties and protects publishers against the risk of court costs and exemplary damages.
> - Support the development of news publishers, through partnerships and collaboration.
>
> Who we are:
>
> - Key to our role as an effective regulator is our governance and structure.
> - Our board is made up of journalists, experts and specialists with a wide range of experience and skills. They are selected by an Appointment Panel. We also maintain a Code Committee, that is responsible for advising the board on our Standards Code.

- IMPRESS has a small staff team, based out of our office in central London.
- We are growing quickly. Our membership is currently made up of more than 150 regulated publications from across the country, collectively reaching more than 15 million readers each month.

How we operate:

- As a regulator for the public, IMPRESS is committed to openness and transparency in everything we do.
- All IMPRESS's audited annual reports are made public and can be downloaded from the IMPRESS website.
- Our organisational and regulatory policies are also published on our website.'

THE REGULATION OF BROADCAST CONTENT

The Ofcom Code

For all broadcasters there is the Ofcom Code by which you must abide if you are going to keep your licence. The BBC has its own Producer Guidelines which supplement the Ofcom Code.

Ofcom is required by statute to draw up a code for television and radio, covering standards in programmes, sponsorship, product placement in television programmes, fairness and privacy. This is known as the Ofcom Broadcasting Code. The key provisions of the Code for our purposes are Section 5 ('due impartiality and due accuracy'), Section 7 ('Fairness') and Section 8 ('Privacy').

Paragraph 7.1 of the Ofcom Code states: 'Broadcasters must avoid unjust or unfair treatment of individuals or organisations in programmes.'
Paragraph 7.9 provides as follows: 'Before broadcasting a factual programme, including programmes examining past

events, broadcasters should take reasonable care to satisfy themselves that:

- Material facts have not been presented, disregarded or omitted in a way that is unfair to an individual or organisation; and
- Anyone whose omission could be unfair to an individual or organisation has been offered an opportunity to contribute.'

Paragraph 7.11 is a key provision for dealing with potential PR crises emanating from a broadcaster: 'If a programme alleges wrongdoing or incompetence or makes any other significant allegations, those concerned should normally be given an appropriate and timely opportunity to respond.'

I set out in Chapter 7 how these provisions can be deployed either to prevent a PR crisis happening altogether, or at the very least to mitigate its potential damage. One of the joys of dealing with broadcasters is that you generally get at least a number of days to deal with a potential PR crisis – time which can be put to immensely good use if you know what you are doing. As a species they are also rather more evolved than Fleet Street in the sense that they exhibit some sense of their responsibility towards their viewers.

The Ofcom Code applies equally to Sky, Channel 4, Channel 5 and ITV, as it does to the BBC. I can tell you, as a programme lawyer, that the provisions of the Code are taken very seriously (and rightly so) by broadcasters.

SKY

The different mindset of which I have spoken in the broadcasting world is well illustrated by this paragraph from the first page of the Sky guidelines: 'Our reputation as a news organisation is our most valuable asset so it is vital that our journalism is always of the highest quality. If it isn't, and we make bad decisions, poor judgements or mistakes – we put at risk the trust of our audiences and the potential damage will resonate well beyond the newsroom. So, we must ensure that we always act responsibly, with our customers' and potential customers' interests at heart.' Amen to that! Fleet Street, please note.

The role of the programme (editorial) lawyer is set out helpfully in these paragraphs:

'Sky News has its own dedicated lawyer based in the newsroom to assist with all legal issues who is available to provide training and specific advice. Regular media law training sessions are held throughout the year and it is your responsibility to attend these to ensure that you remain up-to-date with the law.

Where there may be doubt or uncertainty over a legal issue – in the first instance check with the Head of Home News or Head of International News as appropriate.

Remember: if in doubt, do not proceed, broadcast, or publish.

Always refer upwards.'

Here some important provisions in the privacy section: 'We cannot and should not breach anyone's privacy without an exceptionally good reason. Any proposal to do so must be authorised in advance by the Director of Newsgathering or the Director of Content and our legal team.'

Sky is also rightly concerned to comply with its data obligations: 'Sky News takes data protection seriously and it is important that we comply with the General Data Protection Regulations ... fines for data breaches are significant.'

Sky is also alert to the risks of being the subject of a defamation claim: 'There are a number of defences to defamation . . . Each of these sound relatively simple but they are not; they are highly complicated legally – and we may end up having to argue our case in a court of law. Therefore any story involving potential defamation needs to be subject to rigorous editorial scrutiny ... If you become aware of a potentially defamatory statement on any platform then it should be raised immediately with the relevant Head of Home or International News and our dedicated lawyer. If in doubt, refer up.'

Section 11 deals both with accuracy and impartiality – the latter being a concept entirely absent from any of the 'regulations' applicable to Fleet Street. The first sentence reads: 'Sky News must always be duly impartial and duly accurate.' As the guidelines warn, 'The consequences of mistakes are extremely serious from a reputational and financial perspective.'

These provisions also apply to Sky News journalists when they use social media. They are obliged to do so, 'Responsibly, adhering to the principles of fairness, accuracy, impartiality, legality. You are personally responsible for the content you publish on social networks.'

CHANNEL 4

The Channel 4 Factual Programme Guidelines include these important provisions:

'Right to reply:

- If a programme makes significant allegations against an individual or organisation, those concerned should be given an appropriate and timely opportunity to respond.
- Right to reply letters are drafted by the producers with input from the commissioning editor and lawyer. They should include the programme description, transmission date where known, sufficient information to enable those concerned to reply properly and a reasonable deadline for the reply …
- The timing of a right to reply will depend upon the nature and seriousness of the allegations, the extent to which they are already in the public domain and the ability of those concerned to respond …

The programme should fairly represent the substance of the individual or organisation's response, but it is not normally necessary, in the interests of fairness, to reproduce a response in its entirety.'

ITV

ITV's editorial and compliance policies and procedures are set out in its *ITV Producer's Handbook*. Again, viewer trust is stressed: 'ITV has a relationship of trust with our viewers. If programmes fall short of our high standards, this can damage our reputation and our relationship with our viewers.'

This is what it said on the issue of accuracy: 'Respect for due factual accuracy is essential. ITV programmes should not be economical with the facts simply to make a show more entertaining or convincing.'

For our purposes, the paragraphs under the heading 'Opportunity to Contribute and Right of Reply' are of greatest value. Here are the key paragraphs:

'It is a basic cornerstone of professional journalism to offer those against whom significant allegations are made an opportunity to respond. It is also often a requirement for the legal defence of a libel claim (*see also* Chapter 4).

Practice 7.11 [of the Ofcom Code] says, "If a programme alleges wrongdoing or incompetence or makes other significant allegations, those concerned should normally be given an appropriate and timely opportunity to respond".

When offering that opportunity, producers must provide sufficient information about the content of the programme and in particular all of the material allegations made against the person or organisation to enable them to respond. You should also always give a date by which you expect a response.

There is no requirement to provide all of the actual evidence you have collected against them, for example, covertly filmed footage. In most cases it will be sufficient to give a *full, fair and accurate summary* of the allegations to be made and a full explanation of the evidence you have supporting them ...

It should be remembered that seeking responses is often part of the fact-checking process, and programmes sometimes can and must change significantly as a result of responses received. Therefore producers should not complete editing before receiving these responses, and should not leave sending out "right of replies" letters too late in the production process.

Where a response to significant allegations has been provided, care must be taken to reflect that response fairly in the programme. That does not mean that the response has to appear verbatim, nor that material irrelevant to the issues needs to be included. But the gist of the response, insofar as it is relevant to the issues and allegations made, must be reflected fairly [emphasis added].'

As with all other broadcasters, ITV programmes are all 'legalled out' by compliance/editorial lawyers. In the media law section there are some important indicia as to ITV's appetite for risk: 'Defending a libel action is expensive, whichever side is eventually successful, and very demanding and time-consuming for the producers, reporters and participants involved in the programme, who may be called to give evidence.'

The BBC

The BBC has its own 'Editorial Values and Standards' document. It is worth setting out the introductory paragraph:

'The BBC's Royal Charter specifies the BBC's Mission, which is to act in the public interest, serving all audiences through the provision of impartial, high-quality and distinctive output and services which inform, educate and entertain. It also establishes our independence from government, guarantees our editorial and artistic freedom ...'

Later in the document, you will find this: 'In our journalism in particular, we seek to establish the truth and use the highest reporting standards to provide wide coverage that is fair and accurate.'

The 'Accuracy' section stipulates, '... all BBC output, as appropriate to its subject and nature, must be well-sourced, based on sound evidence, and corroborated ... The BBC must not knowingly and materially mislead its audiences. We should not distort known facts, present invented material as fact or otherwise undermine our audiences' trust in our content. We should normally acknowledge serious factual errors and correct them quickly, clearly and appropriately.'

BBC's Watchdog gets it badly wrong

Ofcom regulation does not guarantee accuracy from the broadcast media. As an example of the public interest being engaged when the media gets it wrong, one of my corporate clients had invested substantial sums of money in creating a sugar-free and pH-neutral version of one of their popular children's drinks, which therefore had no deleterious effect on children's teeth. It had then spent another large sum of money launching it. BBC's Watchdog then ran a package suggesting that in fact the drink would damage children's teeth.

On my instruction by the substantial multinational which owned the brand, I asked if I could spend a day with the scientists so that I could establish who was right. By the end of the day, I was left in no doubt that the BBC's science was faulty. The effect of this misinformation was that mothers trying to dissuade their children from ruining their teeth by imbibing sugary drinks were robbed of any motivation to substitute this safe product for one which would definitely rot their children's teeth. For that reason alone the company had a civic duty to correct the misinformation – in addition to obligations to its employees and shareholders to protect its business. Alas, in that case, I was not instructed prior to transmission. Had I been, I believe I would have prevented the broadcast of this errant Watchdog package.

BROADCAST AND PRESS CONTRASTED

As I hope is clear, the editorial and ethical values espoused by the broadcast industry are significantly superior to those of the print press, which is why I always recommend people to place more trust in broadcast news than print journalism. That is also the reason why you will have a great deal more threats to reputation emanating from the print press than from the broadcast media. The key purpose however of my outlining of all of these regulatory provisions (for both the print and broadcast media) is that they should form the building blocks of challenges to threatened stories which are both inaccurate and damaging to your reputation/brand.

It is worth adding that the National Union of Journalists' Code obliges journalists to 'strive to ensure that information disseminated is honestly conveyed, accurate and fair'. The NUJ Code also requires journalists to do their 'utmost to correct harmful inaccuracies'. No ex-journalist who has genuinely defected to the PR profession should therefore have any hesitation in deploying the available regulatory and legal mechanisms to prevent publication of falsities – and to correct them if they occur.

THE LEGAL LANDSCAPE FOR CRISIS PR

The other essential building blocks for effective crisis PR are the various legal provisions which are there for the protection of both corporate and individual reputations, along with confidentiality for companies and privacy for individuals. Where the issue of corporate libel occurs vis-à-vis one of the major Fleet Street titles there should never be any reluctance for a large corporation to flex a little financial muscle. The current turnover of Associated Newspapers (over £50 million), Reach (£700m) and News Corp (over $10 billion).

Few of my corporate clients enjoy that degree of financial clout, though thankfully some exceed it. But these news organizations employ teams of lawyers and legally trained personnel and use their purchasing power to drive down the charge-out rates of those solicitors' firms which, in exchange for regular instructions, are prepared to act free of any moral or ethical restraint.

DEFAMATION – THE KEY POINTS

Defamation is subdivided into libel and slander. Libel is in a permanent publication such as newspapers and television programmes, along with social media. Slander is primarily spoken and unrecorded words. There are special rules that apply to slander which make such actions rare and difficult.

Defamation proceedings must be started within a year of publication and, where the publication is online, a year from the date it was first published. There is a theoretical power for a court to extend the limitation period, but in practice it rarely does.

The required elements
A defamatory publication is one made about you to a third party which:

- lowers you in the estimation of right-thinking people;
- substantially affects in an adverse manner the attitude of other people towards you or has a tendency to do so; and
- has, in fact, caused, or is likely to cause, serious harm to your reputation.

The court determines the first two elements by distilling out of the article what we in the trade call the 'defamatory meaning' of the publication. That process is begun by the court determining what is called the publication's 'natural and ordinary meaning'.

To introduce this slightly esoteric concept I cannot do better than borrow the analysis of the judge in charge of the Media and Communications List, Mr Justice Nicklin. This makes me feel rather old as I used to instruct him when he was a young junior at the libel bar in the early 1990s. I inadvertently instructed him for his first-ever trial and well remember his turning around to tell me this as the judge walked in on the first day. He went on to win the case at a canter.

I will set the scene with this helpful analysis, which I expand below, taken from one of his recent judgments, which I have annotated to make it easier for a non-lawyer to understand:

'Natural and Ordinary Meaning: the Law

1. The law I apply in relation to resolution of the first preliminary issue [which I am going to determine] is well settled ... The meaning that any individual publishee [i.e. reader] understood a particular Email to bear, whilst likely to be highly material to any assessment of serious harm to reputation under s.1 Defamation Act 2013 [which stipulates that you must establish that your reputation has either suffered serious harm or is likely to do so], is nevertheless irrelevant to the determination of the [separate issue of the] single natural and ordinary meaning [of the publication].

2. The approved practice when the court [i.e. the judge] comes to determine the natural and ordinary meaning of the publication in a defamation claim is to read the words complained of without reference to the parties' contentions or submissions. The purpose of doing so is "to capture the Judge's initial reaction as a reader". Only after doing so have I considered the parties' pleaded cases and arguments [on the issue of natural and ordinary meaning].

3. In [a recent case] Warby J [Nicklin J's predecessor as the judge in charge of the Media and Communications List] noted:

   [24] The overriding rule when dealing with both meaning and the question whether a statement is factual or opinion is always a question of how the reasonable reader would respond to the words.
   [25] One important principle that follows from that overriding rule is the need to avoid unduly elaborate

analysis. This is a constant theme of the jurisprudence. It applies to the arguments of Counsel, to the reasoning process undertaken by the Judge, and to the reasons to be given by the judge when explaining his or her conclusions on meaning.

4. As to whether a meaning found by the court is defamatory at common law [before the statutory requirement of "serious harm" comes to be assessed], the principles are [that a] statement is defamatory of a claimant if, but only if, (a) it imputes conduct which would tend to lower the claimant in the estimation of right-thinking people generally; and (b) the imputation crosses the common law threshold of seriousness, which is that it substantially affects in an adverse manner the attitude of other people towards him/her or has a tendency to do so.'

There is no better way of understanding the law of defamation and privacy than to read some judgments. The media list judges are all of high quality, experts in the field, and their judgments are usually well-readable by lay folk. For example, the judgment of Mr Justice Eady in the Max Mosley v *News of the World* case of 2008 is fascinating. Its subject matter is an orgy and it contains at least one good joke; it also gives a lurid insight to the degree to which that newspaper was rotten to the core.

It is also in stark contrast to how the *News of the World* reported the judgment, which was grossly misleading – as reports by newspapers of litigation which they have lost often are. Associated Newspapers published a report of the breach of confidence claim successfully brought by Michael Douglas and Catherine Zeta-Jones against *OK! Magazine* over publication of pictures of their wedding with a headline claiming that they had lost the case.

I set out an anatomy of a civil legal claim in Chapter 9. There are, however, some distinctive elements of a defamation claim and some important principles underlying this fascinating area of law which it will be helpful to understand.

THE PUBLICATION IS ASSESSED AS A WHOLE

In the law of defamation, the court does not look just at a specific sentence, headline or paragraph of a piece, but the article or programme as a whole. If there are a number of subject matters, then the court will look at the whole of the portion of the programme or article which refers to the claimant rather than any section within it, though the rest of the programme may impact on how the portion which is the subject matter of a libel action is interpreted. If you are featured in a programme which has racism at its subject matter, anyone watching the minutes which feature you is likely to have this in mind.

A court will not look at a headline of an article in isolation. It applies what is called the 'bane and antidote' principle. That means that in some circumstances a headline may imply something which the reader of the entire article will realize is not what the publication as a whole is communicating. This is what the judge in charge of the Media and Communications List has said on this issue:

> 'The publication must be read as a whole, and any "bane and antidote" taken together. Sometimes, the context will clothe the words in a more serious defamatory meaning (for example, the classic "rogues' gallery" case). In other cases, the context will weaken (even extinguish altogether) the defamatory meaning that the words would bear if they were read in isolation (e.g. bane and antidote cases).'

Again the court will look at the article as a whole, but where there is a strong implication of wrongdoing in a headline and that is not clearly dispelled in the rest of the article, then as a whole the article may be potentially defamatory in that it lowers the claimant in the estimation of right-thinking people. A court will then go on to decide whether the article has inflicted or is likely to inflict the requisite 'serious harm' on the claimant. If not, you may still have a lesser remedy from Section 1 (i) of the IPSO Code which obliges newspapers not to publish headlines not supported by the text.

How the defamatory meaning is established

A court will distil what is called the 'defamatory meaning' or 'sting', which it does by first establishing what is called the 'natural and ordinary meaning' of the publication. This is often the most critical issue in a defamation claim and accordingly will generate vigorous debate in front of a judge.

As you can see from the extract taken from Nicklin J's judgment, the court will not allow in any evidence as to what people thought the article or publication at issue meant. This is determined entirely by reference to what is known as a legal fiction – the impression that the publication will have on a 'reasonable reader'.

It has been judicially determined that the hypothetical reasonable reader is not naïve, but they are not unduly suspicious. They can read between the lines. They can read in an implication more readily than a lawyer and may indulge in a certain amount of loose thinking. But they must not be avid for scandal and not select one bad meaning where other non-defamatory meanings are available. A reader who always adopts a bad meaning when a less serious one is available is not reasonable. To always adopt the less derogatory meaning would also be unreasonable; it would be naïve.

This is primarily determined by a judge reading the article or watching the programme, which as Nicklin J observed, he or she will do before they have heard the arguments on either side as to what the defamatory meaning is, so the judge can form their own view independent of any arm-twisting by the opposing lawyers. Here are some other of his guidance points:

- In order to determine the natural and ordinary meaning of the statement of which the claimant complains, it is necessary to take into account the context in which it appeared and the mode of publication.
- No evidence, beyond publication complained of, is admissible in determining the natural and ordinary meaning.
- The hypothetical reader is taken to be representative of those who would read the publication in question.

The court can take judicial notice of facts which are common knowledge, but should beware of reliance on impressionistic assessments of the characteristics of a publication's readership.

- Judges should have regard for the impression the article has made upon them themselves in considering what impact it would have made on the hypothetical reasonable reader.

Serious harm

The 'serious harm' stipulation was brought in by the 2013 Defamation Act, which was effectively the codification of the otherwise largely judge-made law of defamation. It is the product of intense lobbying by Fleet Street to make libel claims more difficult; which should have been told that it can secure its preferred changes to the law of defamation only when it agreed to be regulated by a Leveson-compliant entity.

When the act came into force on 1 January 2014, we practitioners wondered what, in practical terms, the 'serious harm' stipulation would mean in practice. The answer came in a case called Lachaux, which made it all the way to the Supreme Court. One of the defendants was the *Huffington Post*, for whom I acted (*see also* Chapter 9).

The bar is set low

To the disappointment of the print media in particular, the 'serious harm' threshold was set low in that case in that it is perhaps less of a bar both to individual and corporate claimants than I suspect was originally anticipated when the statute was passed. It was clear to me as I sat in front of the Court of Appeal in Lachaux that the three judges sitting in that court did not like the statute and were determined to limit its impact.

The obvious advantage of being able to make a credible threat of a libel action is because a defamation claim carries with it the threat of a financial penalty in terms of both damages and costs. Often a threatened publication by a national newspaper or broadcaster concerning products or services being provided by a company is likely to generate 'serious harm' to a company's finances, so that claim can be credibly set out as means of discouraging such a publication.

THE DEFENCES

If you are able to establish that a publication is defamatory of you both in the common law and statutory senses, the question then arises as to whether there are one or more defences available to the publisher. There are three primary defences to a defamation claim:

1. Truth – where a defendant can show that the allegations are substantially true (2013 Defamation Act, Section 2).
2. Honest opinion – where the publisher can show that the statement was one of opinion, the statement indicated the basis of that opinion, and an honest person could have held that opinion on the basis of any fact which existed at the time that the statement was made. The defence will fail if the defendant is shown not to have held the opinion (2013 Defamation Act, Section 3).
3. Publication on a matter of public interest – where the statement was or formed part of one on a matter of public interest, and the defendant reasonably believed that publishing the statement was in the public interest, taking into account all the circumstances of the case (2013 Defamation Act, Section 4).

An important recent judgment[7] has highlighted how the court will assess whether this defence is made out. There are three issues for the court to determine under Section 4(1):

i) was the statement complained of, or did it form part of, a statement on a matter of public interest? If so,

[7] https://www.5rb.com/wp-content/uploads/2021/07/Lachaux-v-Evening-Standard -2021-EWHC-1797-QB-Final-for-hand-down.pdf

ii) did the defendant believe that publishing the statement complained of was in the public interest?

iii) If so, was that belief reasonable?

This is the guidance which Mr Justice Nicklin gave as to how the court would go about answering (iii), in particular:

> 'Defendants seeking to rely upon such a belief – whether in support of a s.4 defence or otherwise – would be well advised to ensure that they are able to demonstrate that they reasonably believed that publication would be in the public interest and how, and with whom, that was established at the time. My confidence that the Court is not setting unrealistic targets is also somewhat fortified by the fact that the current Codes of both IPSO and IMPRESS both impose substantially the same requirements as the old PCC Code of Practice ... The IMPRESS Code, particularly, contains a very clear explanation why it is good practice to retain contemporaneous documents that record important decisions about the public interest justification for publication. As an explanation of the importance of contemporaneous documents, it can hardly be bettered.'

At the same time, they identify a 'need' for editors to (a) 'demonstrate' that they believed that publication would serve, and be proportionate to, the public interest; (b) 'explain' how they reached that decision 'at the time'; and (c) 'demonstrate' that their belief was a reasonable one.

THE ABSURD EFFECT OF THIS DEFENCE

I suspect that Mr Justice Nicklin has set the bar high here because an extraordinary aspect of the Section 4 defence is that it can arise in circumstances where the allegations engage the public interest, are ones of fact (rather than of opinion), defamatory and untrue. Once invoked by a newspaper or broadcaster the effect of the defence – whether it succeeds or not – is that a court will not even address the question of whether the allegations are true or false.

So it is that a newspaper can publish highly defamatory allegations which have not a shred of truth, and then elect not to substantiate them by deploying this defence which merely scrutinizes the decision to publish them. At that point – even if the defence fails – the claimant's right to vindication is extinguished, as is the public's right to learn whether the allegations are true or false. All that the court determines is whether those responsible for the publication of the allegations 'reasonably believed [their] publication ... was in the public interest'; not the slightest use to society as a whole.

This is utter madness; the law being an ass of the first order. Even the IPSO Code – written by and for the press and for its benefit – does not have a public interest exception to the obligation both not to publish inaccurate or misleading material or the obligation to publish a correction should that occur.

As Lord Hobhouse said:

'No public interest is served by publishing or communicating misinformation. The working of a democratic society depends on the members of that society being informed not misinformed. Misleading people and the purveying as facts statements which are not true is destructive of the democratic society and should form no part of such a society. There is no duty to publish what is not true: there is no interest in being misinformed. These are general propositions going far beyond the mere protection of reputations.'

This defence should only impact damages and potentially reduce them to a modest sum where a newspaper has done all it can to get a story right, but still gets it wrong, and where it accepts that it has got it wrong. In fact, such a defence already exists in the form of the 'offer of amends', outlined on page 93.

What it should not do is rob us all of the right to learn that we have been misled about a matter of public interest; that being obviously contrary to the public interest – as it is for a person or entity to suffer wrongful reputational damage for which there is no remedy.

This defence is also incompatible with Article 8 of the European Convention on Human Rights (ECHR), which stipulates:

There shall be no interference by a public authority with the exercise of this right except such as is in accordance with the law and *is necessary in a democratic society* in the interests of national security, public safety or the economic wellbeing of the country, for the prevention of disorder or crime, for the protection of health or morals, *or for the protection of the rights and freedoms of others* [emphasis added].

It is manifestly not 'necessary' for the protection of immense commercial entities such as News Corp and Associated Newspapers that they are free to defame individuals and companies and then be immune from a judicial finding that they have both done so, robbing individuals and companies of their right to vindication.

As to the 'rights and freedoms of others'; Article 10 enshrines the right of individuals to receive information – in this case that they have been misled, a right of which they are robbed by this provision.

The law has taken this course – that this defence serves the public interest – despite the fact that it is irreconcilable not only with the IPSO Code, but also those published by the NUJ, IMPRESS and Ofcom, all of which say that where inaccurate stories are published, they should be corrected. You might think this was blindingly obvious, but apparently our legislators (and those advising them) have fallen under Fleet Street's thrall and believe they know better.

There are two other important defences to defamation claims:

1. Privilege: public policy requires that certain statements should enjoy special protection. Some statements made in Parliament or during legal proceedings will enjoy *absolute* privilege. Others such as employment references will enjoy *qualified* privilege, which means the defence will fail if the statement can be shown to have been 'malicious';

i.e. mendacious or with a reckless disregard for its truth
or falsity.

2. Offer of amends: the level of damages can be cut by up
to a half if a publisher makes what is called an 'offer of
amends' which is essentially a white flag which a publisher
can wave where they concede that the allegations at issue
are false, they offer to publish a correction and to pay
damages and costs. If the amount of damages cannot be
agreed, then it can be determined by a judge who will
do so by first assessing what the level of damages would
have been without the offer of amends, and then apply
whatever discount they think is appropriate, which can be
up to 50 per cent.

DAMAGES

Estimating the amount of damages which would be awarded in
a defamation (or privacy) claim is difficult and normally done by
a specialist barrister, though an experienced solicitor can make
an informed estimate. All you can do is to look back at earlier
awards, especially those from the Court of Appeal and Supreme
Court, and make an informed guess about what sum will be
awarded in your case.

Unusually, in the law of defamation, the award is based not only
on the virulence of the allegation and the extent of publication,
but can be increased if the defendant's conduct *after* publication
is deemed to have been aggravating and to have exacerbated the
damage caused by the original publication.

The current maximum in what we call 'general damages'
is around £300,000, which would only be awarded for a very
serious allegation which had been published (say) on the front
page of a national newspaper. Where there has been financial loss
which can be directly attributed to a defamatory publication, this
can be recovered by means of 'special damages', for which there
is no top end.

DEFAMATION INJUNCTIONS

It is in theory possible to secure an interim injunction to prevent the publication of defamatory material. In practice it is very difficult because on the basis of a seminal nineteenth-century case called Bonnard v Perryman, where a defendant credibly asserts that they will rely on a substantive defence, then a court will not grant an injunction.

At the end of a libel trial in which the claimant is successful, the court will usually make an order in the form of a permanent injunction that the defeated defendant must not repeat the allegations at issue.

My tiny footnote in legal history

I have only once attempted to secure a libel injunction to prevent publication of defamatory material. In that instance I was successful because I was able (with the assistance of a skilled QC) to persuade the duty judge that my client was the subject of blackmail.

My client was a high-profile female musician whom a journalist had accused of going 'commando' at one of her concerts. She had successfully protested to the newspaper at this story and had thereby incurred the ire of the freelance journalist who had sold the story when he lost his fee, which he was then trying to extort from her.

After securing the order preventing him from publishing some very ugly material about my client, I secured my minute footnote in legal history by obtaining permission from the judge to serve the injunction by email. Fortunately, he was a young member of the judiciary who was clearly tech-savvy and he accepted our argument that since we only had an email address for the journalist there was no reason in principle for him to decline our application to serve the order via that address.

I later learned that this was the first such order to be made anywhere in the world and it received some modest press coverage back in 1996. It was ironic that the greater success was getting the injunction rather than securing what was then a novel means of serving it.

When the unfortunate journalist checked his emails and discovered that one of them was a High Court order to which he was subject, he duly caved and withdrew his threats.

There is a useful provision at Section 13(1) of the Defamation Act 2013, which allows a court to order that a non-party cease communicating a defendant's defamatory statement. Such orders are made after a claimant has obtained judgment, and can be against a website operator requiring them to remove the statement (Section 13(a)), or any person who was not the author, editor or publisher of the defamatory who is distributing, selling or exhibiting material containing the statement (Section 13(b)).

Business libel – a case study

A good example of what can be achieved in a PR crisis via legal action was the work I did for Ayman Asfari who was the Chief Executive of Petrofac, a leading provider of services to the oil and gas industry in the Middle East.

The *Mirror* had wrongly alleged that Mr Asfari and his company Petrofac were covertly dealing with the brutal Assad regime in Syria. The context of this allegation was a forthcoming general election and Mr Asfari was a Tory donor – he was therefore inevitably in the crosshairs of the leftist *Mirror*.

My instruction came from a leading corporate PR firm after the City law firm from whom they initially sought advice had advised there was no legal solution. They were entirely wrong. A few weeks later, I was able to read a Statement in Open Court exonerating both Mr Asfari and Petrofac[8].

---

[8] https://inforrm.org/wp-content/uploads/2015/03/asfari-v-mgn-sioc.pdf

THE STATEMENT IN OPEN COURT

A Statement in Open Court is the usual outcome of a defamation claim which has been settled by the publisher by negotiation. It is a formal statement made in front of a judge at the High Court which formally exonerates the claimant in a defamation claim.

Here are the key paragraphs:

1. Mr Asfari is the Group Chief Executive of Petrofac ... Mr Asfari is also a supporter of the moderate opposition to the regime of Bashar al-Assad.
2. The *Daily Mirror* published two articles referring to Mr Asfari ...
3. The last paragraph of the Articles stated that Mr Asfari had 'courted controversy by dealing with [the] Assad regime in Syria ...' The print version of the Article also referred to a photograph which featured both Bashir al-Assad and Mr Asfari.
4. Mr Asfari has never had any dealings with the regime.
5. Mr Asfari abhors the violence being meted out to his fellow Syrians by the Assad regime and has committed much of his time and resources to alleviate that suffering. He was therefore profoundly distressed and angered at the suggestion made by the *Daily Mirror* that he in any way had supported the regime of Assad.
6. Mr Asfari is however grateful that the *Daily Mirror* has now agreed to the reading of this statement on his behalf retracting the allegation and that it has also agreed to make a contribution to the humanitarian work in Syria.

MAKING INFORMED DECISIONS ABOUT
DEFAMATION CLAIMS

There are a number of key things to understand about the law of defamation in addition to the strict legal principles if you are to be able to make an informed decision about whether and how to deploy it as part of crisis PR; and fully to understand any advice that you are given.

Defamatory meaning

The first is that many defamation claims turn on what the court determines to be the 'defamatory meaning' of a programme or article which is the essential allegation complained of. This therefore needs to be authoritatively determined right at the outset of any prospective claim, the success or failure of which may well turn on this issue.

In the bad old days, newspapers in particular would conduct disingenuous defences of libel claims by advancing bogus defamatory meanings which they claimed that the article (because this was especially the practice of newspapers) bore. This was to grind down the claimant financially and psychologically by forcing them to go all the way to a trial.

DIRTY TRICKS FROM THE *MIRROR*

This was done some years ago by the *Mirror* in the defamation claim which I successfully brought against it for the bestselling author Paul McKenna, where it was only on the first day of the trial, after proceedings which had run for well over a year, that the *Mirror* finally undertook a volte-face and admitted that it had made an allegation of dishonesty against Paul McKenna about his US doctorate – an allegation which the trial judge found was unfounded. Prior to that, the paper had disingenuously denied any allegation of dishonesty; something for which both its internal and external lawyers must take responsibility.

EARLY DETERMINATIONS OF MEANING

Such malpractice is no longer an option because the practice in the Media and Communications List is for the court to determine the defamatory meaning of a publication at the outset of a libel action, which can lead to the early settlement.

If a judge determines that the defamatory meaning of the publication is grave, then the defendant may conclude that there is no viable defence to a claim. If the judge determines that it is mild, and accordingly the defendant is likely successful to defend the claim, then the claimant may throw in the towel.

An alternative means of resolving a defamation dispute is where both sides (with good sense and goodwill) agree jointly to instruct a senior barrister to determine the defamatory meaning of a publication which allows both sides to consider their positions with the benefit of that decision, which is made binding contractually. I have used such a method successfully in the past to secure an early resolution of a defamation claim.

Nearly all libel actions settle

The second key point about the law of defamation is that many defamation claims are resolved prior even to the issue of proceedings, let alone at a point at all proximate to a trial. A well-judged and carefully drafted Letter of Claim (which in any event is required by the Civil Procedure Rules) can be sufficiently persuasive to entice a newspaper or broadcaster to save themselves the expense of the issue of proceedings and resolve a defamation claim prior to that point being reached.

The secret is often to offer reasonable settlement terms at the outset. For companies, for whom damages will rarely be a priority, its entitlement to damages can be traded in whole or in part (as can costs) for the potency of the exoneration.

An alternative to a libel claim, and one which does not require the proof of 'serious harm', is a 'malicious falsehood'. The difficulty is that unlike in the law of defamation you have to prove both that the allegation is false and that it was made maliciously (i.e. there must be some form of bad faith). This is the UK equivalent of the US law of defamation, which is why so few defamation claims succeed in the US.

BREACH OF CONFIDENCE AND PRIVACY –
THE KEY POINTS

A common cause of a media crisis is where confidential information belonging either to an individual or a company finds its way into the media. There are sound legal and policy reasons why the media should have the liberty to report information sourced from whistle-blowers, though some are merely hell-bent on revenge for a perceived wrong and may make false or selective leaks which give a misleading picture of the company as a whole.

My work for TV legend Noel Edmonds and a substantial number of other Lloyds Banking Group fraud victims was only made possible by the courageous actions of a whistle-blower, whom the bank then treated unlawfully and brutally. It was later obliged to apologize and compensate her. Shame on both their internal and external lawyers who did the bank's dirty work for it, exhibiting the same lack of personal integrity which I have often encountered in lawyers working for Fleet Street.

Even before the Human Rights Act 1998 came into our legislature, when I was a partner at Schillings, we would use the law of breach of confidence as a means of protecting the privacy of individuals. This became much easier when Article 8 was brought fully into our legal system via the Human Rights Act and for a period there was a flurry of what the media mis-described as 'super injunctions' but were in fact merely privacy injunctions.

THE QUEEN'S ETCHINGS MAKE LAW

The law of breach of confidence goes back to the nineteenth century. A wonderful early example was when in 1849 Prince Albert brought an action which began the development of the law of confidence in the UK.

Both Queen Victoria and Prince Albert had ordered a series of prints of etchings which they created together as a hobby. The printer ran a series of illicit copies of the etchings, which were about to be exhibited – which means, like the Duchess of Sussex in her claim against the *Mail On Sunday* in 2021, they could also rely on a breach of copyright claim.

Prince Albert sued for the surrender of the etchings and for the prohibition of the exhibition. The court granted him an injunction restraining the malefactors from exhibiting the unauthorized copies.

When Parliament passed the Human Rights Act 1998, which formally brought into our law the European Convention on Human Rights, it was in complying with their obligation to give effect to Article 8 of the Convention that our judiciary began to fashion a law of privacy – much to the outrage of Fleet Street and in particular Associated Newspapers, who wrongly blamed 'unelected' judges for the development of a law of privacy. The press hates the fact that, unlike politicians whom they can intimidate with threats that they will be driven out of office, they wield no such power over judges.

Naomi Campbell v the *Mirror*

The court's jurisdiction around breach of confidence and privacy are in some senses distinct, but they also overlap, which meant that early privacy cases while the law was unclear would also be brought as breach of confidence claims. It would take a major case brought on the basis of privacy to achieve the situation that we now have: a fully-fledged law of privacy. This case was courageously brought by supermodel Naomi Campbell against the *Mirror*, whose editor at the time was Piers Morgan. The paper had reported Naomi's attendance at a Narcotics Anonymous meeting.

As the son of a probation officer who spent most of his professional life dealing with the fallout of drug abuse and helping addicts to get clean, I well understand why Naomi was determined to take this claim forward – though she inevitably incurred the ire of Fleet Street in so doing, most of whom made the self-interested claim that the action was a mistake – just as they did in the Duchess of Sussex case against the *Mail on Sunday*.

Piers Morgan's much-vented outrage at being sued by a mere celebrity is expressed at length in his book *The Insider*. In his evidence at the trial he said that Naomi had been 'invading her own privacy for years'.

Naomi Campbell won at first instance. All three Court of Appeal judges found against her and the case ended up at the House of Lords (the predecessor to the Supreme Court). I remember standing over the fax machine as it printed out the speeches of the five Law Lords. It came to the point where two had found in her favour and two had found in favour of the newspaper, so the outcome of the claim turned on the last judge, who found in her favour.

Had that case failed, then (as Fleet Street earnestly hoped) the privacy jurisdiction of the High Court would have been strangled at birth. As it was this was the case which created a viable law of privacy in the UK.

One of the extraordinary aspects of the case is that the mathematically minded among you will have noticed that Naomi Campbell won her case despite only four of the nine judges presiding finding in her favour and five finding against her. That illustrates how difficult this area of law is even for practitioners who are expert at it. I spoke to a top QC about a possible privacy claim for a music mogul, who admitted that such was the state of the law even he did not know what the correct answer was in that instance.

BREACH OF CONFIDENCE IN THE BUSINESS CONTEXT

A breach of confidence case in a business context brought in 2007 illustrates what can and cannot be the subject of a privacy injunction. Lord Browne of Madingley sought an interim injunction against Associated Newspapers to prevent them publishing a 'kiss and tell' by his former partner, a Canadian called Jeff Chevalier, with whom he had had a four-year relationship. The *Mail on Sunday* threatened to publish revelations about his personal life and relationship with Chevalier.

The court distinguished between information in which Lord Browne did and did not enjoy a reasonable expectation of privacy. The information that Browne had used company resources to set Chevalier up in business was information of the type on which the shareholders and board members had a right to make a judgment. Conversely there was a reasonable expectation of privacy in private conversations in a domestic context between Browne and Chevalier about Browne's relationship with his colleagues. The bare fact of the relationship was not subject to a reasonable expectation of privacy. The revelations forced Lord Browne to resign early as BP's chairman.

THE DIFFERENT APPROACHES OF IPSO AND THE LAW ON THE ISSUE OF PRIVACY

If you are raising an issue about your privacy to a regulator, another factor taken into account is the extent to which you have already disclosed the relevant information.

This is Paragraph 2 (ii) of the IPSO Code: 'In considering an individual's reasonable expectation of privacy, account will be taken of the complainant's own public disclosures of information and the extent to which the material complained about is already in the public domain or will become so.'

As this passage illustrates from the judgment of Warby J in the Duchess of Sussex's privacy case against the *Mail on Sunday,* while the courts continue to recognize that public domain disclosures of similar or related information may weaken or undermine a claimant's reasonable expectation of privacy, the law on this issue has evolved:

'At one time it was thought that disclosures in a given "zone" of a person's private life could defeat or at least greatly reduce the weight of any claim for privacy in respect of other information in the same "zone". That theory has been discredited. In the modern law, it is recognised that the respect for individual autonomy that lies at the heart of Article 8 means that the starting point is a person has the right to exercise close control over particular information about her private life: to decide whether to disclose anything about a given aspect of that life and, if so, what to disclose, when, to whom.'

The courts conceive of distinct areas of private information. Those which are often recognized as deserving of greater protection are your sexual relationships, your medical circumstances, significant financial matters and information concerning children. A court will be very willing to step in to protect private medical information.

HAVING TO INJUNCT THE *SUN* TO STOP IT FROM PUBLISHING PRIVATE MEDICAL INFORMATION

A client of mine who is one of the UK's biggest television stars, although young in years, was diagnosed with cancer. For entirely understandable reasons he did not want this to be splashed across the front page of a tabloid – as would have been inevitable.

Tragically only a very small circle of close friends and family knew of the diagnosis, which meant that my unfortunate client was confronted with the fact that he had a traitor in that group who had contacted the *Sun* in an attempt to sell the story. Showing not a scintilla of respect for its regulatory obligations or the human rights of my client, rather than sending the individual away with a flea in their ear, the *Sun* 'bought up' the miscreant and made a concerted effort to run the story.

The *Sun* contacted my client's agent late on a Sunday morning, who then contacted me. Its intention was to publish the story in its Monday edition. I spent the whole of Sunday afternoon arguing with the *Sun* that there was no justification whatsoever of this information being published against my client's will because it was not only directly contrary to Section 2 of the IPSO Code, it was also the most blatant misuse of my client's private information. Unfortunately, because the client is one of the most popular TV personalities in the country, the *Sun* was holding on to this story like a dog would a bone.

By the latter part of the afternoon, it became clear to me that the *Sun* was trying to talk this issue out – i.e. they were maintaining a pretence at negotiation but the intention was to get to a point where it was too late for me to make an application for an injunction and the story would then be published by default.

Around 6 p.m. I explained this to the client's agent and said that a decision needed to be taken at that point whether, if the *Sun* stood its ground, we were going to apply for an injunction. That decision was made and so I lined up one of the country's leading media QCs to ready the application. I duly briefed him and then told the *Sun* that if they did not undertake by 7 p.m. to abandon the story, then an application would be made for an injunction.

No such undertaking was offered and so a telephone application was made to the duty judge, during which time the QC instructed by the *Sun* shamefully put forward a litany of absurd justifications for the newspaper to act in this obviously unlawful way and the judge had little hesitation in granting the injunction. The story did not run and, some days later, the *Sun* grudgingly agreed to undertake not to publish the story and pay my client's costs.

INJUNCTIONS

A great deal of self-serving nonsense is written about injunctions – especially by *parti pris* print journalists who misstate the law either by ignorance or design. These generally centre on the small proportion of them who go wrong for one reason or another. Other journalists have sunk so deeply into a pit of self-serving cynicism that they cling to the nonsensical belief that anyone seeking a privacy injunction must be trying to cover up wrongdoing.

It is true that during the height of the period of the so-called 'super injunctions', several were sought to prevent tales of celebrity adultery appearing in the tabloid press, though I have never sought one for a client in those circumstances. But Article 8 obviously covers sexual activity and where there is no genuine public interest in the lives if not only the sexual partners but many individuals around them be wrecked by a tabloid exposé, then an injunction should obviously be granted.

On the one occasion where one of my clients found themselves potentially at the wrong end of one of these stories I advised what is called a 'soft landing' – i.e. doing a mild version of the story with the client's co-operation. I did this because, though sure that I would secure an injunction at the outset, I was by no means convinced that I would be able to keep hold of it because the incandescent paramour herself was hell-bent on the story coming out. The story passed like a ship in the night and has long since been forgotten.

Securing an injunction, if the facts are right and you prepare the case properly, is reasonably straightforward. But if you are confronted by a tabloid with scant respect for the law (i.e. all of them) and you have a third party who is determined to get the story out there, assuming there is also a dim MP who has no respect for the law or the constitution, you risk ending up like Ryan Giggs or Philip Green.

While always critical of others doing so, newspapers are perfectly happy to deploy this legal remedy when it suits them – as News UK did to permit the 'Fake Sheik' to go on doing his dirty work, such as his appalling treatment of my client, singer Tulisa Contostavlos, whom he wrongly accused of dealing drugs. By a glorious stroke of justice it was he rather than Tulisa who ended up in jail.

THE FIRST INCARNATION OF AN INJUNCTION

The term 'interim injunction' is used because an injunction may have three incarnations. The first is an interim injunction, which may be obtained very rapidly, but will have a very short duration. Such an emergency injunction will be time-limited by the judge to a few hours, or a day or so at most, at which point there will be a second hearing at which (unlike the first) the defendant will have an opportunity fully to argue their case with the benefit of enough time to prepare.

The second stage is also an interim injunction which is obtained where, at that second hearing, the parties argue about whether an injunction should hold the line up to the end of the trial. This is the critical hearing because if at that point the injunction application fails, then, subject to an appeal, confidentiality in the information and/or privacy of the individual is irretrievably lost and the only remedy (if any) will be in damages. If the claimant is successful at that second hearing, the second incarnation of the injunction will hold the line until trial. However, in practice, if a newspaper has thrown everything that it has in at the second stage and failed, it will normally throw in the towel at that point.

The third incarnation is a 'final injunction', which will be awarded to a successful claimant after a trial – as was granted to the Duchess of Sussex against the *Mail on Sunday*. It would probably be better termed an indefinite injunction because a court can always lift it if the defendant goes back to court successfully claiming that because of a material change in circumstances the injunction should be lifted.

An interim injunction (an urgent application to a judge for an order which, in this sphere, prevents publication by a newspaper or broadcaster of confidential or private information) can be obtained at any time of the night or day. The fastest that I ever succeeded in securing an injunction, with the assistance of two excellent barristers, is within an hour of being instructed.

An injunction is what we call a 'discretionary remedy', which means that the court is under no obligation to grant one. If the application is made without notice, the claimant and his solicitors owe particular duties to the court, including that they must make a fair presentation to the court of the material facts and the law relevant to the application – i.e. the court must be told about anything that would incline it not to grant the injunction. Even if the application for an injunction is made on notice, the court will expect a high standard of conduct and disclosure.

An applicant for an injunction will usually be required to give what is called an undertaking in damages. This is a formal undertaking to the court to compensate the defendant for any losses that it has suffered as a result of the injunction being granted at the interim stage should it be lifted at a later stage.

An injunction for the Duchess of York

The most dramatic circumstances in which I ever secured a breach of confidence injunction was when I was acting for Sarah, Duchess of York in a case which was of such worldwide interest that there were film crews outside the offices of Schillings (where I was then a partner). One even managed to fight its way into the reception area. Every stage of it was played out in the press, and where they could not glean information, they simply made it up – a common practice especially but not exclusively in the lower end of Fleet Street. I would repeatedly read things about my work for the Duchess that were complete fiction.

I was instructed to seek an injunction against a publisher which was going to publish a book written by the business partner of the Duchess' financial adviser, with whom she had had an affair, notwithstanding the fact that he had signed a confidentiality agreement. The initial application was made before the duty judge whom at my suggestion was persuaded by the QC that the fact of the injunction should also be kept out of the public domain – the QC being far from sure that we would get such an order. That may have been the first 'super injunction'.

The application for the second stage of the injunction took place on a Friday, where I was quaking behind the QC at the court, convinced my career was hanging by a thread and would crash and burn if I failed to hold on to this injunction in the face of the most vigorous and angry opposition by the lawyers acting for the publisher. Neither the Duchess nor I were spared the vitriol of the publisher's lawyers, whose QC was puce with outrage that the two of us had apparently managed to rob his client of such a huge publishing scoop.

After granting the second stage of the injunction, the judge asked my opponents about the current status of the book. He was told that it was contained in discs which were being flown over from the United States and would arrive during the course of the weekend. Late that afternoon I sent an email off to my opposite number dealing with some housekeeping matters and explaining that I expected to have a copy of the book early the following week as part of the publisher's disclosure obligations.

To my astonishment my opponent emailed back saying that I was not entitled to this material and was only entitled to a copy after it had been edited. As a matter of law this was nonsense since the discs themselves contained the confidential information which was the very subject matter of the claim, the disclosure of the information by the first defendant to his (second defendant) publisher being a flagrant breach of his duty of confidentiality.

Despite my explaining this in words of one syllable, he stood his ground, so I asked if he would at least provide me with an undertaking over the course of the weekend that the discs would not be tampered with and I put him on notice that I would be making an application on Monday morning for an order that a copy of the discs should be made available to me. In so doing I was only asking him to abide by his professional and legal obligations not to tamper with evidence.

To my further astonishment he refused even to give that undertaking so I told him that I was going to make an immediate application for an injunction obliging both him and his client not to tamper in any way with the core evidence in the case. It was an absurd stance to take since in the circumstances we were 100 per cent certain to get the order that we needed. But this is par for the course with a dedicated 'free speech' lawyer – a term which I explain fully in Chapter 4, but a lawyer who I define as dignifying doing the dirty work of unprincipled commercial media outlets by claiming moral high ground to which they have no right.

I needed the order urgently so that it was in place by the time the discs arrived at the defendant publishers. By then it was early evening and all the judges had left the elegant Royal Courts of

Justice in the Strand for home. That meant that we were going to have to make our application to the duty judge, who is available on a 24/7, 365-day basis. He was unlikely to be happy with the defendants disturbing his Friday evening because of their bone-headed truculence.

I rang my long-suffering QC to explain that I was about to ruin his evening because we were going to have to make an application that night for an order obliging the publisher not to tamper with the discs. He invited me around to his elegant home where over a light supper we prepared the application, which we were then to make over the phone in a process whereby we set out our case to a judge, who would then ring the other side and summarize it to them to enable them to respond, which response he passed back to us for our comment before judgment was delivered. However, before that was done, we needed to fax certain key documents to the duty judge. The first problem was that my QC's fax machine would not work. I set about the device with my limited technical knowledge, but managed to fix it.

However, the judge then told us that *his* fax machine had broken and he asked us to fax the immensely confidential documents to his next-door neighbour, where he promised he would be standing over the fax machine. All of this meant that we eventually secured our order at approximately 2 a.m. the following morning.

For an injunction really to bite, it must have what we call a 'penal notice'. That means that there are possible criminal sanctions for anyone who breaches the injunction. For the court order to have that effect the injunction must be served personally. My trainee had long since fallen asleep in his chair, so I sent him home and called a minicab to take me to the offices of the publishers.

When I arrived at the business park where the publisher's offices were located, I was confronted by high walls and a wrought-iron gate around three metres high. By then I had been working for about seven hours to obtain this injunction and I was not going to be defeated in achieving my aim by a mere gate. So I shinned up the side of it and, to steady myself as I swung my legs over it, I put my arms around the large stone ball set on one of the pillars holding the hinges of the gate. To my horror this thing came away in my arms. Turns out it was not attached to anything but merely sat in a cup – rather as does an egg. So I quickly released it, hoping it would not topple down and land on me as my feet hit the ground, feeling rather like Wile E. Coyote as he observes the spreading shadow of the boulder that is about to flatten him.

Mercifully, it did not. So, I hurtled across the quad to try to find the door with the brass plaque indicating that it was the registered office of the publisher. But I had only taken a couple of steps before a battery of lights and alarms went off. I had obviously triggered the security system.

I next expected an Alsatian guard dog (or similar) to attach itself to my behind, so I ran even faster until I found the right door, posted the court order through the letterbox and belted back to the high gate, taking care to clamber over without disturbing the stone ball. I dropped down the other side to see the minicab driver standing next to his car, gazing at me in astonishment, and suggesting that we should probably make a rapid getaway – which we did.

Ryan Giggs and Philip Green

Two instances are often cited where injunctions properly granted by the court were then breached, entirely improperly, by MPs who plainly do not understand the constitutional importance of respecting the decisions of judges – even when they don't agree with those decisions.

Neither Ryan Giggs nor Philip Green were the most fragrant of claimants so their 'outing' by an MP might not seem such a bad thing. However, both MPs fundamentally breached vital constitutional principles, substituting their own judgment for one which had been taken with the benefit of knowing the law and the evidence. An injunction is an important power that the court has to protect the rights of both individuals and companies. When it comes to privacy, in both cases the judges were applying statute – i.e. law passed by Parliament.

Not one of the injunctions that I have secured has failed to have the desired effect and when my advice has been sought about seeking an injunction where I do not think I would be able to hold on to it, I have advised against making the application. Not one of them has been lifted by the court.

The Giggs and Green cases are extremely unusual and are no reason not to seek an injunction when both the law and good sense militate in favour. By their nature most commentators will not be aware of the many privacy and/or breach of confidence injunctions which have had the desired effect.

To illustrate how well these things can work, this is what Mr Justice Tugendhat said at the hearing of the second stage of the privacy injunction that I secured for Tulisa Contostavlos: 'The steps taken have been so successful that, at the time I heard the application, the evidence was that people were making postings on the internet complaining that they could not find on the internet a copy of the video or videos the subject of my order.'

PJS v News Group Newspapers – aka the David Furnish case

Since he has been identified in the Wikipedia entry for this case, I have after some hesitation decided to name David Furnish as the claimant in an important and controversial privacy case which was both misrepresented and misreported by the press at the time it was decided in 2016.

In January 2016 David Furnish applied for an injunction to prohibit publication of the details of a sexual encounter between him and two others by the *Sun on Sunday* (aka the *News of the World*). The application was refused primarily on the basis that some overseas publications accessible in the UK had already published the story.

David Furnish applied to the Court of Appeal and was initially successful in overturning the High Court decision. However, in

April 2016 the Court of Appeal changed its mind and ruled that the injunction should be lifted as the allegations had been published widely both abroad and online, saying, 'Much of the harm which the injunction was intended to prevent has already occurred. The court should not make orders which are ineffective.'

David Furnish then appealed to the Supreme Court, which in May 2016 decided to reinstate the injunction by a majority of 4–1. These were the observations of Lord Mance:

'3. The Court is well aware of the lesson which Canute gave his courtiers. Unlike Canute, the courts can take steps to enforce its injunction pending trial. As to the *Mail Online*'s portrayal of the law as an ass, if that is the price of applying the law, it is one which must be paid. Nor is the law one-sided; on setting aside John Wilkes' outlawry for publishing *The North Briton*, Lord Mansfield said that the law must be applied even if the heavens fell: R v Wilkes (1768) 4 Burr 2527, 98 ER 327 (347). It is unlikely that the heavens will fall at our decision. It will simply give the appellant, his partner and their young children a measure of temporary protection against further and repeated invasions of privacy pending a full trial, which will not have been rendered substantially irrelevant by disclosure of relatively ancient sexual history.

[...]

32. the starting point is that (i) there is not, without more, any public interest in a legal sense in the disclosure or publication of purely private sexual encounters, even though they involve adultery or more than one person at the same time, (ii) any such disclosure or publication will on the face of it constitute the tort of invasion of privacy, (iii) repetition of such a disclosure or publication on further occasions is capable of constituting a further tort of invasion of privacy, even in relation to persons to whom disclosure or publication was previously made – especially if it occurs in a different medium ...

Privacy is not necessarily lost because the information has appeared in other news outlets.'

Breach of confidence and privacy distinguished

The key thing to understand here is the distinction between a breach of confidence claim, which this was not, and a privacy claim, which this was. Despite the fact that the information at issue was to some extent already in the public domain, the Supreme Court (rightly) treated every further disclosure of private information an infringement of David Furnish's rights, and that of the children of his marriage to Elton John as protected (the court observed) by the IPSO Code.

It was blindingly obvious to the court – though apparently not to much of the media – that there was major qualitative difference between the modest level of publicity that the information had already received and it being splashed all over the front pages of the *Sun on Sunday*. The court made it clear that the civil wrong of misuse of private information protects different values to breach of confidence and an injunction can still have value even if the information it protects is known to some.

The majority of the Supreme Court was strong on the lack of public interest in 'kiss and tell' stories, even questioning whether the mere reporting of sexual encounters with a view to criticizing those involved falls within the concept of freedom of expression under Article 10 at all.

Three more recent privacy cases

In Sicri v Associated Newspapers 2020, Warby J considered whether publication by the *Guardian* of the claimant's identity in connection with his arrest diminished his right to privacy and held that 'a person's privacy rights are not defeated by the mere fact that information is accessible'. He also noted there was minimal overlap between the readership of the *Guardian* and *Mail Online* and so the *Guardian* article did not 'end the claimant's reasonable expectation that the defendant would not publish the Information' – i.e. his identity and arrest in connection with the Manchester terrorist attack.

In the second case, Associated Newspapers subsequently agreed to pay substantial damages after revealing that an actress had made a rape complaint to the police about a film director. Sand Van Roy said she intended to stay anonymous – which is her legal right in France, as in England – but had the choice taken from her (she has now waived her right to anonymity).

Details of the complaint were reported in the French press and the *Mail Online* was the first UK title to report the allegation. The *Mail Online* accepted the articles were a breach of Van Roy's privacy as she had not waived her right to anonymity. The third case is ZXC v Bloomberg, where the issue before the court was whether a right of privacy exists for the subject of a police investigation before either arrest or charge. Agreeing with the first instance judge and Court of Appeal the Supreme Court found that it did, though it accepted that there may be specific circumstances where the public interest required the information to be made public.

How an ill-judged injunction application can backfire

A large American corporate client rejected my advice and sought an injunction against a broadcaster, which application was turned down both at the first instance and the Court of Appeal.

I had spent most of a precious Sunday afternoon explaining to the client, whose employees had been recorded by secret cameras operated by a leading current affairs programme joking about how they were ripping off customers, that there was no way that I would be able to secure an injunction to prevent transmission of the programme. I took my fulminating clients in detail through the relevant principles of the law of breach of confidence and explained that even though the material was confidential because the footage was taken in their offices, the public interest defence which the broadcaster would undoubtedly run would defeat any breach of confidence claim.

When my advice was rejected I took the client to a consultation with the country's leading QC in the field of corporate breach of confidence, the awesomely clever Antony White QC, who acted for Associated Newspapers in the breach of confidence/privacy and copyright action brought by the Duchess of Sussex. Surely, I thought, the client would listen to him.

Both he and an excellent junior counsel robustly confirmed my advice that any application for an injunction would fail. He was promptly fired, as to my great relief was I. I had no desire to try to prevent the transmission of an excellent investigative journalism programme by which serious corporate misconduct was going to be exposed.

So it was that another partner at my then firm (Lewis Silkin) took my place for the hearing itself, where predictably the application was rejected and given short shrift by the Court of Appeal later that day. Needless to say, the broadcaster then trailed the programme as the one which the company in question had tried to ban.

THE IMPORTANCE OF NON-DISCLOSURE AGREEMENTS IN BREACH OF CONFIDENCE CLAIMS

There is one other important aspect of the law of breach of confidence which anyone contemplating seeking an injunction should know. In ordinary circumstances, and as illustrated by the failed application for an injunction that I have just described, the test which the courts use is whether there is a sufficient public interest in the information coming into the public domain for the obligation of confidentiality to be set aside.

However, where the confidential information is about to enter the public domain in breach of a non-disclosure agreement, the courts apply a different test – which is whether there is sufficient public interest in the information coming into the public domain to override the public interest in parties to an agreement being obliged to abide by that agreement. That is a much stiffer test for a defendant to such an application to overcome.

That is one of the reasons why HRH Prince Charles succeeded in securing summary judgment of his breach of confidence claim against Associated Newspapers and securing an injunction to stop it publishing his *Hong Kong Diaries*.[9] That meant that the court found in his favour

[9] HRH Prince Charles brought the case when the *Mail on Sunday* published extracts of a dispatch titled 'The Great Chinese Takeaway' which he had written about the transfer of sovereignty of Hong Kong to China, and had been handed out to friends. The Prince described the Hong Kong handover ceremony as an 'awful Soviet-style' performance and 'ridiculous rigmarole' and the likened Chinese officials to 'appalling old waxworks'.

without requiring the case to go to a full trial at which he would have had to give evidence. A fascinating twist to the Duchess of Sussex case is that the judge, Warby J, was the QC who unsuccessfully defended Associated Newspapers in that case brought by her father-in-law.

This order is made where a judge concludes that on the evidence before him there is no realistic chance of a defence succeeding. It was the same order as was made by Warby J in the Duchess of Sussex's claim against the *Mail on Sunday*. The same order can be made against a claimant where a judge finds that there is no possibility of a claim succeeding, in which case he will grant summary judgment to the defendant.

Trouble with a laptop

I cannot leave the subject of protecting confidential information without recounting one unconventional way by which I did so. One of my clients, a well-known film and TV actor, had decided to upgrade his laptop. He then advertised his old laptop for sale on eBay. Unfortunately, he had not wiped the contents before selling it. This handsome gentleman lived a colourful lifestyle and some of that was recorded in photographs which were on the laptop when it was sold.

Fortunately the individual who was sold the laptop contacted my client, rather than a tabloid newspaper. The client's agent contacted me and asked me to deal with the issue. I advised that there was the conventional legal route of seeking an injunction, but thought that in these circumstances a better option was to make a generous offer to the individual who had purchased the laptop, to buy it back, and to include a strong non-disclosure agreement in the contract for the purchase of the laptop.

I reasoned that this individual did not want to deal with the tabloid press (mercifully) and that if he came away from the transaction feeling that he had reaped a good reward for his honesty, then he would abide by the agreement. If I had used the legal process there was always the risk that the story would break to the great embarrassment of the client. That was more than 10 years ago and the material on the laptop has never seen the light of day.

4

How the Media Operates

As I have explained, the British media is far from being homogenous and this must be factored into crisis PR work. There is a pronounced and divergent scale of ethical and editorial values in both its institutions and individuals.

One thing which informs my crisis PR work is whom I am dealing with at the other end, both in terms of the entity and the individual. Though they tend to be of the same hue as their employers, the character of the managing editors along with the internal and external lawyers will significantly impact my approach to dealing with a potential adverse story, as will the media entity for which they work.

At one end of the scale is a *Guardian* editorial lawyer who is ex-BBC, with whom I have worked for years on publication issues, and who was a co-speaker with me at a media conference and said that she welcomed a warning from me if her title was about to publish something incorrect. It matters to her that her title gets things right. At the other end there are the editorial lawyers who are not remotely concerned whether what their title publishes is true or false, who in turn will seek out external lawyers who will be content to assert under their letterhead that the earth is flat – I have received many such letters – if that is what they are instructed to do.

THE COMMON FACTORS

There are however some common elements to all the commercial news media outlets:

- They are nearly all to a greater or lesser degree bound by some form of internal and external regulatory code, and an important recent judgment has highlighted the risks of departing from those codes.
- They are all bound by certain legal provisions, principally the laws of defamation, privacy and copyright.
- These regulatory and legal provisions have been created by government and/or the media industry for the very purpose of protecting the rights of those who would otherwise fall victim to mistreatment by the news media, and to protect the public from being misled by the news media.
- These provisions are however of virtually no use to those confronted by possible ill-use by the news media unless they are invoked.
- In order to monitor their compliance with the applicable codes and laws, news media outlets employ lawyers and compliance officers, and train journalists in those laws and regulations.
- Virtually every element of journalistic content that you see or hear from the news media has been assessed as to whether it is compliant with the applicable regulations and laws.
- The primary role of the person undertaking that responsibility is to assess risk – i.e. how likely is it that the paper/broadcaster will be held to account for this story via the available regulatory and/or legal forums; and if so, what is the likely outcome?
- There are a number of factors taken into account in that risk assessment, one being the track record of this company or individual in taking steps to protect their brand/reputation/privacy. Where this has been done assiduously in the past, the story becomes high risk and will therefore be least moderated and possibly dropped altogether.

- By contrast, if that company/individual has consistently failed to hold publishers/broadcasters to account when they have been targeted, then the story will be deemed low risk and be liberally 'legalled' accordingly. This may also mean that a story initially legalled with a degree of caution may be reiterated at a later date in a more virulent form if no challenge is forthcoming.
- Another factor in the mind of the individual doing the 'legalling' is the level of resources enjoyed by the prospective objector to the story. A huge multinational or high-net-worth individual will be treated with much greater caution than (say) a small company or reality star – unless they are a Kardashian.
- The perceived risk of publishing a story will rise dramatically if the individual tasked with 'legalling' it receives a clear signal that the story is to be subject to robust scrutiny by someone of their own skill set, with the real possibility of the veracity of that story being challenged (in whole or in part) in some regulatory and/or legal forum.
- At very least that will prompt a more cautious editing of the story, which is likely to lead either to the gravity of the allegations being diminished and/or some of the more serious ones being dropped. It may result in the story being dropped altogether if the challenge is administered with sufficient detail and cogency.
- The only type of PR practitioner who can achieve such a quantum leap in perceived risk to a publisher/broadcaster is a PR lawyer. This is not only because they have the required skill set, but also because their pre-publication deployment sends the clearest possible signal that this company/individual is serious about protecting their reputation/brand/privacy.
- The likelihood of a publisher/broadcaster adhering to their regulatory and/or responsibilities is greatly increased if they are provided with a credible deterrent from breaching them.

THE WIDELY DIVERGENT ATTITUDE WITHIN
THE MEDIA TO RISK

In deciding strategy both prior to and during a media crisis, another key factor to take into account is the appetite of this broadcaster or this publisher for risk. If you are a PR professional, you need either to know or at least be able to assess this informedly if you are to best serve your client; as it is if you are making your own crisis PR decisions.

The media grows ever more diverse and its attitude to risk covers a wide spectrum. No broadcaster or publisher wants to be embroiled in a defamation or privacy claim – with the possible exception of Associated Newspapers which seems to enjoy flexing its financial muscles in the courts; just as it enjoys flexing its editorial muscles via its news pages, website, social media and in the high corridors of power.

Defending litigation and (to a lesser extent) regulatory disputes take up precious legal, managerial, creative and financial resources – as I know because I have done it. But as a media publisher, if you want your factual content to have some bite, then you must be prepared to invest in some risk. Many smaller publishers/broadcasters have insufficient finances to allow them such a luxury. On the whole, book publishers are very risk averse.

Media publishers have widely divergent attitudes to litigation, depending on a number of factors:

- Finances;
- Editorial agenda;
- Editorial mindset;
- Editorial lawyers' agenda and mindset.

FLEET STREET

In Fleet Street there is a wide divergence of attitude towards litigation risk. At the reasonable end of the scale, you have titles like the *Guardian* and the *Independent*. Both will make considerable efforts to avoid having court battles – partly because of their relatively low hubris quotient and the modesty of their finances. Titles like the *Star* and the *People* are run on shoe-string budgets and therefore are also very risk averse.

For local papers, specialist and trade magazines, glossies, etc., their finances preclude them from engaging in the luxury of litigation. So if you can present them with a viable claim (i.e. that they are about to or have just published false and defamatory material) and convince them that you are fully prepared to commence proceedings if a correction is not made, then you will normally find them compliant.

At the other end of the scale there is the publisher of the *Mirror* titles which, guided by its aggressive but gaffe-prone legal team, has in the past made catastrophically bad decisions about what cases to fight and what not to fight – especially when it comes to phone hacking – which have massively increased both the financial and reputational damage they have suffered; albeit justly.

Associated Newspapers has both the immense financial resources and ego to allow it the luxury of fighting cases in which they are blindingly obviously in the wrong, as they were in the Duchess of Sussex privacy and copyright claims. Again this is driven ultimately by a hubristic editorial and legal mindset which (as with the *Mirror*) I have encountered on a number of occasions and against which I have had to fight hard.

As for the broadcasters, the rarity of libel or privacy trials concerning broadcasters indicates the lack of appetite on their part for major legal battles – though their better regulation and greater respect for truth is also a major factor in keeping them out of the courts.

The BBC came badly unstuck in the Cliff Richard privacy claim[1] (and rightly so), but is rarely embroiled in legal proceedings over its

[1] Cliff Richard sued the BBC over footage that it had transmitted of a police raid on his home as part of an investigation into historical child sex allegations which proved to be groundless.

content – despite the immense volume of its output. When I have come up against the BBC, either in terms of libel or copyright, they have demonstrated a strong aversion to being sued. When I have worked with them, I have been surprised how editorially cautious they are.

I cannot recall the last time ITV fought any content litigation to trial; similarly, with Sky. I know from my work as a cub lawyer for Channel 4 and subsequent dealings with it, that it is, of all the prospective broadcast defendants, the most likely to take you on in a fight. Its legal team is the toughest among broadcasters.

Taking witness statements from stage-struck criminals

In 1990 Channel 4's *Dispatches* was sued for libel by the business owner of a company which sold garden statuary. The programme alleged that he was arranging items to be stolen to order.

As a trainee I found myself taking a witness statement from a man whose entire shaved head was covered with a spider tattoo, who was telling me how he stole statues to order for the owner of a garden furniture business, who then sold them on to his customers. If a customer asked about a particular piece of statuary which the business did not have, they were asked to come back a few days later – at which point this colourful character was dispatched to go and find one to steal.

I asked whether he was not concerned at giving evidence in defence of Channel 4 which might leave him open to criminal prosecution. But he was apparently so enamoured of being involved in legal proceedings for a TV programme that he said he was not bothered.

The owner eventually abandoned the claim when confronted with this evidence. Not all broadcasters would have fought the claim with such vigour.

THE PRINT AND BROADCAST MEDIA CONTRASTED

The first distinction to be made is between what we still tend to call the 'print' media, despite them being increasingly online broadcasters, and the broadcast media. Broadly speaking, my practice has been to sue the print press and defend the broadcast media. They are two very different species, though slightly less divergent in character than they were when I started out at the beginning of the 1990s. This is to do with both their history and the way in which they are regulated. For every errant news media crisis that you have with a broadcaster, you will have at least 50 with newspapers.

THE PRESS

For that reason I will start with the press. However badly you imagine some sections of the press behave I can assure you that they actually behave worse – as one Fleet Street lawyer once told me over a drink, which they did knowing that my professional experience had already exposed me to activities which are truly shameful and which (as well as many others) has had a devastating impact on clients of mine.

This has included attempted suicide, mental and physical breakdowns, financial ruin, profound trauma and injustice – such as that meted out by the *Sun* to my client Tulisa Contostavlos, who was falsely accused of drug dealing by a journalist at that title; the now-infamous criminal Mazher Mahmood – aka the 'Fake Sheikh'.[2] It devastated her life, but the *Sun* has never even seen fit to apologize to her; let alone compensate her for the wrong done to her.

I have also acted for a client who was the wife of an *EastEnders* star whose special needs son was asked, through the letterbox, about the state of his parents' marriage by a reporter from the same title.

---

[2] Mahmood was convicted of tampering with evidence in the drugs trial of singer Tulisa Contostavlos and jailed for 15 months for conspiring to pervert justice. The *Sun* has refused even to apologize let alone compensate Tulisa for the trauma to which she was subjected by Mahmood.

Another *EastEnders* star client discovered that a *News of the World* reporter was approaching her neighbours, offering them £5,000 in cash if they would sign a statement saying she was a bad mother.

We all know about the tragic suicide of my client Caroline Flack, driven to it by the tabloid press – which seems to be particularly brutal towards women; especially women of colour like Meghan Markle.

The British rightly set a high value on having a 'free press'. We also pay a heavy price for what would better be described as a commercial press which is inadequately regulated, and for which there is therefore a constant temptation to prioritize profit and editorial agendas over its overarching obligation to serve the public interest. The result is that newspapers routinely dish out 'fake news', some of which is shamelessly made up.

The press consistently refuses to be answerable to anyone but itself – the clearest possible indication that very limited trust should be invested in it. There should also be no hesitation on the part of anyone to challenging it when it is about to peddle damaging fiction about you, your products or services.

Much that the press in particular gets away with is because of a lack of knowledge, especially on the part of PR professionals, about the tools and means of deploying those tools to stop companies and individuals from falling victim to fake news. Some of them – especially those who are ex-print journalists – appear to be ambivalent about standing up to a newspaper and telling it that because a particular story is wrong, it has a regulatory and/or legal obligation not to publish it.

If the newspaper is regulated by IPSO, then it owes that regulator a contractual obligation not to publish inaccurate or misleading material. But the protection that its Editor's Code provides is most unlikely to be of any practical use unless, at the appropriate moment, a paper is confronted with this obligation and told that it must abide by it.

Effective reputation management can only be undertaken by the astute deployment of the regulations and laws with which the unruliest element of our commercial media is supposed to comply.

I say this not only on the basis of my experience as a PR lawyer but also as an editorial lawyer – though one who has never sought or undertaken work for a Fleet Street title; not that any of them would hire me!

'YOUR ENEMY STALKS ABOUT LOOKING FOR SOMEONE TO DEVOUR'[3]

The great Christian philosopher C S Lewis said this:

> 'The greatest evil is not now done in those sordid "dens of crime" that Dickens loved to paint. It is not even done in concentration camps. In those we see its final result. But it is conceived and ordered in clean, carpeted, warmed and well-lighted offices, by quiet men with white collars and cut fingernails and smooth-shaven cheeks who do not need to raise their voices. Hence, my symbol for Hell is something like the office of a thoroughly nasty business concern.'

For 'a thoroughly nasty business concern' read Associated Newspapers, News UK and Mirror Group Newspapers. All three are capable of doing their job well, and sometimes do so. Associated Newspapers' outing of the killers of Damilola Taylor was greatly to their credit. But they also exhibit a serial, cynical and cruel disregard for human rights.

The most extraordinary aspect of the Leveson Inquiry was not what emerged in the form of serial criminality on the part of some newspapers – much more of which has emerged since. To anyone who has dealt with Fleet Street for long enough, none of the revelations came as any surprise. It was rather that these activities ever saw the light of day.

Another reason why Fleet Street remains free to abuse its privileges is that it generally operates a strict system of *omertà*[4]

---

[3] Apostle Peter – 1 Peter 5:8
[4] Code of silence among the Mafia about criminal activity.

about its own wrongdoing; with the honourable exception of the *Guardian* which courageously led on the phone-hacking story while under fire from some of its angry peers. Fleet Street also pays vast sums to lawyers to cover up its wrongdoing.

Anyone who has dealt with the tabloid element of the press in particular will be able to give their own accounts of appalling misconduct by some of our popular national newspapers; the real reason why they so vigorously resist any form of effective or independent regulation. I could fill a book of accounts of such activity just taken from my own practice. Just a selection is included in this one.

THE *SUNDAY MIRROR* DRIVES A CLIENT TO ATTEMPT SUICIDE ABOUT WHICH THE *SUN* THEN REPORTS, AFTER BRIBING THE POLICE

Another *EastEnders* client was contacted by the programme's press office on a Friday afternoon to be told that the *Sunday Mirror* was going to 'out' him as a closet homosexual. Whether or not that was true – I believe it was not – it was none of the newspaper's business, rather an entirely private matter for my client.

This was a blow my client could not bear and the following day, after buying himself a knife and a large amount of paracetamol, he booked himself into a hotel where he made a serious attempt to take his own life. Fortunately, later in the day a friend rang him and my client confided in him that he had attempted suicide.

The friend called the emergency services and my client was rushed to hospital and the police were called. An officer then contacted the *Sun*, which paid him £1,000 for the story.

My client was in intensive care on the following Sunday after his stomach had been pumped and his slashed wrists treated, waiting to find out if he would live or die. The doctors had told him that they were not sure whether they had emptied his stomach in time before the paracetamol had been able to destroy his liver.

While waiting to learn his fate he was told by the *EastEnders* press office that they had been contacted by the *Sun* to say that they were going to run the story of my client's attempted suicide in their Monday edition. Is it any wonder that the publishers of the *Sun* are so set against any form of effective regulation – as are Associated Newspapers and the Mirror Group[5]?

The fate of Milly Dowler's parents, shared by countless others

Much condemnation has rightly come the way of News UK for its cruelty towards the parents of Milly Dowler, the teenager abducted and brutally murdered in 2002[6]. The decision by Associated Newspapers to bribe the father of the Duchess of Sussex into providing them with a copy of a deeply personal letter to his daughter and then weaponizing him as a witness against her in the subsequent proceedings has not attracted the same level of opprobrium in the British media as its relentless criticism of the Sussexes for a seemingly endless list of much lesser failings. This is how those standards play out in practice.

THE ASTONISHING CRUELTY OF ASSOCIATED NEWSPAPERS

One late December night I was on stage at Holy Trinity Church Brompton, where I was playing bass in a jazz quintet for one of their Alpha course[7] suppers. Playing tenor sax was the legendary Steve Gregory, who among other stellar work, played the iconic solo on George Michael's 'Careless Whisper'.

---

[5] Mercifully my client survived and went on to make a full recovery. I secured a six-figure sum for him in damages against the Metropolitan Police.
[6] *News of the World* journalists accessed Dowler's voicemail after she was reported missing, giving her parents false hope that she was still alive. The resulting outcry contributed to the closure of the paper and led to a range of investigations and inquiries into phone hacking and ethics in British media.
[7] The Alpha course is an excellent introduction to Christianity which has been adopted by Christian denominations worldwide: https://www.alpha.org/.

At the end of our second set, one of the curates came up and asked me to ring a client who he said was extremely distressed. She had not been able to reach me because I had switched off my phone while playing the gig, because previously I found myself playing bass with my left hand and holding the phone with my right advising on a Duchess of York privacy claim.

My client – a talented actress – had rung HTB (as it is popularly known) not because she knew I was there that evening, but because she knew that I was often there and she could not reach me at home. I have no idea how she managed to get through so late in the evening. I immediately rang her back. She was evidently in a very bad way. I told her to meet me at my flat, which was only a mile or so away from hers. She sat on the floor of my living room literally shaking with fear. I made her some cocoa and listened as she told me her story.

Over the last few weeks she had been meeting up with a *Daily Mail* journalist who she thought was courting her. He had initially contacted her for a story. Caroline Quentin's agent Sharon Hamper Management Limited had gone into liquidation owing the *Men Behaving Badly* star more than £100,000. My client was also represented by that agency, hence the interest from the *Mail* journalist, who had also discovered that my client had disappeared from the entertainment business for many months and pressed her to tell him why. Eventually, once he had won her trust and assured her that he would treat anything that she told him as confidential, she disclosed to him how she had been viciously stalked and put in such fear of her life that she fled to a commune in India to escape the man responsible.

The stalker was an ex-boyfriend whom she had dumped when she realized that he was a psychopath, which she did after he was involved in a road-rage incident while driving her in his car. He later smashed down the door of the block of flats where she lived, sent her pills with the suggestion that she commit suicide and slashed her car seats with a knife. Once he beat her senseless and was caught by a passer-by trying to manhandle her unconscious body into the boot of his car. Had that not happened I imagine he would have killed her and dumped her body. She was too frightened to go to the police at a time before the introduction of the Protection from Harassment Act in 1997, at which time stalked women had nothing like the requisite protection by the authorities. Fortunately, my client had a special forces friend who visited this individual to discourage him from further harassment, but she continued to live in terror of this man.

My client called me immediately after she had been contacted by the journalist to tell her that he had written up the story for the newspaper and it was to be published in the next day or so. She begged him not to let the story run, explaining that if it was published, she was sure her stalker would come after her in revenge. But her pleas fell on deaf ears.

I was able to calm her fears by telling her that I would ring the newspaper the following morning and that I was sure that when confronted with the risks that publication would expose her to, it would relent. Eventually, after many more tears, she went home comforted.

First thing the following morning I rang the Associated Newspapers legal office, confident that I would be able to persuade the *Daily Mail* to have mercy. After all, I reasoned, the newspaper already had the full account of what she had suffered and would only be intent on publishing it if they accepted that it was true, so surely it would not place my client's safety at risk from a man who had already tried to kill her once?

How wrong was I?

I knew the senior lawyer at Associated Newspapers but could not get through to him, so I spoke to one of his team who was a woman. My heart leapt. Surely, I reasoned, she would recognize the plight of a fellow female and do something to help? As I explained to her, if it published an account of her experiences, as the stalker had threatened, he might kill her and her elderly parents.

How wrong was I again? As I explained the situation I was confronted with a flinty indifference. I stressed that I was not asking the newspaper to drop the story primarily on a legal basis, but as an act of compassion. Eventually I was told that the issue would be sent up to the managing editor and that I could speak to him later in the day.

My client was too terrified of being attacked again by her stalker to return to her flat, which the stalker had once broken into, so she had started to sleep at her parents' small flat and spend her days in a meeting room or in the reception area of our offices (Schillings) where I brought her drinks and sandwiches.

When I was eventually able to speak to the managing editor, my client was in our offices. Ordinarily I would never allow a client to speak to a newspaper. But in this case the situation was so desperate, I decided that I would bring her in on the call. My reasoning was that whereas the paper might not listen to a media lawyer, it might listen to my petrified client.

Fortunately, Keith Shilling was away so his office was free. I took her in and briefed her about what to say and what not to say, and we had what proved to be an extraordinary conversation with the managing editor.

I introduced my client and explained the purpose of and background to the call. My client then explained in greater detail what she had suffered at the hands of this violent man and how she was terrified that if the story was published he would once again break in to the building where she lived and not only kill her, but also kill her parents who were elderly and frail.

The managing editor appeared to be completely unmoved by any of this. He then said something truly extraordinary. He had evidently learned from the reporter that my client had fled to India to escape her attacker and his suggested resolution was that she went back abroad a day or so before publication of the story.

Astonished, I asked him what she was supposed to do for money to pay for this travelling, when was she supposed to return and what benefit that was to her frail parents. None of these issues appeared to have occurred to him. So it was that, at the end of that phone call, nothing was resolved, but at least it appeared to me that publication of the article was not imminent.

Another day passed by which time it was 23 December. It is difficult (though not impossible) to secure an injunction during the court's Christmas holiday, so I knew that if that proved to be necessary I needed to get a move on. I rang the managing editor again and asked whether the newspaper had decided to publish this story. Despite the obvious urgency of the situation, he said no decision had been made. I then asked whether he would give me a holding undertaking that they would not publish in the period between Christmas and New Year. At least he would grant me that, I thought. Again, I was wrong. I told him that in those circumstances I would have no option but to make an immediate application for an injunction.

As I did so, I wondered how I was going to get the court order my client so obviously needed. I also knew that practically speaking I had to get one that day. First, for all I knew the newspaper might run the story in tomorrow's edition. Second, there are not many good media barristers who work on Christmas Eve.

I was happy to be working for my penniless client without charge, but I could not reasonably expect a barrister to do likewise. In those days you could still obtain civil Legal Aid, though I had never applied and had no idea how to do so. But I found a number for the Legal Aid office and God must have engaged an angel to answer the phone because a kind man talked me through the whole process and granted me an emergency certificate over the phone to make the application for an injunction that very afternoon.

Armed with a Legal Aid certificate I found a good barrister to make the application, whom I briefed initially by phone. We arranged to meet at what is known as the 'Bear Garden', a kind of Dickensian hall in the Royal Courts of Justice in the Strand, around which there are a number of small courts (but no bears). In one of them sat a Queen's Bench judge, to whom you made emergency applications – you just turned up at the court, explained briefly to the court usher why you needed an emergency appointment and roughly how long you would be. You were then duly sent in and made the application 'on the hoof'.

When I told the managing editor that I was going to make an application for an injunction, he told me that he wanted a letter from the newspaper to go before the judge. One was duly faxed to the office from one of the paper's lawyers. It was an extraordinarily cruel and ugly missive which I had no doubt was going to make my job easier rather than more difficult.

While waiting outside the courtroom I was able to brief the barrister more fully. When we made our application I duly handed the judge the *Mail's* letter and his expression told me what he thought of it. Not only did he grant our injunction without hesitation, very unusually he did not set what we call a 'return date' – i.e. a date on which we would have to go back to the court with notice to the newspaper to secure the second stage of the injunction; namely one that should stay in place up until the date of the trial.

I duly served the injunction and was able to calm my client with the knowledge that she was at least safe until the New Year. However, unbeknown to me, in addition to her evident mental distress, she had started to suffer a complete physical breakdown. As the medical expert would later explain to me, her whole body was shutting down.

This had another consequence. Because she had been out of circulation for so long, my client's showreel (essential for her to get new work) was out of date. She had no money to pay for a new one, but had persuaded a friend who ran a studio to edit together some of her more recent work into a new showreel over the Christmas break so that she could try to pick up some work in the New Year. However, she was rendered incapable of doing anything during that period, so that essential means of her restarting her career was lost.

So it was that in the first week of January I wrote to Associated Newspapers and asked that the dispute be resolved on the basis of the *Daily Mail* providing an undertaking not to publish the story and that it would make a payment of £5,000 to my client – a minute sum for that vast entity. I explained that this was made up of £3,500, being the value of the studio time that she had lost, and £1,500 to allow both her and her parents a brief holiday in which to recover from their ordeal. I also explained that I was not looking to the newspaper for any legal costs. This offer was angrily turned down by the newspaper, which would still not even give an undertaking that it would not publish the story.

I had no option but to take the legal action forward and mercifully the Legal Aid Board was sympathetic, and so began the most unpleasant piece of litigation which it has ever been my misfortune to conduct. It went on for several months and involved a number of very grim hearings. In the end the *Daily Mail* backed down, and though it never undertook not to publish the story, it formally told a judge that it had no intention of doing so, which was the next best thing.

A number of incidents during the course of the litigation bear recording in this book, though it is impossible to do justice to how badly the *Daily Mail* and its lawyers behaved towards my client during that time. One of my practical difficulties was that I had a client who had suffered a catastrophic breakdown not because the publication of her stalking ordeal had gone ahead, but because its publication had been threatened. I wracked my brains to try and think of a precedent case which I could use to try and recover damages for my client who had been mentally and physically incapacitated by the appalling actions of the newspaper. Then I remembered from my student days an old authority called Wilkinson v Downton. This wonderful old 1897 case was the first one in which our law recognized the civil wrong of intentionally inflicting mental shock. This is what happened to Mrs Wilkinson ...

Thomas Wilkinson was the landlord of the Albion pub in Limehouse. One of his regular customers, whose name was Downton, decided to play a cruel practical joke on his wife. One day Mr Wilkinson went off to the races and left his wife to manage the pub. Mr Downton then told her Mr Wilkinson had suffered a serious accident; that he had been trampled by horses and suffered two badly broken legs, which in those days was a grave injury.

The effect of this news on Mrs Wilkinson was devastating; a violent shock to her nervous system, which caused her to vomit, her hair to turn white, and there were other more serious physical consequences which entailed weeks of suffering and incapacity, as well as expense to her husband for medical treatment. Mrs

Wilkinson succeeded in her claim for the intentional infliction of mental shock by Mr Downton.

My research however told me that this was a case which had scarcely ever been followed in the subsequent hundred years and I was by no means sure that I could succeed in an action for my client against the *Mail* in these circumstances. So I took a leading media QC out to lunch and ran the idea past him. Rather to my surprise he thought we could make the claim stick and so I began proceedings against the newspaper on that basis.

This case was some way out of my practice area as a media lawyer, because it was effectively a personal injuries case and I had never conducted one. Fortunately, I had a cousin who was an excellent personal injuries solicitor, so I rang him for help. I was also very reliant on counsel.

One of the consequences of bringing a claim of this sort was, as my barrister warned, I was going to have to obtain a medical report for my client to prove that she had suffered medical and psychological injuries as a consequence of the *Mail*'s brutality towards her. I broached this to her as gently as I could, but in her broken state the prospect terrified her; especially because she was going to have to relive her stalking experiences as part of the process. It was only after she had cried many tears in my office and with great difficulty that I eventually persuaded her that she had to go through this process if we were to take her claim forward against the newspaper, which at that time had not changed its position on whether it would publish the story.

This took me even further out of my comfort zone. Not only was I doing my first case on Legal Aid, but I had never dealt with a medical expert because you do not have need of them in the type of work I did. But I found a directory of medical experts and identified one who looked as though he was suitable, and my client attended an appointment with him.

Shortly after he had finished examining my client, he rang me. He was so concerned about her mental and physical state that (as I understand it – without precedent), he had decided that he must also treat her using his skills as a psychiatrist. She was in a very bad way, he warned.

His report made grim reading and I hoped desperately that when I sent it over to the newspaper their attitude towards my client would change. Again, I was wrong. They not only said they did not accept the contents of the medical report, they insisted my client be examined by their own expert.

When I raised this prospect with my medical expert, he was unequivocal. He told me that under no circumstances could she go through this ordeal. After that I spoke with the barrister, who said that he saw no option if we were to take the action forward, but that she would have to go through with it.

My client was even more distraught when I told her she would have to be examined by the newspaper's medical expert than she was when I had told her that she must be examined by ours. Initially she flatly refused. Later, she said that she would only go if I went with her. Gently, I explained that the newspaper would never allow this. I asked her whether she thought she could go through with it if she were accompanied by her own expert. Eventually, she agreed that she would do so on that basis and so I wrote to the paper explaining the situation and asking that my client's own expert, who – I also explained – was so concerned about her that he was treating my client, could attend the appointment.

The reaction of the newspaper's lawyers was what I had now come to expect. Absolutely not! You will find if you take on titles like the *Mail* and the *Mirror*, their lawyers adopt a policy of 'whatever the question is, the answer is no' – which is pursued to grind down their opponents and run up costs.

A stand-off ensued, during which time I threated to make an application to a judge (having no idea whether I had a basis to do so) for an order that my client's expert should attend the appointment with their medical expert. Eventually the newspaper backed down and we were given the name of the psychologist whom my client was to see; the only psychiatrist in the world whom I knew and who was a friend of my younger brother. They had been medical students together and I knew this individual to be somewhat

colourful. However, because I knew him, I comforted myself that
he would assess my client fairly and write an honest report.

I well remember the day when my client was due to meet with
the psychologist because I was so worried for her. The appointment
was only supposed to be a couple of hours long. After that, when
I heard nothing, I started to ring her mobile regularly to check she
was alright. By chance, she answered literally as she was walking out
the door of the consulting room. She was in good spirits because
(as she explained) the psychiatrist had concurred with her medical
expert on every point, and had concluded that she had indeed
suffered a complete breakdown and that the cause was the actions
of the newspaper.

I asked her to pass her phone to our medical expert, who
confirmed that this was what the psychiatrist had said. My client
was elated, but I feared the newspaper would find a way around
this problem.

We then waited six months for the medical report to be served.
When it came in, its conclusions were the polar opposite of what
the psychiatrist had said at the end of the consultation. It seems
that the poor man had been browbeaten by the newspaper's
lawyers over the period of that six months into performing a
180-degree volte-face, which appears to be serious breach of
conduct on the part of the lawyers at least, though they deny any
such conduct[8].

I have no idea what pressure the psychiatrist was put under, or
what he was told in order to persuade him to do this. Whatever it
was, it was a despicable exercise. But I do know that the newspaper
was alleging that I was having an affair with my client as part of a
black propaganda that it was spreading in an attempt to defeat the
claim. Also, I know what the first draft of the report would have
said; as would the newspaper and its lawyers. Rather than offer to
settle the claim, they fought on.

---

[8] From the SRA (Solicitors Regulation Authority) rule book: 'You do not seek to influence
the substance of evidence, including generating false evidence or persuading witnesses to
change their evidence.'

Just as Thomas Markle was introduced into the Duchess of Sussex's privacy action as an extra-legal deterrent to his daughter holding the *Mail on Sunday* to account for its actions, so in my case Associated Newspapers tried to introduce the stalker into the proceedings that I was bringing against them. This is how they did it.

I was handed a fax containing a court order which had been made against a private detective of whom I had never heard requiring him to provide all his files to the newspaper's lawyers. This order had apparently been sought because Tessa Dahl (Roald Dahl's daughter), who the paper knew was a friend of my client, had said in an interview that she had a great private detective whom she recommended to all her friends.

The newspaper's lawyers knew of my client's friendship with Tessa because I had served a witness statement from her as part of my evidence. She had heard the reporter assure my client on speakerphone that he would not write up her stalking ordeal in the *Daily Mail*. The paper also knew from our evidence that my client had found the home address of her stalker via a private detective.

The paper's lawyers had not only made their application for this order without notifying me – for which there was no justification – they had also misled the judge in the supporting evidence by stating that the issue of stalking was a central issue in the case, which it was not, because the paper was not disputing the fact that stalking had taken place, which it could hardly do while insisting that it should be permitted to publish the story. When a claimant applies for an order against a defendant in their absence there is a 'duty of full frank disclosure' to the court. The *Mail*'s lawyers rode a coach and horses through that one.

The paper's lawyers then breached the undertaking that they had given to the court that they would serve the order very shortly after it was made; they did this so they could get hold of the detective's client list before I had time to apply to set aside the order. As it turned out, it was a waste of time and money because this was not the private detective that my client had used.

The newspaper's lawyers began to make the litigation *ad hominem*[9] – a common tactic in Fleet Street. Standing outside a courtroom, I was threatened by the paper's QC with a personal costs order against me when I had to make an application alone because I did not have the funding for a barrister.

The application was defended by that QC, accompanied by a partner at the solicitors acting for the paper, her assistant and an assistant to her assistant; all accompanied by the senior lawyer at Associated Newspapers. One Friday afternoon I was sent six letters by the paper's lawyers to ensure the obliteration of my weekend. I was eventually able to persuade the paper not to publish the story, but was unable to secure damages for her.

More cruelty by Associated Newspapers
and their lawyers

The same newspaper and its lawyers behaved similarly badly to another client of mine, whom I can name because she has placed her own experiences in the public domain.

Danielle Hindley is a beautician and hardworking single mother towards whom over a long period the *Mail on Sunday* and its lawyers behaved with studied cruelty. The paper had wrecked her life by wrongly accusing her of being a rogue beautician who put the health of her clients at risk. Showing immense courage and tenacity, Danielle had managed successfully to pursue an IPSO complaint against the paper. She now needed a libel lawyer to secure compensation from the paper because of the ruinous effect that its article had had on her life, that of her son and her business. I was asked by Hacked Off, a pressure group which campaigns for greater accountability in the press, to assist her when two lawyers had told her there was no viable libel action.[10]

[9] A Latin term which here means that the newspaper had resorted to personal attacks on me in an attempt to deter me from acting in my client's best interests.
[10] https://hackinginquiry.org/

Here, she describes her suffering at the hands of the *Mail on Sunday* and their lawyers:

'I was a victim of press abuse towards the end of 2017. I have since been diagnosed with PTSD and continue to suffer from anxiety. I have felt suicidal and attempted to take my life more than once during my legal battle against the *Mail on Sunday*, which wrote an inaccurate and misleading story about myself and [a] small business which I run from home. A journalist entered my house under a false identity and used a hidden camera to film myself, another client and even my young child.

For months after the article I lived in bed 24/7, on cups of tea, without taking care of myself, in a dark bedroom. My son began having nightmares of me being murdered.

I would often go into panic attacks, losing my movement of hands and arms and even lost my vision briefly on 4 occasions. My physical health deteriorated and I started suffering with acne and insomnia.'

I offered Danielle a 'no-win, no-fee' agreement, secured appropriate insurance for any adverse costs order, and wrote a libel claim letter to Associated Newspapers in November 2018. They replied that they would provide a substantive response by the end of November – which they did not; which was a ruse to try to ensure that we missed the one-year limitation period for a libel action. A second letter promised that the company intended to resolve the dispute 'in a just and equitable manner'. It also acknowledged 'the high level of distress and anxiety' already caused.

Ten weeks after my letter Associated Newspapers finally responded, denying libel and stating its intention to defend its reporting in court despite having admitted in the IPSO correction that it 'did not have a basis to suggest that Ms Hindley had "botched" treatments'.

Associated Newspapers thereby asserted in effect that it had not meant what it said in the correction. It said it had 'offered to publish a correction in the terms set out in order to reach a compromise' and had been 'required to publish' this under its IPSO contract, but it insisted it was beyond IPSO's remit to 'determine whether Associated Newspapers Limited reasonably believed that publishing the article was in the public interest'. On these grounds, it claimed the correction did not amount to an admission of responsibility.

For four months it maintained its warlike stance – among other things obliging Danielle to raise £2,500 for court fees – and then, at the moment when it was obliged to present a plausible defence (having secured two extensions), it eventually admitted liability. Associated Newspapers then haggled over damages and costs to a such degree that Danielle eventually accepted an offer some way below what she felt she was entitled to. Professor Brian Cathcart (Professor of Journalism at Kingston University) wrote an account of my work for Danielle.[11]

Associated Newspapers' record of misleading the public on medical issues

Associated Newspapers also has form for making assertions on issues of intense public interest which are catastrophically false and therefore grossly irresponsible. This was well illustrated by the Hacked Off article, which was re-published by the media blog site Inforrm in November 2020.[12]

In 2002, the *Daily Mail* published an article wrongly, linking autism and bowel disease to the MMR jab.[13] It took 17 years for the newspaper to undertake a belated U-turn.[14] They only accepted fault over this article, which must have changed very

[11] https://bylinetimes.com/2020/02/25/the-beautician-and-the-beast-danielle-hindley-v-the-mail-on-sunday/
[12] https://inforrm.org/2020/11/29/the-daily-mails-coronavirus-coverage-contained-serious-distortions-the-governments-failure-to-criticise-it-is-pathetic-and-dangerous-hacked-off/#more-47573
[13] https://www.dailymail.co.uk/health/article-123482/New-MMR-link-autism.html
[14] https://www.bmj.com/content/367/bmj.l6487

much for the worse the lives of many children and their families, in November 2020.[15]

ASSOCIATED NEWSPAPERS' RECORD OF MISLEADING THE PUBLIC ON LEGAL ISSUES

My favourite 'trousers around the ankles' moment for the *Mail* titles, which also gives the clearest insight into the complete disregard for truth of that arrogant organization, is the 100 per cent fake news story it published online about the notorious Meredith Kercher trial, which was reported only in the *Guardian*.[16]

The *Mail's* website initially mis-reported that Amanda Knox has lost her appeal against her conviction for murdering Meredith Kercher when, in fact, she had been successful. The article, written in anticipation of the verdict, included quotes attributed to the prosecutors apparently reacting to the guilty verdict and the description of the reaction in the courtroom to the news, stating that Knox 'sank into her chair sobbing uncontrollably while her family and friends hugged each other in tears'. It further stated that the family of Meredith Kercher 'remained expressionless, staring straight ahead, glancing over just once at the distraught Knox family'. The article was a complete work of fiction and was later replaced by one reporting the correct outcome of the trial[17].

It is this unethical and hubristic mindset which requires those who undertake crisis PR vis-à-vis the press to be the sturdy equal of those who fight the corners of newspapers with immense resources and without qualms, in terms of knowing the relevant regulations and laws which, if deployed as intended, at least to some extent hold these unaccountable entities in check.

---

[15] https://www.bmj.com/content/bmj/331/7525/Reviews.full.pdf
[16] Meredith Kercher was a British student who was murdered in Perugia, Italy. Police charged Kercher's American roommate, Amanda Knox, and Knox's Italian boyfriend, Raffaele Sollecito, whose prosecutions received international publicity.
[17] https://www.theguardian.com/media/greenslade/2011/dec/09/pcc-dailymail

You also need to be of a robust disposition to dare criticize

Few journalists have the courage to hold Associated Newspaper and its brutal regime to account. One such publication is *Byline Investigates*, which I am proud to count as a client.

The *Mail* titles assert a near-absolute right to say exactly what they want about any subject they choose. They take a different view about their small band of brave critics. In March 2017, they instructed the same lawyers who brutally enforce their right to free speech to curtail that of one of their critics to write a letter threatening a libel action against *Byline Investigates*, who instructed me to defend them.

The hypocrisy in that letter starts right from the top, where it says, 'Not for publication' – this from a newspaper that routinely flouts the confidentiality and privacy of others in its news pages, an instruction rightly ignored by my client. The prospective claimants were: Mr Dacre, then editor of the *Daily Mail* and editor-in-chief of Associated Newspapers Limited (ANL); Mr Wright, editor emeritus at ANL; and Elizabeth Hartley, Head of Editorial Legal Services at ANL.

The complaint was that *Byline Investigates* had alleged that these individuals 'suppressed evidence from the Leveson Inquiry in order to mislead the Inquiry about the real extent of ANL's dealings with [a private investigator who was up to no good]'.

It is difficult to know where to begin here. In no particular order:

- Associated Newspapers was one of those who lobbied hard for the introduction of the 2013 Defamation Act – cited in the letter, which included the 'Publication on a Matter of Public Interest' defence, to which the articles at issue were plainly entitled.
- *Byline Investigates* is regulated by the fully independent and Leveson compliant IMPRESS, which is where these individuals should have taken their complaint if – as the letter claims – their primary concern was to secure a

correction. Instead they wielded their massively greater financial power and threatened a libel action.

- By contrast, it will have been primarily via the decision of these three individuals that Associated Newspapers chose to be regulated by IPSO, which entirely lacks independence, credibility or legitimacy.
- The letter states: 'It is extremely important to our clients that these defamatory allegations, which have already been republished by third parties, are *immediately* removed from your website and that the record is set straight [emphasis added]'. Anyone who has dealt with the *Mail* titles, and as Warby J observed in the Duchess of Sussex case, will know they will do everything they can to avoid taking down inaccurate material – let alone publish a correction – even when it is proven wrong.
- The letter threateningly demands to know who are the individuals responsible for the publications, which can only be so they could be sued personally. There would be howls of outrage from Associated Newspapers if anyone of similar financial might had the temerity to sue one of its journalists personally, accompanied by screams of press censorship.
- The letter concludes, 'We look forward to hearing from you as a matter of urgency.' Anyone who has dealt with the *Mail* titles knows that any such stipulation sent to them will invariably be ignored.

The response from *Byline Investigates* was to publish the claim letter and put up a robust defence of their allegations in a letter which I immensely enjoyed drafting – with help from the excellent Hugh Tomlinson QC.

My final missive to the Associated lawyers included this paragraph: 'So far as our clients are concerned, they stand by every word of the Articles. They will not be silenced by groundless threats of legal action by your clients such as that set out in your correspondence, and nor will they be prevented from continuing their investigations into the conduct of both your clients and [Associated Newspapers]'.

Needless to say there was no libel action, from which you can draw your own conclusions.

MIRROR GROUP NEWSPAPERS APES ITS LARGER AND RICHER RIVALS

Mirror Group Newspapers, as we now know, hacked phones in the same industrial quantities as did News UK. While they were doing this, the senior lawyer presiding over the newspaper's lack of adherence to the law was Marcus Partington who it has been alleged in court knew about criminal activity and failed to prevent it.

Here is an extract from a letter sent to me by Marcus in response to a claim letter I sent to the *Mirror* on behalf of bestselling author Paul McKenna: 'If your firm were foolish enough to advise your client to issue proceedings, and if your client was foolish enough to accept that advice, then ... he will learn to his immense personal and financial cost that he has picked the wrong fight over the wrong article with the wrong newspaper.' This was described by the trial judge as 'armchair machismo' in his judgment, as he found in favour of my client.

THE *NEWS OF THE WORLD* BLACKMAILS ONE OF ITS SOURCES

The tabloid press as a species will have no hesitation in turning on its sources even if it suits their purposes. In Mr Justice Eady's judgment following Max Mosley's successful privacy action against *News of the World*, he suggested that the approach adopted by the newspaper amounted to blackmail.[18] This is

---

[18] Commenting on evidence given by *News of the World* journalist Neville Thurlbeck who had threatened two women with exposure if they did not co-operate with the paper, Eady J said this: 'It seems that Mr Thurlbeck genuinely did not see the point. Yet it is elementary that blackmail can be committed by the threat to do something which would not, in itself, be unlawful.'

because one of the women featured in the sting footage was told that she would be identified and her photograph put in the newspaper unless she co-operated with the *News of the World*. Apparently, no one at the paper thought there was anything wrong in this.

The *Mirror* steals a story from one of its sources and then sues her

In another of my cases, the *Mirror* published something entirely false and defamatory about a premiership footballer client and was trying desperately to justify the unjustifiable in the defamation proceedings which I was bringing against it. The case had arisen when the ex-partner of my client, who felt that she had been spurned by him, approached both the *Sun* and the *Mirror* to sell her story.

As was inevitable, the *Mirror* was outbid by the *Sun* by whom she was duly 'bought up'. The *Sun* then took this woman to a hotel in what was a form of solitary confinement and pumped her for information over a lengthy period until they extracted from her the story which they wanted to run – which caused them to pay substantial damages both to my footballer client and his new celebrity girlfriend.

The *Mirror* also published the story without this young woman's permission, based on the conversation that she had had with the title while it was discussing whether it would buy her story from her, so I also sued it on her behalf too.

In an attempt to force this young woman into siding with the *Mirror* in the libel proceedings I had commenced against it, it joined her as a third party – i.e. they started an action against her which had the effect that if, they had been forced to pay damages and costs, they could recover those damages and costs against this young woman; a single mother of modest means from whom they had stolen the story.

Because it's your turn

The reason why I quote the Apostle Peter's warning about a lion looking for prey at the start of this chapter is that the same hubris and complete disregard for the public interest on the part of entities like News UK, as evidenced by their wholly unwarranted 'QUEEN BACKS BREXIT' headline as published by the *Sun*, can be turned on you or your company for no apparent reason. More than once I have been told by a press insider that an organization or an individual has suffered the destructive attention of a national title merely 'because it was their turn'.

I was once on an expert panel for a debate on media regulation at Imperial College London. One of the other panel members was a high-profile Fleet Street editor. An audience member asked if he had ever considered as part of a publishing decision what the impact of a particular article might be on its subject. With little hesitation he replied in the negative.

And yes, even the *Guardian* too when it has an editorial agenda to pursue

Even more honourable Fleet Street titles such as the *Guardian* have on occasions elected to pursue its editorial agenda at the expense of both the truth and public interest – though in its defence the events that I now relate took place some 15 years ago and under a different legal and editorial regime.

In 2004 Colonel Campbell-James was wrongly accused by the *Guardian* of being involved in the appalling abuse of Iraqi war prisoners in the Abu Ghraib jail. Not only was he not at the jail at the time, he was not even in Iraq. This was not only a false allegation against a distinguished army office, it was also a serious allegation against his regiment, the British Army and the British State, the effect of which was to place other British soldiers serving in Iraq at risk of reprisals.

To its shame the *Guardian* initially cited the then common law Reynolds public interest defence (now Section 4 of the 2013

Defamation Act) as its justification for refusing to retract the allegation. Had it elected to run that defence, Colonel Campbell-James would have been robbed of his right to vindication and a false story staining him, his regiment, the British Army and the nation as a whole would have stayed uncorrected. So much for it being a 'public interest' defence.

As Mr Justice Eady observed in his judgment, which merits reading in full and was damning of the *Guardian*: 'It was not simply a matter of good journalistic practice [to publish a prompt retraction]; it was a matter of elementary human decency.'[19] Only grudgingly and belatedly did the paper retract the allegation and only paid damages when ordered to do so by a court.

To its credit, the *Guardian* later acknowledged its failure to do right by the British officer in an acceptance of fault unlikely to come from any other Fleet Street title.[20]. Then editor Alan Rusbridger stated: 'In general we do try to correct errors swiftly. In this case, for a number of reasons, we didn't publish an apology as early as we should have done, which was very unfortunate. We very much regret the distress caused to Colonel Campbell-James and his family, and would like to apologise again to him, as we have already done in the newspaper and in open court.'

Since this was an aberration on the part of that title, when dealing with the *Guardian* I adopt a different approach from how I would when dealing with either the *Mirror* or *Mail* titles. The *Guardian* lawyers I have dealt with are courteous, ethical and fair-minded and I only ever deal with them on Christian name terms; as I do some of the other Fleet Street lawyers with whom I can deal, knowing that they will conduct themselves properly. The newspaper is reasonable to deal with if it gets things wrong and also has sensible and courteous readers' editors who will generally correct minor inaccuracies when asked to do so.

[19] https://www.5rb.com/wp-content/uploads/2013/10/Campbell-James-v-Guardian-QBD-12-May-2005.pdf
[20] https://www.theguardian.com/media/2005/may/13/pressandpublishing.iraq

THE ROLE OF A FLEET STREET LAWYER IN WORKING AGAINST THE PUBLIC INTEREST

One of the reasons why I have never acted for a Fleet Street title, or sought to do so, is that for most of them you will be expected to advance arguments and make assertions which no honest part of you could believe are true, and defend and/or cover up wrongdoing which you know perfectly well should come into the public domain.

It was no surprise that some senior Fleet Street editorial lawyers were summoned to give evidence at the Leveson Inquiry and that Lord Justice Leveson had serious doubts as to the extent to which he was being told the truth by some of them. Some have subsequently had to leave their posts under a cloud. There are some honourable exceptions – fine folk who do defendant work both in the print and broadcast media without abandoning any concept of right or wrong. I will not embarrass them by naming names, but they know who they are.

However, Fleet Street in particular could not get away with much of its wrongdoing if it were not abetted by a small coterie of well-paid lawyers prepared both to cover its tracks and to ensure that the fake news that it disseminates is not corrected. This does an immense disservice to society and press-abuse victims alike.

In the media industry there is an almost complete divide between claimant and defendant lawyers – especially when it comes to Fleet Street, where it is pretty well absolute. That is why I am so privileged to have occupied both camps, though I have never acted for a Fleet Street title. A celebrity client told me of a meeting which he had with former CEO of News International Rebekah Brooks to resolve an issue in the newspaper at which she asked him who was his lawyer. When I was named she apparently put her head in her hands.

THE ARRIVAL OF THE 'FREE SPEECH LAWYER'

Recently some of those that we in the trade used to call defendant lawyers have taken to calling themselves 'free speech' lawyers (FSL). Having seen a website for American attorneys claiming the moral high ground for such work I suspect it is one of those phenomena which has invaded us from the other side of the Atlantic.

However much which is presented as 'free speech' lawyering is in fact nothing of the sort. It is rather the mercenary exercise of saving the face of newspapers, editors and journalists when they publish false and disparaging copy, thereby ensuring that the most important victim of such press activity – the general public – never learns that it has been misled, and victims are robbed of vindication and compensation.

Free speech and *Animal Farm*

The right of 'free speech' is alas by no means fairly distributed. Although there has been some mitigation of this with the advent of social media, when it comes to exercising the right of free speech there remains an immense inequality between the behemoths of Fleet Street and even the highest profile individuals and corporates.

As George Orwell sagely observed in his wonderful novella *Animal Farm*, so far as the ruling pigs are concerned, 'some are more equal than others'. For the free speech pigs read porcine behemoths like Associated Newspapers, Mirror Group Newspapers and News UK. Against the power wielded by such entities even the most powerful of my corporate clients are at a substantial disadvantage, which renders effective crisis PR essential.

The reason that we need both effective press regulation and the protection of reputation and privacy is precisely because without them the money and hubris-driven Fleet Street empires will both mislead us according to their editorial whim and further rob non-porcine individuals and entities even of such free speech audibility as they would otherwise have by telling lies about them.

THE DAMAGE THAT FSL CAN DO PRE-PUBLICATION

What is it that the self-styled FSL of our country do to justify claiming the moral high ground – which not only do they ascribe to themselves but inevitably so do to those whose interests they serve?

An ex-journalist at a leading Sunday tabloid told me how his in-house lawyer had facilitated the publication of more false stories than anyone else he knew – including journalists.

Did FSL at newspaper groups found guilty of serial criminality and human rights breaches regard it as part of their calling to turn a blind eye to, facilitate, deny and/or cover up this wrongdoing? I fear so. As a long-standing editorial lawyer, I cannot understand how anyone of my expertise can be embedded at a newspaper and not know that such serial criminality is rife.

THE DAMAGE THAT FSL CAN DO POST PUBLICATION

It is however not the role of FSL prior to publication which most contravenes the public interest. It is their role post publication, along with the roles of individuals like newspaper apologists such as managing editors, 'ombudsmen' and entities such as IPSO that I want to expose to the harsh light of reality. They are the ones who 'chill' true free speech by trying to prevent those who have been misled from learning the truth – a right which Article 10 ranks no lower than the right to disseminate information.

FSL at IPSO-regulated titles clearly regard their responsibilities as including the prevention of those who have been misled by their titles learning of that fact. They do this by trying first to persuade the acquiescent IPSO that an article which has plainly breached its Code is in fact compliant; and if this fails, to ensure that the corrections are a fraction of the size and prominence of the offending article so as to ensure the minimum people get to know about it. IPSO is itself one of the most potent enemies of true free speech because of its dismal failure as a 'regulator' to ensure that those misled by the titles it 'regulates' learn of the fact.

So it is in an IPSO complaint where there is an argument over the prominence of the correction, it is the complainant's lawyers who are the real FSL because they seek to ensure that those who have been misled by a newspaper article are disabused of that false information, thereby trying to secure their Article 10 rights. Where a paper has stepped outside its Article 10 right by publishing the false information, it has no free speech right to defend.

Every time (for example) IPSO refuses to order the correction of a front-page howler via a subsequent front page it drives a coach and horses through Article 10 by denying the right of the millions of non-purchasers of the newspaper who have been misled by its front page to receive the corrective information in the only place where they will see it. It therefore proves the claim on its website to 'help maintain freedom of expression' to be false and consequently a breach of its own code's injunction against the publication of misleading or inaccurate material.

It must be difficult for those who are employed to be apologists for the same organizations and individuals who cynically blitzed the Article 8 rights of many thousands via phone hacking, blagging, bribing police officers, etc., to place their earnings/bonuses at risk by ever reminding those who employ them of the true nature of free speech. Those in private practice however have much less excuse. It is perfectly possible to make a reasonable living as a media lawyer without ever acting for a Fleet Street title, as I have throughout my 30-year career.

Some of the other ways that FSL ill-serve society

Although I no longer should be, I am still astonished when a reply comes back to a claim letter which is grossly disingenuous and makes a litany of assertions which the writer cannot possibly believe are true; as I am when counsel, instructed by the press, draft defences denying the defamatory nature of an article which is blindingly obviously defamatory and solicitors (doubtless citing free speech principles) sign statements of truth to such documents.

I recall a hearing where Mr Justice Tugendhat, with his customary grace, declaring himself surprised at the assertion made by the defendant paper's lawyers that an article was not defamatory, said that until he had read the defence it had not even occurred to him that the article was anything other than defamatory.

A leading FSL QC was on his feet at the time, who a few weeks later spent a pointless half hour trying to persuade a Court of Appeal judge that the same publication meant other than it plainly did – thereby making a second attempt to rob the readers of his client publisher of their right to learn that its paper had misled them.

It is routine for FSL, both at the Bar or in the solicitors' profession, to promulgate meanings for publications which they blindingly obviously do not bear. The defamatory meaning that they advance is crafted around the facts which the newspaper thinks it can prove, rather than the true sting of the words in the publication.

I have no idea how the barristers who produce such documents and solicitors who sign off on them are able to do so with a clear conscience, or with any sense that they are serving the cause of free speech or society as a whole. This is an exercise in medicating the hubris of editors by preventing those that have read the offending article and been poisoned by its sting from learning that they have been misled, thereby trashing their free speech rights. In those circumstances, the real FSL act for the claimant.

FSL AND A RELIGIOUS MINORITY

A recent encounter with an FSL acting for the *Telegraph* concerned an Islamophobic attack on a moderate and devout Muslim community leader for whom I acted. The FSL sought to deny the readers of that newspaper their free speech rights by insisting, against the plain words of the article, that it meant something other than what a judge subsequently emphatically found was the case and as we had always said that it meant.

When that was brought to an abrupt end at a preliminary trial on meaning, the retreat position was to try to deny the claimant the Statement in Open Court which fulfilled the element of the

Article 10 right which is less popular in Fleet Street; namely the entitlement of the general public to receive information – such as that this individual had been falsely accused by the paper of severe wrongdoing and anti-social activity.

As any victim of falsities promulgated by one of the Goliaths of Fleet Street will tell you, one effective means of robbing an individual or organization of their right to free speech is widely to disseminate damning lies about them. The real free speech lawyer is the solicitor and/or barrister acting for that individual; particularly (as was the situation in this recent encounter with FSL) a faith community leader. In those circumstances not only has the leader's free speech right been undermined, but so too has that of the community that they serve as its mouthpiece.

FSL and the Duchess of Sussex

Sometimes even a gaggle of distinguished lawyers, such as the heavyweight legal team that acted for the *Mail on Sunday* which include two top QCs, advance arguments on behalf of a Fleet Street behemoth which surely should have engaged their consciences.

This collective moral failure by the *Mail on Sunday*'s lawyers of is one of the untold stories from the proceedings; the other being just how vile is Thomas Markle for siding with his daughter's oppressors. They were defending the actions of a newspaper who had (as I assume) bribed the Duchess of Sussex's father to let them publish an intimate letter from his daughter, whom the newspaper then deployed in defence of the indefensible.

That legal team, which will have been around eight in size and cost around £5,000 an hour, rightly received a lashing from Warby J in the judgment in which he found that, despite their ingenuity and creativity, the newspaper had no viable defence to the Duchess of Sussex privacy and copyright case that she brought the paper; a judgment which was subsequently upheld by the Court of Appeal and Supreme Court.

Surely, they must all have known that.

These individuals are all facilitators of the wrongdoing which is endemic in Fleet Street by (as Warby J decries) deploying arguments that are 'tired and illegitimate' – arguments which IPSO will indulge, but which judges will generally not. Fleet Street will continue to conduct itself in the appalling way that it does now while it can find lawyers prepared to lend their support for such wrongdoing.

THE WARBY J JUDGMENT

Here are some examples taken from his judgment of the contempt that Warby J (as he then was) had for many of the newspaper's arguments as advanced by their lawyers:

> 'I am satisfied that this line of defence has no sound basis in law.'
> 'In some respects, the defendant's case is legally untenable or flimsy at best ...'
> 'I would class the notion as fanciful.'
> 'This aspect of the Defence is in my judgment entirely hopeless.'
> 'I am unable to detect in these paragraphs any logical or arguably sufficient basis for disclosing any part of the Letter.'
> 'Thus, it was argued, an accurate court report would gain no protection insofar as it merely recited the incidents and events in court. This seems a remarkable argument for a news publisher to want to advance. Mr Speck cited no authority to support it.'
> 'The defendant's factual and legal case on this issue both seem to me to occupy the shadowland between improbability and unreality.'

THE PROFESSIONAL OBLIGATIONS OF THE *MAIL ON SUNDAY*'S LEGAL TEAM

These are the key obligations of a solicitor as per the SRA Principles[21]: You act:

---

[21] https://www.sra.org.uk/solicitors/standards-regulations/principles/

1. in a way that upholds the constitutional principle of the rule of law, and the proper administration of justice;
2. *in a way that upholds public trust and confidence in the solicitors' profession and in legal services provided by authorised persons;*
with independence;
with honesty;
with integrity;
in a way that encourages equality, diversity and inclusion;
in the best interest of each client. (emphasis added).

As for the barristers, they share similar obligations. The Warby J judgment suggests that none of the lawyers acting for the *Mail on Sunday* were complying with their professional obligations.

FSL AND THE STOKES FAMILY

In August 2021 it was announced that nearly two years after an intrusive and deeply upsetting front page article about them, the privacy claim brought by Ben and Deborah Stokes against the *Sun* had been settled, with the newspaper agreeing to apologise and pay substantial damages. The nonsensical and desperate defence deployed by the paper's lawyers made the one in the Duchess of Sussex seem meritorious by comparison[22].

PRESS ATTACKS ON CLAIMANT LAWYERS

By contrast, the press will not hesitate to take a swipe at leading claimant lawyers if they think it suits their ends. Leading barrister David Sherborne, who alone spoke for phone-hacking victims at the Leveson Inquiry, has suffered personal knocks from the Fleet Street empires that he challenges.

[22] https://inforrm.org/2021/09/13/the-stokes-familys-privacy-claim-why-the-sun-had-to-settle-paul-wragg/#more-50046

News International's then solicitors, Farrer & Co, set private detectives on two of the leading phone-hacking lawyers in the hope of establishing that they were having an affair. Both Associated Newspapers and News International (as it was then) have spent substantial sums on lawyers in an effort to wreck my career; in both cases making allegations which neither legal team could possibly have thought well-founded because of what they knew about me from my dealings with them.

'DOING YOUR BEST FOR THE CLIENT'

Shortly after my long fight with the team of lawyers acting for Associated Newspapers in the stalking victim case which I described earlier (*see also* pages 127–38), I met a junior member of that team at a social event. I asked his thoughts about the case. He gave only the slightest hint that his conscience had been engaged about the work that he had been doing, but defended himself and his firm on the basis that they were just 'doing their best for the client', which he regarded as adequate justification.

I do not. When Scrooge comments to Jacob Marley's ghost that he was a 'good man of business', this is his response: 'Mankind was my business. The common welfare was my business; charity, mercy, forbearance, and benevolence, were all my business. The dealings of my trade were but a drop of water in the comprehensive ocean of my business!'[23]

Surely the *Sun*'s lawyers can have had no doubt of its wronging towards the Stokes family, and no one who acted for Associated Newspapers could doubt the wickedness of which it was guilty towards the Duchess of Sussex; as they cannot in the *Mail*'s appalling abuse of my stalking victim client. There must surely come a point where bigger issues are taken into account by an ethical legal professional. Should they not confront themselves in the mirror and ask whether they really want to be facilitator of and apologists

---

[23] From *A Christmas Carol* by Charles Dickens where Scrooge is visited by the ghost of his erstwhile business partner.

for activity which on any legal and moral basis is wrong, and which would have to cease if no one stepped forward to defend it.

FSLs occupy a unique position of responsibility. The lawyers who tried to conceal wickedness on the part of big business and deny justice to victims in *Erin Brokovich* and *Dark Waters* were dealing with historic pollution in small areas of the US. The wrongdoing of Fleet Street is ongoing and pollutes the whole of society. While there are lawyers who are willing to collude with that wickedness by lending their assistance both to conceal it and prevent the polluters paying proper compensation to victims, Fleet Street will continue to abuse us all.

SUING THE BOY SCOUTS (NOT)

A decision to refuse to lend your professional skills to defend an exercise which fails the 'smell test' not only requires moral courage, but may also cause you financial loss. I met a successful businesswoman at an awards lunch who asked if I could advise her on a possible libel claim – the pursuit of which would have generated good billing. We arranged to meet up for lunch a few days later, during which she explained that she wanted to sue her local Scout troop for defamation. This is what had happened ...

My client's substantial and luxurious home backed on to a London park. She explained that she and her daughter liked to sunbathe in the garden. She had however been horrified to discover that the local Scouts had been given permission to build a new HQ on a small hill overlooking her garden, which she felt meant that she could no longer sunbathe there.

Apparently, my client had marched up to the Scout hut and remonstrated with the leader about the new edifice, but had not been received sympathetically. According to the letter which the Scoutmaster then wrote to the local council, and which was to be the subject of the libel action, my client had then been 'abusive' towards him.

The letter was passed over the lunch table for me to read. I then passed it back to my client and launched into my advice. As I did so, the first clue emerged that acting for this client on this issue was a bullet that I should dodge. I began by explaining that the circumstances in which the letter was sent clothed it with what we in the trade call 'qualified privilege' and that this was a defence which would almost certainly defeat any libel claim against the Scouts.

As I did so, and before I could stop her, my client wrote the words 'qualified privilege' on the (original) letter about which she wanted me to sue for libel. So it would be that when we came to disclose the letter, when that stage had been reached in the proceedings, the lawyers on the other side would learn that I had advised there was a good defence to the claim.

Qualified privilege arises in a number of different circumstances and is a complex area of the law of defamation, so media law textbooks contain long chapters about it. It is easiest to explain by way of an example of when it arises. If an employer sacks an employee for dishonesty and is later approached by another company for a reference for that employee, then a response that the ex-employee is a thief would be highly defamatory. Any libel claim could be successfully defeated by the defence of truth (as was the Johnny Depp claim against the *Sun*)[24], but that is a major exercise which would require a full trial of the facts.

The law takes the view that when providing a reference you must be permitted to be candid. So as long as you do not say something in it which you know not to be true, or something which is wrong and about which you are reckless as to its truth or falsity, your communication will be protected by qualified privilege. In this case the Scoutmaster was writing to the council on a planning issue to do with the Scout hut and my client's objection to it. The letter therefore 'attracted' (another trade term) qualified privilege. To defeat that, we would effectively have to prove that the Scoutmaster was lying, which was most unlikely.

[24] Johnny Depp lost his libel claim against the publishers of the *Sun* over an article calling him a 'wife beater' ... In his ruling, the judge said that while Depp 'proved the necessary elements of his cause of action in libel', News Group Newspapers showed that what they published was 'substantially true'.

I strongly advised my client against suing the Scouts, being confident of where the sympathy of the court would lie. But she was insistent that she wanted to take legal action. Now that I am entirely my own master I would have backed out at that point. But I was a newly qualified solicitor at Schillings and so I felt that I should at least write a letter for her.

Rather to my surprise a letter came back from a top libel firm (bad news for me and my client), which robustly critiqued the threatened claim. But more surprising perhaps was that an offer was made to undertake not to repeat the allegation – one of the stipulations in my letter – and so something had been achieved.

My client was not satisfied, however, and instructed me to issue proceedings. I pressed her more firmly at this point on what had actually happened and prised out of her a partial admission that she might have said some things which could be interpreted as 'abusive'. But she was still determined to have her day in court.

I concluded that it would not be proper to start this claim, which in the light of what I then knew could be an abuse of the process of the court. That being the case, I wanted to decline the instructions. I then went to see my then boss Keith Schilling to ask his advice. To my relief, he agreed with me and gave me permission to do so – despite the fact that there were copious fees lost as a consequence.

Mercifully, I then took the precaution of ringing the ethics line at the Solicitors Regulation Authority (SRA) for advice. After explaining the situation, I asked whether I could decline the instructions. I was told that the fact that my unequivocal advice against pursuing a libel claim had been rejected meant that the 'relationship of trust and confidence' between me and my client had been sundered and so I could decline to act.

When I wrote to the client in those terms, her immediate response was to complain to the SRA about me. Fortunately, because I had been acting on SRA advice, the complaint was quickly thrown out.

FSL ensure continued press abuse

The ugly truth, which I say as a long-standing defendant lawyer, is that where Fleet Street is concerned, there are many who earn a good living by doing the unquestioning bidding of powerful and proven-to-be-corrupt organizations whose hubristic ambition is to say whatever they like without being accountable to anyone. There are of course honourable exceptions. The *Sun* and its lawyers were right to take on Hollywood actor Johnny Depp and prove (on the balance of probabilities) that its 'wife-beater' allegation was true.

It is the determination of entities such as News UK and Associated Newspapers to be accountable to no one but themselves – evading the obligation of responsibility placed on them by Article 10 – which have created yet another hopelessly compromised regulator in the form of IPSO, whose glaring lack of independence is itself a threat to true free speech. None of this would have been possible had not a number of lawyers, who must have known exactly what they were doing, facilitated it. One was an ex-appeal court judge.

THE BROADCAST MEDIA – A DIFFERENT SPECIES

By contrast to the print press, the broadcast media is, while not a thornless rose (it permitted Piers Morgan to get on screen), a very different proposition. The BBC is commendably right at the opposite end of the scale to the tabloid press, which is virtually unable to accept fault. Often the BBC is the first news organization to report on its own failings and tear into its senior personnel.

Anyone who listened in 2012, as I did, to the beating meted out on the *Today* programme by John Humphrys to his ultimate boss, the Director-General of the BBC George Entwistle, will be aware that it takes its public service obligations very seriously. This interview over the Jimmy Savile affair contributed to his resignation only hours later. It also led to Humphrys being awarded a Gold

Sony Award[25]. Such openness and candour is completely absent in Fleet Street, and yet it bombards the BBC with criticism.

All broadcasters must comply with the Ofcom Code, which stipulates both accuracy and fairness, as well as 'balance'. There is no obligation in the IPSO code either to show impartiality, or in any way to be fair. The broadcast media was birthed out of the BBC, with its ethical and public service undergirding. For all its failings, it has been my experience that the most accurate and reliable source of news is the BBC, closely followed by Sky News, ITN, Channel 5 and Channel 4 News – though the latter is sometimes tainted by its 'woke' editorial agenda.

I have crossed swords on a number of occasions with the normally excellent *Watchdog*, *Dispatches* and *Panorama*. I cut my teeth as a cub lawyer doing work for *Dispatches*, and of all the broadcasting legal teams, the toughest is at Channel 4, which also has a greater appetite for risk than either the BBC or ITV. All programme lawyers, however (of which I am one), take the Ofcom Code seriously; not least because Ofcom has the power to fine and ultimately to take away a broadcaster's licence. IPSO also has the power to fine up to £1 million, but there is not the slightest chance of it ever doing so because it is entirely dominated by the press. But it is not just that …

This is how it can be done – a contrasting account from the broadcast media

Boxers Michael Watson and Chris Eubank fought two memorable title fights. The second took place in 1991 and was stopped by the referee in round 12. When Watson reached his corner, he collapsed.

A limp Watson lay on the canvas for eight minutes before receiving any medical treatment. Twenty minutes passed before hospital care was administered with the result that he suffered

---

[25] https://www.bbc.co.uk/news/av/uk-225212190

severe brain damage, which left him partially paralyzed. This did not stop him showing incredible courage by completing the 2003 London Marathon over the course of six days to raise money for charity.

Chris Eubank was interviewed live in the ring immediately after the fight, after having been pummelled and knocked down by Michael Watson. In what I thought while I was watching the coverage might have been a clumsy attempt to compliment his courageous opponent, Eubank said this: 'I want him tested to see if he had anything in his blood because he was too ... He was so strong ... I want him tested because no one is that strong. I want his urine tested because no one is that strong. No one can be that strong.'

Some months later, Michael Watson's lawyer wrote to my client broadcaster threatening a claim in libel over the remarks made by Chris Eubank at the end of the bout, claiming the words meant he had taken banned drugs prior to the title fight or that he was suspected of doing so, and that he tried to deprive Eubank of the title by cheating.

In those days, a broadcaster was liable as a matter of law for any defamatory statement which they had transmitted even though they were neither the author nor the editor of the allegations, i.e. even when the programme was live.

As the broadcaster's external lawyer, I was sent the letter and asked to advise. I rang the in-house lawyer at the broadcaster and told her that I had seen the bout and had thought that Chris Eubank had not actually meant to allege that Michael Watson had taken drugs before the bout. I added that since, in those days, libel actions were decided by a jury, when the jury saw Watson being manhandled down the court steps in a wheelchair, there was only one way they were going to go in their determination – whatever they thought about what Eubank said. In those circumstances I thought that both the right, proper and commercially sensible thing to do was to settle with Watson straightaway. This would mean that he would not have to suffer the stress of litigation and any money which the broadcaster paid out went to him, rather than be dissipated by having to pay both his lawyer and me.

The in-house lawyer agreed and I was instructed to ring Watson's lawyer and strike a deal before I had even responded to the letter. It did not take us long to agree on a figure and by the time the whole action was over our combined costs were only modest. This was a good deal for my client and, equally importantly, a good one for Michael Watson.

An apology read during the Channel 5 news

My experience of the broadcast media, both acting for and against it, is that there is on the whole a sense of responsibility to get their facts right and not mislead their viewers, and that if they err some concession should be made. I managed to persuade Channel 5 to include an apology and retraction to my client Paul McKenna as part of its main evening news.

I well remember the raised eyebrows of the newsreader as he read the apology via the autocue. I have also experienced the opposite determination not to admit error on a few occasions from programme-makers, but that mindset is sadly endemic (though mercifully, not all-pervasive) in Fleet Street.

5

Avoiding a Media Crisis

If you are a business or individual with any kind of public profile, media attention is unavoidable. It is the inevitable consequence of success. Your relationship with the media should enjoy a great deal of care and attention, and when it works well it can be symbiotic. A good PR lawyer recognizes that and does all they can to preserve it. However, while not entirely inevitable in the same way as death and taxes, the threat of a media crisis is a near certainty. Your primary aim should always be to avoid it entirely. The purpose of this chapter is to provide the means of doing so.

The *Daily Mail* test

I sat at a dinner party next to a civil servant who was so senior that he attended Cabinet meetings. He told me that every new policy initiative was subject to what was called 'the *Daily Mail* test'.

Accepting that this is a horrifying example of the media tail wagging the political dog, it is nonetheless a sensible test for senior management to apply to its actions: 'How would this look if it ended up on the front page of the *Daily Mail*?' If a company does not routinely ask this question internally, then it is likely to find that the *Daily Mail* or its equivalent will subject them to rather more public and brutal inquisitions in the years to come.

THE BEST PROTECTION FROM MEDIA CRISES IS DOING THE RIGHT THING

One thing I take from Warren Buffett's quotation about the importance of reputation (*see also* page 42) is that I believe he was thinking primarily about adopting the kind of corporate culture which renders media crisis far less likely than he would be where the corporate culture is rotten.

The great American evangelist D L Moody said this: 'If I take care of my character, my reputation will take care of itself.' That was in the latter part of the nineteenth century and is not entirely true today. However, you do not need to read erudite PR tomes to know that a company which has no or very few skeletons in their cupboard is going to be far less vulnerable to media crises than one where the cupboard can barely contain them all. It has very much been my professional experience that this is the case.

I can think of only one corporate client with an exemplary corporate culture which was the subject of a series of damaging allegations in the media, none of which was true. That client, an ethical investment fund, was just unfortunate to be caught up in the Brexit debate and unjustly become a whipping boy for a number of anti-Brexit campaigners. However, the client adopted a zero tolerance to the false stories using all the available legal and regulatory means and has now largely eradicated them.

Similarly, Julian Richer's retail empire (Richer Sounds) selling music and audio equipment is now in its 42nd year. Many years ago Julian was the drummer, my brother was the guitarist and I was the bass player in a school band. I have therefore known Julian since school days. So far as I am aware he has not suffered a media crisis because he is a man of honour and integrity, and someone who genuinely puts his customers first while taking good care of his staff.

TAKE A CANDID LOOK IN THE MIRROR

Taking a candid look at your policies towards your staff, your customers, the environment, company ethics, inclusion, and in doing so deploying the lens of an investigative journalist, is a powerful hedge against attacks by the media. This job is best done in conjunction with a PR expert from outside your company who would be better able to give you independent and candid advice. I also highly recommend Julian Richer's excellent book *The Ethical Capitalist: How to Make Business Work Better for Society*[1] as a guide to how to make your company less vulnerable to media criticism – legitimate or otherwise.

CREATING A MEDIA CRISIS BY DOING THE WRONG THING

By contrast an organization like the Lloyds Banking Group plc (LBG), which has rightly been at the wrong end of fierce media criticism for a number of years because – *inter alia* – of a fraud that it committed against small and medium enterprises (SME), has found itself in that position because of the appalling way it has treated its SME customers, which it serially robbed and ruined. It could neither have done so, nor covered its actions up for so many years, without a small army of unprincipled professionals willing to do the bank's dirty work for it.

I know a lot about LBG's image problems – which are not nearly as bad as they should be – because I have acted for numerous victims of a massive fraud which emanated from within that company, and in particular its most well-known victim, TV presenter Noel Edmonds. To my delight, I was so vocal in the defence of my clients and critical of LBG that I received a letter from their Magic Circle lawyers (an elite group of major London firms) threatening to sue me for libel, to which I responded in terms of 'go ahead, punk, make my day'. To my disappointment, they did not.

When you conduct yourself in the disgraceful way that LBG has, there is a limit to what any PR company – however powerful – can do to save you. LBG has tried to spend its way out of problems by

[1] https://www.penguin.co.uk/books/111/1115429/the-ethical-capitalist--how-to-make-business-work-better-for-soc/9781847942210.html

investing astronomical sums in their ubiquitous and mendacious 'By Your Side' advertising campaign. The vast cost of this campaign would have been better spent in paying a proper level of compensation to those whom the bank has grievously wronged.

CARPHONE WAREHOUSE

Here is an illustration of a problem which could be solved simply and inexpensively by an ethical in-house lawyer, but can turn into a major financial and PR blow if handled by the obverse. It also demonstrates that crises can emanate from every level of a corporation, and can even be sparked by the actions of a low-level employee.

One of my ex-beauty queen clients is now an 'influencer'. She once picked me up from my office in a magnificent white Bentley convertible to attend a sports arbitration hearing, where she was the star witness against a Premier League ex-boyfriend who was being sued by his agent. Cherie Blair QC was on the adjudicating panel.

My client had discovered small lumps in her breasts which were surgically removed, bringing the risk of scarring. In order to disappear from the public eye during her recuperation, she travelled to the Mediterranean where she had hired a villa, and during the stay she took some pictures of her breasts with her mobile phone to trace the progress of the healing of the wounds.

Sometime later her mobile phone malfunctioned and she took it to a branch of the Carphone Warehouse where she asked for it to be replaced and for the data from her old phone to be transferred to the new one. The man behind the counter recognized my client, and as well as transferring the data from her old phone to the new one, he also transferred it to his laptop. That data included the intimate pictures my client had taken of herself.

This individual then rang around various British tabloids to try to sell those pictures. Fortunately, the publication of those images would have been so obvious a regulatory and legal breach, no one 'bought them up' (the industry term). It was also known that this woman was a client of mine, which will have helped. One of the journalists contacted my client to warn her that these photographs were being touted for sale.

I was instructed and wrote to the Carphone Warehouse and began a dialogue with someone who was apparently their General Counsel. My letter to the shop worker had the desired effect and he promptly waved a white flag, ran for cover and assured me that he had deleted the photos. I had sufficiently frightened him to be confident that he was telling the truth. Unsurprisingly, on the issue of costs and damages he pleaded poverty – especially as he had been sacked.

However, no such pragmatism was exhibited by his employer to whom I wrote asking for some modest payment to my client, principally so that she did not have to bear her legal fees. Her pictures however had been sent around Fleet Street and seen by various people for the purpose of their evaluation and consequently, though to a limited degree, her privacy had been invaded.

There then began an absurd sequence of assertions from this lawyer as to why the Carphone Warehouse was under no obligation to compensate my client. The first was that they did not bear vicarious liability for the actions of their shop worker. This was ridiculous for a number of reasons, including the fact that my client had done business with him standing at the counter of a Carphone Warehouse store. Her defective phone had been purchased from Carphone Warehouse, she had transacted with him for a new Carphone Warehouse phone and had asked him in his capacity as a Carphone Warehouse employee to do the data transfer. Despite sending reams of probative case law over to this individual, he would still not accept that Carphone Warehouse bore any legal responsibility for the actions of its employee.

One of the things which he asserted was that Carphone Warehouse shops never do data transfers. Therefore, the transfer of data was outside the terms of his employment contract with the company, and accordingly not something which fixed the shop with vicarious liability for the actions of this individual. That was plainly wrong as a matter of law, but I was also confident that what this individual did for my client and her phone was done routinely by Carphone Warehouse staff. I was blessed because at that time the BBC was making a documentary called *See You in Court*[2] about celebrities that were taking legal action to protect their reputation and privacy. As one of the media lawyers approached, I was asked whether there was a case which the documentary-makers could follow which could form part of the programme.

When I outlined the case on a no-names basis, the BBC loved it, so I contacted my client to see if she would like to participate, to which she readily assented. We then started filming meetings with her in the office, my reading correspondence from the Carphone Warehouse, my speaking to camera about how I was going to respond to them, the absurdity of their legal position, etc.

At the time I had an excellent trainee whom I decided to send to some Carphone Warehouse premises, starting with the one where my client had been served and then visiting two or three nearby branches. On each occasion he asked whether the branch would transfer data from his old phone to a new one if he bought it there; the answer was unhesitatingly in the affirmative.

Since I was working with the programme-makers, I thought it might be fun to send my trainee on this mission accompanied by a BBC film crew. It worked brilliantly and so we had evidence on film that the assertion made by this errant lawyer about data transfer was a lie. Therefore I was able to respond to his letter denying that they did data transfers with not only the fact that my assistant had been to these shops to prove that that was untrue, but he had been accompanied by a BBC film crew. I received an outraged letter in response, which I enjoyed reading to camera.

Even then, this individual's hubris and stupidity did not allow him to concede defeat. He then instructed his lawyers to make an application for summary judgment, which went spectacularly wrong, and my barrister and I had the pleasure not only of

[2] The programme was a 'fly on the wall' documentary which filmed the progress of these claims and featured meetings between the celebrities and their lawyers, and explanations of the legal processes featured.

speaking to camera before the hearing, but also in rather smug terms afterwards.

The case did eventually settle after it had received damaging media coverage for the Carphone Warehouse, both via the well-rated BBC programme and press coverage, and also cost them a substantial sum. The in-house lawyer was sacked.

None of this would have occurred if the company had just apologized to a customer who had been grievously wronged by one of its employees and paid her a modest sum in compensation. This would have been both the right thing to do and by far the most commercially sensible option. If you are either a company or an individual, if you employ people who have no proper set of personal ethics, then you place your organization's reputation at risk.

6

Preparing for a Media Crisis

One of the challenges of writing this book is that it will (I hope) be read by a wide range of folk, which will include both those who already practice crisis PR and who want to a better job for their clients, and general counsel and board members for whom the subject matter is likely to be new. I must however cater for those who are starting from scratch, so I began by dealing with some fundamental issues; such as the diverse nature of the British media, how editorial decisions are made and what there is by way of regulatory and legal protections for both businesses and individuals who find themselves confronted by PR crises.

THE BUSINESS COMMUNITY IS INSUFFICIENTLY GEARED UP FOR MEDIA CRISES

Despite the immense importance to any company of its reputation, in the early days of my presenting crisis PR seminars it struck me forcibly that many of the blue-chip companies to which I presented invested vast sums of money to protect their intellectual property, their physical property, their financial assets, etc. However, they seemed far less focused on protecting their primary asset – their reputation, and had invested far too little management time in preparing to deal with media crises.

I once presented my crisis PR seminar to the entire comms team of one of the major supermarket chains and was astonished to learn that none of them were aware of the existence of a PR lawyer. Any company that sells directly to the consumer is going to be a favourite target of the media. To have no access to a PR lawyer leaves you with scant protection in such a situation.

A CAUTIONARY TALE

A couple of years into my tenure at Schillings, by which time I had become a partner, I was busy looking after the reputations and privacy of royalty, sports stars, movie stars, rock stars and the like, when I read a remarkable news story which is ultimately responsible for my writing this book.

A number of large companies providing consumer goods and services met at a London hotel to discuss what they could do about the reputation and brand damage they were suffering at the hands of the BBC's *Watchdog*, a thorn in their sides for some 10 years. At the meeting's conclusion, they decided to send a deputation, cap in hand, to seek the assistance of the BBC governors. Predictably, the BBC sent them off with a flea in their ear and leaked the story to the *Daily Mail* which gave it a two-page spread with an interview with a jubilant Anne Robinson, then the main presenter of *Watchdog*, about how this proved just what magnificent a consumer champion the programme was.

I was astonished. Apparently, despite the fact that these were substantial businesses – in several cases multinationals – they did not have access to sufficiently robust and savvy PR support to either provide them with a means of dealing effectively with *Watchdog* when it stepped over the line – as I have successfully done in the past; or to avoid them scoring such a monumental PR own goal, while at the same time strengthening the hand of their tormentors.

It also occurred to me that not only had these companies apparently not been warned against this kamikaze PR stunt, their doomed mission may even have been prompted by errant PR advice. Otherwise, what were they thinking? If there is one lesson to learn here, it is that trying to tackle a potential media crisis without some form of expert advice almost invariably ends badly. I have seen some really horrible attempts to do so.

It also struck me that this was something of a contrast with those of my talent management and PR company clients who looked after top entertainment and/or sports stars, who had generally schooled themselves in the basics of media law, who would have had sufficient media savvy not to make such a spectacular gaffe, and who also knew where to access the kind of robust media professionals who could do the job.

One leading talent agency has even called me in to deliver a crisis management seminar to its celebrity clients. I was also asked by the BBC to deliver the seminar to the cast of *EastEnders* on set – a bizarre but wonderful experience as I realized that all the cast that I met were exactly the same as the characters they played on screen. I felt like an extra during the filming of an episode.

LEARNING HOW TO MAKE USE OF THE CRISIS MANAGEMENT TOOLS YOU HAVE BEEN GIVEN

The legal and regulatory provisions to which I refer here are ones which have been made available either by the media industry itself, or via our democratic process. They should be fully utilized because their very purpose is to prevent the public being misled about (inter alia) you, your products and your services, or those of your clients. This both serves the public interest and that of stakeholders in the business confronted by a media crisis.

The regulatory and legal provisions and methodologies which I deploy in my work are essentially the same for corporate bodies as they are for high-profile individuals. Increasingly, senior management in the corporate realm also need protection for themselves and their families when the media decides they too are fair game for intrusion.

BEING READY FOR A MEDIA CRISIS

If you are a high-profile company – especially one which deals with consumers – or a prominent individual, it is not a question of whether but when you will be confronted with a media crisis.

In an electronic age where media crises can erupt in seconds, it is essential that all the team (internal and external) which you will need are already in place. Ideally, they have already also been given a 'dry run' to ensure that the various elements are in place, efficient and will work seamlessly together.

Your internal team
The decision-making team should be as small as possible – ideally one, but more realistically two, with three as a maximum. All members of that team must be prepared to go into action on a 24/7 basis because time, tide and the media wait for no man. I recently worked for a major entertainment company where each decision had to be approved by a committee of four – it was very difficult to do a good job for them.

I was instructed by an elite sports client on Boxing Day and by a major corporate client the following day. Between them, they needed me to be in action right up to New Year's Day and beyond. I have had to work in my car, in airport lounges, walking in the Alps, by the poolside, having my hair cut and even sitting on the loo. There is no peace, either for the wicked or the PR professional, which can present a challenge for a committed husband and a father, which I have been for most of my career.

It is impossible for a PR professional to deal with a committee in a PR crisis. I have had situations where I have rapidly drafted up a robust response to a threatened newspaper story and sent it off to a client, only for there then to be delays while an internal debate is carried on and/or an attempt made to re-draft the letter in committee. There is little point in investing in top PR professionals only to ignore their advice.

By contrast, to illustrate how well this can work, one of my American multinational clients was confronted by a story originating from an overseas magazine that one of their brand-leading products was carcinogenic – which it absolutely was not. The story had been planted in a European magazine by a commercial rival and had just been picked up by the *Mail Online*. I was instructed by the GC, who was in close touch with his global head of comms. Within minutes, I had drafted a letter to the *Mail Online*, which the GC had approved and was duly sent off and the story taken down.

In those few minutes the *Sun* had enquired about the story and was also ready to run it. I sent the in-house lawyer to the *Sun*, someone with whom I have dealt for over 25 years, a letter similar to the one that I had sent to the *Mail Online* and the story was duly dropped – which would not have happened had I not persuaded the *Mail Online* to delete its article. It was therefore only 'live' for a few minutes on the *Mail Online* and then disappeared without trace.

Had I not got it taken down from the *Mail Online* website within minutes, not only the *Sun* but most of the rest of the media, UK and overseas, would have been running the story, which would have spread like wildfire. The impact on sales of this product would have been catastrophic, which would have been the outcome if the client had merely sent a denial statement. This was not the first piece of work I had done for that client and they have immaculate internal processes in place and they also knew exactly what kind of crisis PR was necessary for that situation.

They also had my mobile phone number.

Your external team
When a PR crisis looms, by far the best outcome is for it to be averted. The professional who is most likely to achieve that is a PR lawyer. Where the prospective PR crisis is of a sort which is susceptible to being killed off, then you need to instruct a PR lawyer as quickly as possible. The best placed professional to judge whether you have a prospect of killing off the story will also be a PR lawyer.

It is impossible to overemphasize how important speed is in these circumstances. It follows then that the time to have established a relationship with a PR lawyer is not when the crisis is looming, or (even worse) after it has broken. That needs to be done as part of your preparations.

You also need both the mobile phone number and email address of an individual, rather than a firm, and that individual needs to be at partner level. As with many aspects of PR, most of what you learn comes from actually doing the job. There is no way that a few years' qualified associate is going to be equal to a situation where a national newspaper is threatening to publish something which could have serious commercial consequences – not least because that associate may be obliged to run all his work past a partner or barrister, but also because they will be dealing with a top-flight media lawyer on the other side with decades of experience.

Do not use your panel firm (or any firm) if it does not have proven expertise in the field of PR. You will be sending in boys to fight men, because the lawyers at the other end will be Premier League in their field who eat, sleep and dream media regulation and law.

Don't hire a Magic Circle firm for media work – or send amateurs against pros

Magic Circle firms will not have the requisite expertise in-house because it is not economically viable in organizations where the partners aspire to earn seven-figure incomes. Do not be fobbed off with a solicitor who is just a litigator with some experience of media work – or worse still, just a litigator. This is because the lawyers (and to some extent, the journalists) on the other side *will* be experts in media law and regulation. In-house lawyers at newspapers know by heart the regulations and laws governing the output of their employers. They attend seminars, receive briefing papers from their dutiful external lawyers and practice in the field all day and every day.

Do not send in an amateur to take on a professional.

Two Magic Circle firms get it badly wrong doing media work

I was delivering a crisis PR seminar to a major city PR agency where I made this point, and at the end of the seminar, one of those present told me that one of his clients was a major high-street bank. On its behalf he had asked its panel lawyer (one of the immense and eye-wateringly expensive Magic Circle firms) whether in the face of defamatory allegations against the bank they could sue for libel. He was told emphatically by the Magic Circle firm that companies cannot sue for libel – which is 100 per cent wrong.

This illustrates the perils of seeking media law advice from non-specialist lawyers – even if they are from expensive Magic Circle firms. I took over a defamation case from a Magic Circle firm where it was being incompetently defended by a copyright specialist – that being the nearest the firm could find to a bona fide media specialist. The consequences for the client were catastrophic because it brought his company down and was close to bankrupting him. After sorting out the claim successfully (the jury awarded no damages to the claimant), I then secured a six-figure sum in negligence damages from the city firm.

Media work is a highly specialist legal practice, requiring deep knowledge of the regulation, applicable law and industry if it is to be done effectively. You cannot dip into and out of it.

ONLY HIRE ONE OF THE ELITE MEDIA LAWYERS

It is not difficult to conduct an internet search to find whether any recommendation by your PR agency has the right qualifications for the job. If (for example) they have not been cited in one of the legal directories as high-tier experts in the field, you should not hire them. Nor should you hire them if they act for any of the Fleet Street titles or are predominantly defendant lawyers. If so, they will inevitably be commercially compromised. Defendant lawyering is also a very different skill.

One large corporate PR company with which I was dialoguing told me that they referred their crisis PR to the law firm which hired them to do its PR. The firm in question had no profile for the kind of work which would be needed and so the interests of their client were being relegated behind their own commercial interests – a good example not to follow.

There are less than a dozen senior PR lawyers who really know what they are doing. Make sure you hire one of them. Even then you cannot be sure of the very best advice if there is an incomplete knowledge of how the media works, which is hard to acquire by external observation only.

Some bad advice

Even a lawyer from one of the elite firms can still get it wrong. I was at a meeting where two related parties were at the wrong end of a major media storm; I was the representing one, while a partner from a top media firm was representing another. The partner advised that the letter of rebuttal over a particular story should be sent in at the last possible moment. As courteously as I could, I explained that this was not correct, which I knew in part from my work as a defendant lawyer.

A news story is like a drying clay pot – the longer you leave it, the harder it is to remould. At a Fleet Street title there will come a point where the newspaper is about to be put to bed and there is little or no time either to abandon or amend an article. A letter sent at that late point has far less prospect of achieving the desired outcome than one sent four hours earlier.

PR lawyers save you money

Another reason why your first port of call should be a PR lawyer is financial. For my large American client and its hygiene products (*see also* pages 176–77), all the necessary work was done in around a couple of hours. I can only guess at the loss of sales that would have occurred if all the national newspapers had reported that this brand-leading product risked causing cancer in children. My bill was about £2,000.

Had the story broken, leaving aside the loss of sales, a massive investment with a PR company would have been necessary to try and mitigate the damage – which in any event would not be possible to erase altogether, especially from overseas websites.

The perspective of an editorial lawyer

When operating as an editorial lawyer I take account of the difference in quality between a letter sent by a genuine media expert and someone who merely dabbles, which is immense, as is its impact.

LBG instructed the partner at a Magic Circle firm with whom I was jousting for my client Noel Edmonds to send me a letter threatening to sue me for libel because I had been outspokenly critical in the media of Lloyds' treatment of Mr Edmonds and my other fraud victim clients. One of the reasons why I did not take the slightest notice of it (apart from sending a very dusty response) was that the writer – a commercial litigator – clearly had no idea what he was talking about.

If that is the impression which is given to a newspaper or programme lawyer, then your chances of preventing the PR crisis from breaking or curtailing it if it is underway are slim.

Checklists for choosing your external team

Unless you are a massive corporation it is unlikely that you will have in your comms team a genuine crisis PR expert, or the capacity to deal with a crisis PR situation which has broken. You must therefore also have established a relationship with an external source of crisis PR before their services are needed, and ensure that you have 24/7 access to an individual who is a genuine and experienced crisis comms expert.

Your PR expert
You should be looking for the following qualities in your PR expert:

1. Someone with extensive experience not only (say) as a
   journalist, but also of doing crisis PR – the two being by
   no means the same skills;
2. An acknowledged expertise in crisis PR rather than
   other forms of PR; so if crisis PR is merely a part of their
   practice then you should avoid them;
3. Identify an individual whose contact details you can have
   and whose credentials you are confident in;
4. Check that they have not represented clients so toxic as
   to sully the reputation of the PR company itself, which in
   turn will reflect badly on you/your client;
5. Ensure they recognize that the best outcome for you is to
   ensure there is no media crisis and offer a credible means
   of achieving that;
6. If you are an individual or small company and they are
   a massive PR firm, then you are unlikely to be a priority
   client, so find a smaller outfit.

Your PR lawyer
This is what you should be looking for in your PR lawyer:

1. Someone whose name and work you can find via Google;
2. They work at a firm which has not acted for such toxic
   clients as to render their instruction something which
   stigmatizes;
3. If they have not appeared as leaders in their field (both as
   an individual and a firm) in the legal directories, don't hire
   them;
4. If either the individual or their firm has acted for a
   national newspaper, don't hire them. I say this for two
   reasons. One is that they are likely to be professionally
   compromised because they will not want to bite the hand
   of the Goliath that feeds them. The other is because of the

extent to which ethical principles must be sacrificed to do that work;

5. If you can find a solicitor who also has a recognized defendant practice, they will be less of a 'red rag to a bull' than some solicitors are to the media and will also be able to do their job better;

6. You are going to be dependent on this professional when making decisions which are likely to impact the viability of your business and/or your own personal circumstances. Therefore, you need to have complete confidence that they are going to advise you with the benefit of a strong set of personal values. If you are a rich and powerful company or individual, you present your lawyer with a strong temptation to make the prospect of fee income a factor in their advice;

7. Find a lawyer therefore who will vigorously talk you out of embarking on litigation which you have anything less than a good prospect of winning;

8. You also need to hire someone who you think, if you put them in a ring, would be the last person standing – going toe-to-toe with Fleet Street in particular is not for the faint-hearted;

9. Ideally, they will be able to touch-type, which is necessary for the sake of speed. They may not have time to send a dictated letter off to be typed.

7

What to Do if a Media Crisis Looms

There is no question but that the best outcome for you or your client is to nip a looming PR crisis in the bud by ensuring any false and damaging allegations which a newspaper or broadcaster threatens to disseminate never see the light of day. Any source of PR support which does not make that its first-line offering is like a doctor who will treat you when you are ill, but will not vaccinate you to keep you well. Fire them!

Missed opportunities and misconceptions in the PR community

For reasons I do not fully understand, this primary service does not appear to feature either in any of the many crisis PR offerings from PR agencies (based on my reading of their websites) that I have read, or articles and/or books on the subject that I have studied as part of my research for this book. I hope this is not because the fees that are earned by killing off a story are a small fraction of those earned by trying to manage it.

Even if it is not possible to force a paper or broadcaster to abandon a false and damaging story entirely, the astute use of the various regulatory and/or legal means available to diminish the severity of the story itself (rather than merely trying to antidote it via a statement or engaging in an unequal competition with the media to contradict it) will not only lessen its initial negative impact. The ancillary benefit of reduction in volume and/or seriousness of the allegations also makes it less likely that other elements of the media will pick it up.

After a negative story has broken, there remains much good work that should be done both to mitigate the damage and to stem the spread of the damaging story, which I deal with in the next chapter. Some issues such as the need to dialogue with key stakeholders are so obvious I do not propose to dwell on them. But in an internet age, bad news spreads like a virus if vigorous and prompt steps are not taken to inhibit its progress. In those circumstances you need a top PR agency with proven crisis PR credentials feeding in antidote into the ether, and a top-notch media lawyer to stem the spread of the poison and to secure prompt corrections from the main media players who have run the story. That is done by using the various regulatory and legal tools which were created for this very purpose.

THE TWO-STAGE EDITORIAL DECISION AND THE KEY ROLE OF THE EDITORIAL LAWYER

To fully understand the methodology for preventing media crises from happening, you must start with how editorial decisions are made. It is a two-stage process:

- The first is whether this is a story we want to include in a television programme or publish in an article – i.e. is it newsworthy?
- If newsworthy, then the second stage is to assess whether the broadcast/publication of the story carries with it a regulatory and/or legal risk. It is on that stage of the editorial decision that the work of a PR lawyer impacts.

The second part of the editorial decision is made primarily by the in-house lawyer at the broadcaster or publisher. Newspapers also employ 'night lawyers' to oversee the publication of stories which crop up out of office hours, or where there are late challenges to stories.

High-profile current affairs programmes such as *Panorama*, *Watchdog* or *Dispatches* have 'programme lawyers' embedded within the overall production team to ensure that the end product complies with the relevant law and regulation, but also that the way in which the programme is made is compliant with the relevant Ofcom Code and the broadcaster's own guidelines.

This is highly specialized and challenging work, but it is also immensely rewarding. It requires a great deal of judgement and a degree of courage on the part of the lawyer; especially when dealing with a subject matter which, if not carefully handled, could bring either a regulatory or legal penalty. More than once I have woken up on the morning after having done this work, thinking, *What have I done? They're bound to sue!* Mercifully, that has never happened – yet.

Michael Jackson

Sometimes an editorial lawyer can be put under immense pressure to green-light material which they know they should not. I was once legalling out a popular late-night talk show which was being recorded as 'live' and in the script was a joke which made an unequivocal allegation against singer-songwriter Michael Jackson that he was a paedophile. This was back in the mid-1990s when there were merely rumours to that effect. I was given a hard time in the 'gallery' by both the star of the show – from which the programme took its name – and its director, who wanted to keep the joke in.

I stood my ground and the joke came out. Not many years later Michael Jackson did sue the broadcaster for libel over a Martin Bashir documentary where it was implied that Jackson was a paedophile. I took the now-notorious Bashir's witness statement on which the defence of the action was based – a fascinating exercise.

Fun with the Church of Scientology and *South Park*

I legalled out a high-profile documentary about Scientology for another broadcasting client. There are circumstances when the subject matter of a programme (or article) is so high-risk and sensitive that external advice will be sought either from an expert barrister or solicitor. In this case, the Scientology cult was known to be highly litigious and intolerant of criticism, as well as having immense financial resources.

This indeed proved to be the case when heavyweight libel specialists Carter-Ruck sent over 20 letters to me while I was doing that work, threatening a slew of copyright claims, privacy claims, defamation claims and Ofcom complaints. Some of the letters had enclosures so massive they had to be sent in the form of a disc. I did not waste time or client money reading the content of the discs which I knew merely contained Scientology propaganda.

The three prospective claimants were the Church of Scientology, its current leader – David Miscavige – and the Hollywood actor Tom Cruise. In addition to my existing knowledge about the cult, my research told me that the evidence of the darkness of Scientology was overwhelming and the many allegations against the Church could be readily proven. It also taught me that David Miscavige was not even allowed to give evidence in legal proceedings, let alone be a claimant in one.

As for Tom Cruise, I had previously passed an episode of *South Park* which had crudely implied that he was gay. Nothing had come of it. Putting myself in the shoes of the Carter-Ruck guys, i.e. considering how I would be advising the actor in these circumstances, I could not see him taking the immense risk taken by Johnny Depp in suing the *Sun*. I therefore made it abundantly clear to my opposite numbers at Carter-Ruck that if Tom Cruise did sue, the case would go all the way to trial and he would spend a very uncomfortable day or two being ferociously cross-examined by a top defamation QC.

There was not a peep out of Carter-Ruck after the programme was transmitted and none of the threatened consequences, despite the fact I had advised not a single second be cut.

Apart from the sheer joy of playing my tiny part in getting this excellent broadcast journalism on screen, I found myself working alongside editorial lawyers at both Associated Newspapers (which is capable of getting it massively right as well as massively wrong) and the BBC as we were all on the same side running similar stories. This enabled me to strengthen my relationships there and to garner further goodwill, which is invaluable to my crisis PR work.

Legalling out *South Park*

It is however rare for an editorial lawyer to enjoy the luxury of time to conduct his own research to supplement the material provided by the programme-makers. I only had a very short time within which to turn around *South Park* between the US and UK transmissions, which meant I had little time to research the allegations against individuals and companies which were liberally scattered in the programmes.

All I had time to do was to follow my instinct and make a risk assessment based on whether the individual or the company had raised objections to this or any other allegation in the past. As I explain later in the book, engaging in robust and deft crisis PR not only pays dividends in the short term, but will impact on the thinking of an editorial lawyer and consequently editorial decisions in the future – some of which you will never learn about.

The 'Golden Hour' principle

Until I began to do research for this book I had blithely thought that I was the first to borrow the medical 'Golden Hour' term for crisis PR – a term which I learned while undertaking courses in

First Aid where it is said that in a medical emergency everything
turns on the actions of the first aider and/or medics in the first 60
minutes after the injury has occurred. I have since learned that it is
in fact, in PR terms, a cliché.

For regulatory and legal reasons, a newspaper or broadcaster will
almost always give you advance notice of a negative story. Ethical
journalists will also do so because they are keen to publish the truth
and will recognize that they are only going to be able to achieve
that outcome if they run the story past its subject for comment.
This is your Golden Hour: don't waste it. If you are properly geared
up to deal with a media crisis, then hopefully you will operate like
a well-oiled machine and follow a well-practiced routine. These are
the most important tasks:

1. Contact a source of external crisis comms and your PR
   lawyer.
2. Assign someone to establish the facts, collate documents/
   links, etc.
3. If you have been provided with insufficient notice of
   exactly what is being alleged against you, then you should
   respond promptly requiring the journalist to give more
   detail – most efficaciously done via a PR lawyer.
4. If you have been given an unreasonable deadline within
   to which to respond to the threatened story, send a
   holding response to the journalist and ideally to the
   editorial lawyer/legal team reminding them of their legal
   and regulatory obligations to provide sufficient notice –
   again best done via a PR lawyer.
5. A broadcaster or newspaper should be reminded of the
   recent decision of a senior media judge who robustly
   criticized a failure of a defendant to provide a full,
   accurate and fair summary of the allegations they
   intended to publish, and the unreasonable deadline that
   they provided for a response.
6. As soon as possible a decision should be made as to
   whether this is a story to try to knock out in whole or
   in part.

7. If it should be knocked out in full, then right from the outset a maximum effort should be made to gather all the evidence which can be released to the broadcaster or newspaper to prove that the story is wrong. This should be accompanied by a robust reminder of the applicable legal and regulatory issues.

8. Once an appropriate deadline has been established, try not to leave your response to the last minute. You have a much better chance either of knocking out the story or moderating it if you send in your rebuttal sooner rather than later.

9. Where you are aiming to knock the story out, your primary objective is to create the perception on the part of the editorial lawyer that if this story is published it will be subjected to at least one form of independent scrutiny (regulatory and/or legal) and that for the cogent reasons that you have advanced, the story will not bear such scrutiny.

10. A decision has to be made not only about how to respond, but who will respond; the second question being a major factor in your chances of knocking the story out or at least attenuating it. Where you are at risk of your rights being infringed via a media attack, the appropriate professional to respond is a PR lawyer, which will come as no surprise to the editorial lawyer or the senior editorial team. Still less will it evoke suspicion. When in my editorial lawyer role, I presume that any savvy company or individual will deploy an expert PR lawyer in their defence because they are best equipped for the job and because deploying the relevant regulatory and legal issues are essential to effective crisis PR.

11. Even when the final communication prior to publication or broadcast is one which accepts the truth of the story, if sent by a PR lawyer it is going to be written up and edited with a greater degree of caution if the perception is created that it will be scrutinized for its regulatory and/or legal compliance post-publication.

When the Golden Hour is in fact 20 minutes

The fastest I have ever had to go into action to kill off a broadcast story is 20 minutes. I was delivering a crisis PR seminar at a London hotel to a top sports management company when, just after the seminar was over, a high-profile e-lender client emailed to say that Radio 4's *PM* programme was to run a very negative package about the company.

I had 20 minutes to draft a letter, get it approved by the client and then send it to the BBC – it being 4.40 p.m. and the *PM* programme goes out at 5. So I opened my laptop in the hotel lobby and went to work. Mercifully I can pretty well touch-type and am able to operate remotely as my laptop is attached to my hip. The letter was approved and sent to the BBC legal department before the programme went on air and the section about my client was dropped.

Securing the cancellation of a TV programme

My client was an international online retailer which was informed by one of our national broadcasters that a programme was in production which was seriously adverse to that company. The commercial broadcaster had been a client and I had a good relationship with the senior editorial lawyer. I studied the compliance letter which had been sent to ensure that the broadcaster's obligation under Section 7.11 of the Ofcom Code was complied with so there was due and timely notice to my client of the impending programme.

I began corresponding with the broadcaster and challenging it on various points. As I did so it became clear to me it had deployed the wrong expert to substantiate the main criticisms it wished to make against my client in the programme. I pressed it hard on this point, knowing that if I were the programme lawyer this would make me uncomfortable. The programme was dropped.

Some more case studies

I was instructed by a store chain which discovered that their trade magazine had published a front-page story saying they were about to close down – which they were not. Needless to say, this did not help in the securing of credit, the purchasing of stock, the hiring of staff, etc. I was instructed to take on the magazine and was able to secure a prompt front-page apology and retraction.

I have acted for a number of blue-chip schools and universities. One particularly prestigious school contacted me because *The Sunday Times* was threatening to publish an article suggesting that there was systematic bullying in the school. I challenged the newspaper hard on this, but it was determined to go ahead with the story. I therefore suggested that the school invite as many as possible of their students to sign a statement asserting that there was not systematic bullying in the school, and seek the support of the parents.

Because I was dealing with a 'Sunday', I had the time to do this. The school went into action with admirable speed and before the Saturday deadline I was able to deliver a document which *all* the pupils had signed and some robust letters from parents to *The Sunday Times* editor. The newspaper was unhappy to be confronted by this and appeared to think that it had in some way been unfairly treated. However, the story was abandoned and the PR crisis averted.

Other successes in my practice include killing off COVID-19 stories for blue-chip schools. This was just as the pandemic was breaking in the UK and the newspapers were desperate to be the first to report that the illness had spread to a school. Twice I was able to persuade different papers that they had got their facts wrong.

Types of PR crises

The catastrophe
PR crises come in all sorts of shapes and sizes, but some are beyond the power of even the best PR lawyer to curtail – such

as an explosion in a factory, a massive oil spill, a train crash or a dangerous product fault. In these circumstances your first call should be to a PR outfit with a top crisis PR team with whom you have an existing relationship and therefore knows your business. You will need a team of people to deal with what may be a tsunami of press enquiries and expert advice about your 'messages' in those circumstances, which must be clear and consistent. The key elements of your messaging should be candour, concern and where you bear some responsibility for what has happened, acknowledging this. No UK judge is going to hold that against you at some later date.

The media coverage should however be carefully monitored and where there is misreporting – usually exaggerating the true scale of the problem, or wrongly attributing blame – the errant broadcaster or publisher must be contacted immediately to put matters right. If that is not done, then the error(s) will be picked up and repeated by other elements of the media.

That is best done by a PR lawyer whose power of persuasion is greater than any other species of PR professional. They should also have the contact details for the editorial lawyers at the paper or broadcaster, and those are the individuals who are likely to secure the changes needed most rapidly. This will also send a clear signal that if the change is not made some form of enforcement action will be taken.

PROBLEMS WITH PRODUCTS OR SERVICES

I reiterate the advantage enjoyed by substantial corporate entities. As a cub lawyer I cut my teeth acting for film and TV stars, elite sports folk, chefs, boy bands, etc. Compared to the financial might of the major Fleet Street titles, these were rank paupers. But despite the massive financial disparity I had to win for them anyway. A FTSE 100 company is an altogether stronger position to get its point across to a recalcitrant newspaper.

If your product or services are as the journalist claims in the warning email, which will almost certainly be sent prior to the story breaking, then it is best to find an elegant and contrite way of conceding that. Lying to journalists is a very bad idea and will almost certainly make matters worse. In these circumstances you may need to win some time to decide what the best response should be. This can best be done by courteously citing the relevant regulatory and/or legal principles which entitle you to that time.

You also want the reporting to be as moderate and accurate as possible. The best way to achieve that is to create a sense of jeopardy on the part of the in-house lawyer at the broadcaster and publisher who will oversee how the events are written up so that they will legal the news output in a way which accords with the facts.

Take effective steps to stem the tide of fake news

In a media crisis such as the cyber-attack on TalkTalk[1] you must be taking effective steps to stem the tide of fake news about the events being played out in the media. I was part of the team dealing with that crisis and my role was to dissuade the media from misreporting the true nature of the stolen data. The press in particular was – as is its wont – wanting to make the biggest drama possible over the crisis.

Getting into the mindset of the editorial lawyer

This exercise requires subjecting the facts which are put forward by the newspaper/broadcaster to the most detailed critical analysis possible to establish – if possible – that some of them at least are wrong; and then applying the applicable regulatory and legal principles which will be breached should they be published. This must be done in the clearest and most trenchant terms.

This is how it works. The key responsibility of the editorial lawyer is to minimize the risk of a story being the subject of a

[1] In 2015 some 157,000 TalkTalk customers had their personal details hacked in a cyber attack.

successful regulatory complaint and/or legal action. You will often see – though may not recognize – in an article what in the trade are called 'lawyer's marks', which are subtle editorial changes made to minimize regulatory or legal risk. The effect of those is to reduce the damaging impact of a story. One of the factors in whether the public interest defence created by Section 4 of the 2013 Defamation Act succeeds in a libel action is the tone of the publication.

That reduction to the impact of the story and the moderating addition of lawyer's marks are only going to occur where there is some perceived risk surrounding the story. If it does not exist prior to 'tee up' email, that sense of risk can only be invoked by a PR lawyer.

Another positive impact of deploying a PR lawyer in any media crisis is that it may induce the lawyer who will therefore inevitably be 'legalling' the story to change what we in the trade call the 'Chase levels' (see below). This is another facet of defamation law with which PR professionals should be familiar.

THE CHASE LEVELS

The Chase levels are the grades of defamatory allegation which can be levelled against a company or an individual. There is some debate as to whether there are three or four grades. I think the better view is that there are four, which are as follows:

1. The MP is a racist;
2. There are strong grounds to believe that the MP is a racist;
3. There are reasonable grounds to believe that the MP is a racist;
4. There are grounds to suggest that the MP should be investigated to establish whether they are racist.

The damage which can be inflicted by an allegation is greatly variable according to which Chase level is deployed and what the tone of the relevant article or programme is. Your aim should be to persuade the newspaper or broadcaster to move the allegation(s) at issue down the Chase scale and moderate the tone of the report.

In my capacity as an editorial lawyer, where I fear that it may become my task to defend an article for which I have been responsible in front of a regulator or judge, I am going to both lower the tone and Chase level of the article to reduce the risk level for the publication. This will make it less negatively impactful on the reader or viewer, and make it less likely that other elements of the media will pick it up.

The concern on the part of an editorial lawyer on the issue of tone comes from the 10 criteria set out by Lord Nicholls in the case that I have already mentioned of Reynolds v *Times* (*see also* page 45). It was these criteria, which have subsequently been approved, which he set out as to whether a publisher should be granted the common law (i.e. judge-made) predecessor to the Section 4 'Publication of a Matter of Public Interest' defence. Here they are:

1. The seriousness of the allegation. The more serious the charge, the more the public is misinformed and the individual harmed, if the allegation is not true.
2. The nature of the information and the extent to which the subject matter is a matter of public concern.
3. The source of the information. Some informants have no direct knowledge of the events. Some have their own axes to grind or are being paid for their stories.
4. The steps taken to verify the information.
5. The status of the information. The allegation may have already been the subject of an investigation which commands respect.
6. The urgency of the matter – news is often a perishable commodity.
7. Whether comment was sought from the claimant. They may have information others do not possess or have not disclosed. An approach to the claimant will not always be necessary.

8. Whether the article contained the gist of the claimant's side of the story.
9. The tone of the article. A newspaper can raise queries or call for an investigation. It need not adopt allegations as statements of fact.
10. The circumstances of the publication, including the timing.

You will find under number 9 the tone of the article will be a factor in whether the judicial 'get out of jail free' Section 4 public interest defence is upheld, as will be whether the publisher adopts allegations or merely reports them. You may be astonished – as I am – that the truth or otherwise of the allegation is apparently irrelevant; it not appearing as a factor in these 10 criteria.

Another benefit of persuading a newspaper to downgrade the virulence of a story is that it will probably be moved further back in the paper and be shorter in content, which will further reduce the likelihood of the allegations being picked up by other elements of the media and social media.

You need to get inside the mind of the editorial lawyer to convince them that on this occasion their advice should be (ideally) that the story/programme be dropped altogether, or at least substantially cut and toned down. This can only be done by presenting the prospect of some kind of regulatory and/or legal scrutiny, and by making the strongest possible case that if the article or programme is subjected to such scrutiny then its content will be found wanting.

LEARNING FROM PIERS MORGAN?

Loath as I am to quote him, Piers Morgan provides a helpful vignette about the relationship between the editor element of the news cycle and the role of the editorial lawyer in his book, *The Insider: The Private Diaries of a Scandalous Decade*.[2] The background to the

---

[2] A book written in diary form by Piers Morgan documenting his time as editor of the *News of the World* and *Daily Mirror*.

story is ironically not a legal threat posed by the subject of a news story, but by a rival publisher.

The story was about the ex-England Rugby captain Will Carling in the context of his alleged affair with Princess Diana. Here, I am going to use Piers' own words to tell the story:

> 'A legal letter arrived later from the *Mail on Sunday* saying they had an exclusive interview with Will and Julia Carling and we must keep our grubby hands off. It's the usual futile effort papers make to stop everyone lifting great chunks of their scoop later in the night, and I laughed when I read it. As if we're just going to sit there, read this great interview, agree not to run a word of it and go to the pub.
>
> To save time, I just shouted to our lawyer across the newsroom: "Hey Tom, how many fingers will this cost us if we nick it all?" He flicked five fingers at me: £50,000 maximum damages, well worth a front page and two spreads inside.'

Tom Crone

The lawyer in question was Tom Crone, who was at the *News of the World* at the time. It is hard to overstate the key role that these individuals play in the editorial process. Crone was immensely powerful at News International and occasionally even authored articles for the *News of the World*. It was he who tried very hard to cover up the phone hacking there. I generally got on well with Tom because you knew exactly what you were dealing with when you engaged with him.

So far as I know I only angered him once when having settled a defamation claim for a respectable sum in damages and costs, Tom was dragging his feet about sending over a cheque. After my chasing letters were ignored I sent over a statutory demand for the sum, which is the first stage in a winding up petition.

Tom apparently did not find at all amusing the prospect of News International being wound up by a PR lawyer, so after sending a bike round with a cheque he cancelled our forthcoming lunch.

The PR/editorial lawyer dialogue

The role of the PR lawyer is to communicate with their opposite number (i.e. the editorial lawyer, compliance officer or managing editor) that the publication of this story/broadcast of this programme carries with it a real regulatory and/or legal risk. This can only be done effectively with the benefit of a complete understanding of the relevant regulations and law, a reasoned and cogent explanation of why the facts which are going to be alleged are incorrect and a good understanding of what/who you are dealing with at the other end.

For a PR lawyer it is essential to have at least a working relationship, and ideally a good one, with the senior editorial lawyers both in the broadcasting and Fleet Street worlds. I will nearly always write to the in-house lawyer directly on a legal issue, address them by their Christian name if I know them personally – as I usually do – and write as courteously as is possible in a letter which is contemplating a regulatory or legal challenge. This allows me to stay on good terms with them despite the fact that we are on opposite sides. It is also important to know something about their personality and how, therefore, they will react to any particular situation. It is also helpful to know whether or not they abide by a set of personal standards. Some definitely do and others definitely do not. Either way, it is essential never to mislead them.

Winning and retaining the trust of editorial lawyers

I wrote a letter to a newspaper on behalf of a high-profile client who I later learned had misled me about the content of an article. I had no reason to believe they had done so at the time, but nonetheless wrote to the lawyer in question to apologize for inadvertently misleading them. I received a most gracious reply.

On another occasion, some way into a piece of litigation that I was conducting against the BBC, the lawyer on the other side whom I knew well and was an ethical and courteous opponent (would that they all were) rang early one evening to warn me of what was coming in by fax.

The BBC had discovered that the contracts on which I was suing were effectively forgeries. The first thing that I did, when I read the letter and evidence which clearly proved this, was to pick up the phone and to apologize to that lawyer for having served forged documents. She was kind enough to say that it had never crossed her mind that I knew the documents were forged.

I was called by a newspaper editor about a story the paper was going to run about a high-profile client who had apparently attended something akin to an orgy. After thanking him for his call, I said that I would take instructions and get back to him. I then asked why he had called me rather than the client's agent.

'Because I know you won't lie about it,' he said.

It is impossible to overstate the value of having such relationships with the people that you deal with when undertaking crisis PR.

WHO DOES THE MEDIA TAKE NOTICE OF?

The first challenge when confronted with a looming media crisis is to get the attention of whoever makes the decision as to whether or not the storm will break, and if it does how severe the storm will be.

As I have explained, the editorial decision which determines the weather pattern is a two-stage one: the first being editorial and the second being legal/regulatory. It is on that second element that you are seeking to impact.

HOW DOES AN EDITORIAL LAWYER ASSESS CRISIS COMMUNICATIONS?

In my capacity as an editorial lawyer when a letter comes in about a programme or article that I am 'legalling' – i.e. prior to its publication – then this is the order in which I assess it.

Who has sent it?
In ascending order of impact:

1. Internal comms: because this injects no sense of
   jeopardy that the forthcoming article or programme
   may be the subject of independent scrutiny, I will
   assume either the finances, expertise or will is
   lacking to take the appropriate action to hold my
   client to account.
2. Management: ditto; I have seen some truly dreadful
   letters drafted by senior management which – as
   politely as possible – I have had to bin in their entirety.
3. External comms: ditto; a crisis comms expert is
   unlikely to persuade me that I need to change my
   original editorial decision because they do not create a
   credible risk of independent scrutiny.
4. In-house lawyer: I will treat this as indicative of either
   an unwillingness to make the necessary investment
   to protect the reputation and/or brand at issue, or a
   lack of expertise in media law/crisis management; or a
   lack of resolution on the part of the company to take
   effective steps to protect its reputational brand. I will
   therefore take little notice of it.
5. External lawyers who are not media experts: I will
   take this as indicating that the company does not
   appreciate the importance of hiring experts in the crisis
   PR field and will assume therefore that it will not be
   expertly represented on the issues arising, should the
   matter become contentious. It will also tell me that
   this lawyer's judgement is poor and that they have little
   concern about the best interests of their client. If they
   were truly intent on doing the best for their client,
   they would find a lawyer to do the work who is an
   expert in the field. It is also easy to spot a letter which
   has been drafted by a barrister for a solicitor who lacks
   the requisite expertise to write it themselves. I will treat

that as further indication of the wrong mindset on the part of my opponents.

6. A known specialist media with a track record of dealing successfully with the media: then I know I am going to have to adhere to the applicable regulations and law, and make sure that I have my facts both right and have at least some evidence to support them. I must also ensure that the tone of the piece is not too hyperbolic or the allegations beyond what the facts justify so as to give my client the best prospects of seeing off any regulatory or legal challenge.

How much money does the prospective complainant have?

1. Cynical though this may seem, I can assure you that when acting as an editorial lawyer, if my prospective assailant enjoys a turnover of billions whatever the subject matter of the letter, my attention has been grabbed.
2. Newspaper lawyers have to operate within a budget. They will be aware that libelling this company may consume all of it in legal fees alone; they are also aware of the management and journalist's time and energy that can be taken up by a determined and properly resourced exercise to correct error and seek redress.
3. Of even greater concern to me would be the financial risk that my client would be taking if by defaming a large company 'serious financial loss' was the consequence. All of that loss would be recoverable in damages against my client broadcaster or publisher.

What is the content of the letter?

1. I will learn a lot from the content of the letter about the expertise of its author. A letter which without detailed factual and legal analysis (especially if the latter is defective – as I have often seen) merely says in

effect, 'If you publish/broadcast this then we will sue', it will not impress me. If your lawyer ever writes such a letter, then you should fire them.

2. If the letter sets out a detailed, credible and well-evidenced response to the allegations at issue, then the publisher/broadcaster is presented with a genuine regulatory and/or legal risk that is going to inform my editorial advice – which at the least is going to be to tone the article/programme down. It may be that the programme/article should be abandoned altogether.

STRATEGIES TO PREVENT PUBLICATION OF DAMAGING FALSE MATERIAL

By far the best thing you can do for you, your company or your client is to prevent negative material emerging to cause a media crisis. The first question to address therefore when one looms is whether there is a real prospect of killing a story off. Your strategy of dealing with a true story should be very different from a false one, which is why that issue needs to be determined at the outset and as rapidly as possible. Here, I am dealing with prospective stories, which are false in whole or in part.

Whatever the type of story, the best results are going to be obtained if you engage not only with the journalist/editor, but also with the editorial lawyer, who has the power to exert considerable influence over editorial decisions.

Avoid the telephone
Never try to deal with a potential media crisis over the telephone. For a number of reasons, it is essential that when confronted with a potential media crisis that you oblige the journalist to commit their questions and/or allegations to writing. The reasons include:

1. The mere fact that the journalist is obliged to do so will concentrate their mind and instil in them a realization

that they must watch their step – an important start to
the process. It may also buy you time.

2. You need to know the exact form of the negative story if
you are to deal with it effectively. The detail is often vital,
and it is more difficult for a journalist to fudge it in writing.

3. It gives you the contact details of the journalist and will
tell you whether they are staff or freelance.

4. In any subsequent regulatory or legal dispute it is essential
to know exactly what the paper/broadcaster has said prior
to publication and what has been said in response.

Key issues when the prospective story comes in
When the email from a newspaper and/or news programme comes
in which threatens a reputation-damaging story, there are a number
of factors to consider:

1. Who is the journalist?

   i)   Check out the journalist from their past work. Are
they bona fide, or merely an indiscriminate wielder
of hatchets?

  ii)   This should inform how you deal with them because
if bona fide they are more likely to be impacted by a
reasoned explanation of why they are wrong.

2. Is the journalist staff or freelance?

   i)   Where the journalist is staff they have to account for
their time. A newspaper has also already invested in
the story because of the income which it has paid
to the journalist in question. The paper is therefore
going to be reluctant to bin that investment by
abandoning the story.

  ii)   If you are dealing with a freelance journalist, the
position is reversed. A freelancer is trying to sell a
story into a newspaper. That means that in addition
to any disincentive which you communicate to the

paper via the freelancer (any communications to the freelancer should be copied to the in-house lawyer to make sure that the warnings are heeded), the additional negative motivation is that the freelancer does not have to be paid if the story is dropped.

3. Is the journalist a big or small fish?

    i)   A newspaper will be more indulgent towards and supportive of one of its high-profile journalists than someone who is just starting out.

    ii) One in-house lawyer pleaded with me that the journalist in question, a doyen columnist, could not be asked to retract a false story which they had published because of their exalted status. You can imagine how sympathetic I was to that argument.

4. Has a reasonable time been given to respond?

    i)   If the prospective publisher is an IPSO-regulated title, Section 1(1) of the IPSO Code requires the paper to 'take care not to publish inaccurate or misleading material'. This includes both putting the prospective story to its subject and providing that subject with an opportunity to respond.

    ii) Similar conditions apply where the title is regulated by IMPRESS.

    iii) If this is a prospective broadcast story, then Section 7.11 of the Ofcom Code which says this: 'If a programme alleges wrongdoing or incompetence or makes other significant allegations, those concerned should normally be given an appropriate and timely opportunity to respond.'

    iv) If it is a prospective BBC programme, then this is the relevant paragraph from Section 6.1 of the BBC Producer Guidelines: 'When our output contains allegations of wrongdoing, inequity or incompetence or lays out a strong and damaging critique of an identifiable individual or organisation, those criticised should normally have a right of reply, unless there is an editorial justification to proceed without it.'

v) Whoever is the prospective publisher of the story, there is clear judicial authority that the subject of the story must be given sufficient and accurate detail about the story to enable them to respond, and given a reasonable time to do so.

vi) When operating pre-publication, I deploy observations made by Mr Justice Nicklin about the second defendant's conduct in a case called Turley v Unite.[3] Nicklin J criticized, among other things, the second defendant's failure to set out a full, accurate and fair summary of the allegations that he intended to publish and the unreasonable and self-imposed publication deadline for a response.

5. Is there sufficient detail to be able to respond cogently?

i) Most of the above points apply equally to this question.

6. Are the alleged facts true or false – or a mixture of the two?

i) If some of the points put to you are true, these should not be denied. One reason is that they may have been put to you in a way which conceals the fact that the publisher or broadcaster has incontrovertible proof of them and the intention may be to elicit a provably false denial.

ii) In responding to those elements of the prospective story that are true, care should be taken to inform the journalist what the legitimate boundaries are of the

---

[3] Anna Turley brought a successful legal action against Unite the Union and Stephen Walker, the publisher and editor of the left-wing blog, *The Skwawkbox*, for libel, breach of the Data Protection Act and misuse of private information/breach of confidence.

story, and a warning issued against exceeding those boundaries.

iii) Those elements of the prospective story which are false should be addressed robustly and in detail.

iv) If they are all true in substance, then a succinct statement should be prepared for publication which minimizes the adverse PR effect that the news will have. This should be done with expert professional support and sent over in a way that communicates that the reporting of events must comply with the applicable regulations and laws.

7. Is the journalist lying?

i) On one particularly busy Friday – always the busiest days for PR pros because you are dealing with both the Saturdays and the Sundays – I spent eight hours dealing simultaneously with a story about mouldy cakes that *The Times* wanted to run about a popular café chain; and inappropriate language used towards women by a TV star, which the *Sun* was threatening. In both cases it emerged that the journalists were lying.

ii) In the case of *The Times*, a key figure put to my client was proven wrong when an email emerged from the same journalist which had an entirely different figure for the same subject matter, which he had changed in an effort to make his story stand up.

iii) The *Sun* journalist claimed that he had heard a recording made by a production company backing up the allegation he wanted my client to admit to. It emerged that no such recording existed.

8. Is this a features piece or part of a serious investigation?

i) One of the divisions in newspapers is between journalists who are feature writers and those who are specialist investigative journalists. The former can ply

their trade without having to generate controversy or
risk; the latter cannot.

9. How much evidence is there to support the story?

i)   Some of the stories which might create a media crisis
     are wafer-thin, a careful reading of which will show to
     be little more than speculation on a flimsy factual and
     evidential basis. This should be pointed out robustly
     to the journalist, along with the applicable regulatory
     and/or legal principles, and this should be sufficient
     to see the problem off.

ii) At the other end of the scale, you may get a two-/
     three-page email with numbered paragraphs and a
     litany of serious allegations accompanied by indicia
     that they are supported by copious evidence. So
     will it often be where there has been some form of
     whistle-blowing.

iii) I have encountered the work of whistle-blowers
     who, having justifiably been terminated by
     their employers, in a fit of pique try to avenge
     themselves on their employer by digging out and
     misrepresenting material – which may also be
     obsolete – while at the same time trying to extract
     payment from a newspaper. My most recent
     experience of that led to a story emerging, but I was
     able to communicate robustly with the newspaper
     which meant that a piece which would have taken up
     most of a page ended up being only a few lines long.

iv) When confronted with such a situation you are
     entitled to insist firmly on sufficient time to produce
     a detailed and comprehensive response to the
     allegations, as I was able to do in this case. Good
     use was made of the time and the story was dialled
     down from a Richter scale 9 media crisis to one which
     barely registered 2 and was not picked up by any
     other media outlet.

10. How credible is the source(s), if known?

    i) This can be an important factor in whether you succeed in preventing a media crisis occurring because it is an important factor in the law of defamation.

    ii) If the journalist does not disclose their source, then there is no way that you can force them to do so. Journalists have both a legal entitlement and (under the IPSO Code) a moral obligation to protect the identity of sources. Were this not the case, much good and important investigative journalism would be impossible, though it can also cause great injustice where the source is mendacious.

    iii) If you are able to undermine the confidence of a journalist in their source, you go a long way towards persuading them and their employer not to run the story. I persuaded the *Mail on Sunday* that their primary source for a story that they were going to publish about a very senior Anglican clergyman had been a communist revolutionary. It was dropped.

    iv) The primary reason for this is legal. Section 4 of the Defamation Act 2013 provides a defence which is called 'Publication of a Matter of Public Interest'. The first limb of the defence is that the story's subject matter must be one of public interest. The second is that the publisher 'reasonably believed' that the publication served the public interest. The word 'reasonably' means that this is an objective rather than a subjective test.

    v) One of the criteria by which a court will decide whether a journalist's belief in the public interest of this story being published is reasonable will be on the credibility of their source, and particularly (to quote the relevant judgment) whether that source has an 'axe to grind'.

vi) One potent tactic is therefore to place on record prior to publication that there are good reasons *not* to believe the information emanating from the source. Should the matter end up being the subject of libel proceedings you will have undermined the ability both of the journalist and the newspaper to persuade a court that their belief in the public interest of this story being published was 'reasonable'.

11. How much evidence is there to rebut the story?

i) Where you are confronted with a false story, the process should begin immediately of gathering rebuttal evidence. No editorial lawyer is going to take much notice of a mere 'if you publish this, we'll sue' blast, even if accompanied by an erudite exposition of the relevant regulatory and legal principles. To successfully kill off a story you have to advance credible evidence that it is wrong.

ii) One of the traps for the unwary here is to respond in so much detail that you effectively provide the journalist/newspaper/broadcaster with new material to add to the story. This is a matter of skill and judgement based on both a full understanding of the law and regulation, and years of experience in doing the job.

iii) One of the most difficult situations is where the information which you need to rebut a story is confidential to your clients/customers and cannot therefore be disclosed to the media. I have a number of healthcare provider clients and this is a common problem when they are threatened with stories which would create a media crisis.

iv) There is no easy answer to this. You just have to make the best use of such material that you can deploy and undermine the story put to you as best you can. Sometimes you can establish that it is

internally inconsistent, or not credible, or rebutted
by a regulator's report, etc.

12. If the story is false to any degree, does it concern events
which mean that some media coverage is inevitable?

   i)   The most likely scenario is that some unfortunate
incident has occurred and the media is casting
around for someone to blame.

   ii) In these circumstances it will not be possible to
prevent media coverage. However, any response
should robustly deal with the issue of blame if the
journalist proposes wrongly to ascribe it.

   iii) Both the press regulatory codes compel journalists
to distinguish clearly between conjecture and fact.
Citing these provisions will usually help.

13. If not, how big a story is it? For example, how hard is
the paper/broadcaster going to fight to hold on to it?

   i)   There is an element of luck in dealing with a
potential media crisis. It is going to be much easier
to knock out a story on a day which is news-heavy
than one when it is news-light.

   ii) It follows then that a story which may be
substantial on one day may be of little value
on another.

   iii) One of the skills of a PR professional is to
persuade the newspaper or broadcaster that
the news item in question is of little editorial
value. During a friendly conversation with a
TV journalist, I was able to persuade him that
the story that he had put to my corporate client
for comment about an apparent failure in its
regulatory systems was of lesser public interest
than the lack of effective government regulation
covering the same issue. The package was run
including an interview with the aggrieved

individual, but the finger of blame was pointed at the government rather than my client, which was not mentioned in the piece.

iv) One piece of research you should do is to try to find out whether a similar story has already been published. If you can persuade the journalist that they are regurgitating an earlier news item, that may persuade them to abandon the story.

v) If you can show that the story has previously been considered and dropped, or retracted by another publisher, then that is also a potent way of persuading a journalist to drop the story.

vi) If it really is a 'scoop', then you have to be realistic – the newspaper (or broadcaster) is going to be very hard to persuade to abandon it. In those circumstances, you must judge your response accordingly.

14. If it is a newspaper or magazine, is it part of the IPSO or IMPRESS regulatory system and therefore bound by the terms of their respective codes?

i) Part of the reason why Fleet Street news coverage is so errant is that insufficient people, especially PR professionals, know how to hold newspapers to account via the applicable editorial codes. No effective crisis PR is possible without a working knowledge of the applicable regulatory regimes and their respective codes.

ii) If a newspaper or magazine is part of the IPSO or IMPRESS scheme, they have a contractual obligation to abide by the terms of its code. They are however far more likely to do so if they are reminded of that obligation and presented with the possibility that if they breach that obligation then a regulatory complaint will follow.

iii) They should also be reminded that a failure to
adhere to a relevant regulatory code may also
render them more vulnerable to successful legal
proceedings.

15. If not regulated by either body, what are the title's
editorial standards/policies?

   i) Newspapers such as the *Guardian, Financial Times*
   and *Independent* have publicly available editorial
   standards and policies. These should be quoted
   back to the paper at a point where it appears likely
   that they are about to be breached.

   ii) A breach by a newspaper of its own editorial
   guidelines will render that title more vulnerable to
   a successful defamation claim because they are less
   likely to avail themselves of the Section 4 public
   interest defence. That should be pointed out as well.

16. If dealing with a broadcaster, is there a prospective
breach of the Ofcom Code?

   i) Having long done the work of a programme lawyer
   I know the Ofcom Code is taken very seriously
   by broadcasters; not least because Ofcom has the
   power to fine and, unlike IPSO which will never
   fine anyone, Ofcom does levy them. Ultimately
   it also has the power to withdraw a broadcasting
   licence.

   ii) As with publishers, an infringement of the Ofcom
   Code will also make a broadcaster more vulnerable
   to a defamation action.

   iii) I once successfully deployed the Section 7.11
   provision of the Ofcom Code when an e-commerce
   client received notification from *Watchdog* late
   on a weekday afternoon that they were going to
   be the subject of a very damaging package in the
   programme, which was to be transmitted the

following day. There was nothing that I could do at that point to rebut the content of the package. However, the BBC had provided insufficient time within which to prepare a proper response to the allegations that were going to be made in the package. I responded to *Watchdog* in those terms and told them that in those circumstances they could not transmit the package as part of the following day's programme. The package was duly dropped. The agenda for the programme the following week was different and the package was never run.

17. What additional regulations and/or editorial standards can be deployed beyond the Ofcom Code?

    i)   If the programme at issue is being made by the BBC, then in addition to the Ofcom Code the relevant provisions of the BBC Producer Guidelines should be cited in any response to a prospective adverse story.

    ii) Like the Ofcom Code, and unlike the IPSO Code, the BBC Producer Guidelines also include a concept of 'fairness', which can be deployed to good effect.

18. Is there a viable argument that the material at issue is confidential and/or private and that a court would therefore grant an injunction to prevent the material entering the public domain?

    i)   Whereas no pre-emptive injunction is generally available for defamation, it is where there is a prospective breach of confidentiality or misuse of private information.

    ii) This is a question which needs immediate, careful and expert judgement because a decision must be made rapidly; and an ill-judged application for an injunction against a programme or newspaper can add profile to the news story. But if the material is confidential and/or private, you should immediately seek the advice of a specialist media lawyer to see if this remedy is available.

iii) The primary reason why Max Mosley's injunction application against the *News of the World* failed was because, as the judge commented, by that time well over 100,000 people had read the story and in those circumstances the horse had bolted – though a recent Supreme Court decision on a privacy issue suggests a possible different outcome now. He was let down by his lawyers. Lord Justice Warby (as he now is) was the QC leading the *News of the World*'s defence of that action.

iv) The other reason is that an injunction is a discretionary remedy, unlike damages which are the automatic entitlement of a successful claimant in privacy and/or breach of confidence. To persuade a court to grant a discretionary remedy, you must abide by certain additional principles – one of which is that the application is made as soon as possible.

19. Is the prospective story defamatory or just inaccurate?

i) You have a much better prospect of persuading a publisher or broadcaster not to run a story if you can persuade them that it is defamatory of an individual and/or a company.

ii) If you believe that it might be defamatory, then immediately seek expert advice from a recognized defamation expert who should then be the one that responds on your behalf.

iii) If you are a company threatened by a prospective article and/or programme (newspapers and broadcasters work in tandem to save costs) and

you can credibly predict a substantial financial hit
if the story is published, then the newspaper and/
or broadcaster can be told that any such loss can
be recovered from the publisher/broadcaster in the
form of 'special damages'.

iv) One of my multinational clients contacted me when
a news agency approached them with a story that
one of their leading baby products caused chemical
burns. Fortunately, this is a long-standing client,
which operates like a well-oiled machine in the
face of a PR crisis. It began immediately providing
me with the relevant science which disproved the
story, which I was able to understand and apply,
remembering my school chemistry lessons. The
agency, which was part of the IPSO scheme, was
therefore notified robustly by me that the sending
out of this story to most of the British media would
infringe its IPSO obligations. It was also told that
it would expose the agency to a massive damages
claim on the basis that baby products which
allegedly cause chemical burns do not sell well. It
therefore became an existential decision on the part
of the agency whether to proceed with the story or
abandon it. It chose the latter.

v) A word of warning: had this client merely sent
a denial statement back to the agency, the story
would have gone out to the entirety of the British
media with the statement tacked on at the end.

20. If defamatory, does it defame individuals and/or a
company?

i) As I have explained, for both companies and
individuals you have to persuade a court that
'serious harm' has been inflicted or is likely to be
inflicted as a consequence of the publication, so in
a pre-emptive communication to the publisher or

broadcaster a strong case must be made that this
will occur.

ii) Where the prospective claimant is a company
trading for profit, you have the additional burden
of persuading the broadcaster that the 'serious
harm' will occur in the form of financial damage.

iii) Sometimes you can assert that allegations made
against a high-profile company are in effect also
made against its senior management. An example
would be if serious allegations of impropriety were
to be made against the elements of the Virgin
empire which were still run by Richard Branson,
then the likelihood is not only would the company
be defamed, but so too would Branson.

21. Is it actionable because it is both false and malicious?

i) An alternative claim to defamation is malicious
falsehood. Here you must prove that the allegation
in question was both false and made maliciously
– i.e. the author either knew it to be false or was
reckless as to whether it was true or false.

ii) The advantage of this claim is that you do not
have to prove 'serious harm'; the disadvantage
is the weighty burden of proof, especially to
show malice.

iii) Malicious falsehood is effectively the mirror image
of the American law of defamation, which is why
so few defamation actions are brought in the US –
and still less succeed.

22. What is the editorial mindset of the company or
broadcaster/programme/production company; what
appetite do they have for risk and conflict?

i) There is a huge divergence in appetite for risk
within the media, and preparedness to stand by
stories in the face of litigation.

ii) Any decision in the face of a media crisis must be taken with knowledge of the robustness of the entity with whom you are dealing.

iii) When dealing with a broadcaster, even though the programme may be being made by an independent production company, the compliance is handled by the commissioning TV channel. It is primarily to that channel that you should look to answer this question.

iv) There are some programmes that, because of their robust investigative journalism ethic, will take a great deal of persuading to abandon a story, or an element of a programme. This especially goes for *Dispatches*, *Watchdog* and *Panorama*.

v) By contrast, if you are dealing with an entertainment programme, daytime TV or a programme and/or broadcaster with no need to include controversial elements in their content, you have a much better chance of persuading them to abandon the damaging material.

vi) Book publishers are normally very risk-averse. Recently, one abandoned – entirely unnecessarily – a whole biography of Kate Winslet after a letter was sent by her lawyers.

23. A related question: what is their financial status?

i) When you are dealing with media behemoths such as Associated Newspapers or News UK, they can afford to be profligate with their vast wealth and stand their ground even when they know perfectly well that they are in the wrong – as both are wont to do by deploying their army of FSLs.

ii) By contrast, a regional newspaper or magazine, a trade title or Fleet Street titles at the lower end of the financial scale are going to be eminently more persuadable of the wisdom of abandoning a story

about which they are likely to be challenged either
by the regulatory procedures or in the courts.

24. What is the mindset of the editorial lawyer?

    i)   One of the things which you need to do to give
yourself the best chance of seeing off a media crisis
before it occurs is to move the decision-making
from the desk of the journalist to that of the
in-house lawyer. This can only be done by a PR
lawyer, and the moment that it has been achieved,
the process of at least moderating the relevant
article or programme has begun.

    ii) Like judges, it is inevitable that in-house lawyers
have their own baggage when it comes to dealing
with editorial decisions, in which they are hugely
influential. They are sometimes overruled by editors,
but that is the exception rather than the rule.

    iii) Some in-house lawyers enjoy greater stature within
their organizations than others. It is useful to know
how influential the lawyer that you are dealing
with is.

    iv) The mindset of in-house lawyers varies immensely
according to their characters. Some are ethical,
courteous, recognize the responsibility that comes
with publishing to millions and also act as a
lawyer should – which is to maintain a degree of
professional independence in providing advice
to a client.

    v) At the other end of the scale, you have in-house
and defendant lawyers who are mendacious,
confrontational, hubristic, with a complete
disregard for their professional obligations and not
the slightest bit concerned if society is misled by
the newspapers or broadcasters they act for. The
damage to society inflicted by this small number of
well-paid individuals is incalculable.

vi) You need to know where in this scale of professionals the editorial lawyer in particular stands and decide the tone and content of your communications accordingly.

25. Should we just send over a robust and well-evidenced rebuttal and demand that the story be pulled, or hedge our bets by adding a short statement?

    i) This is can be a difficult judgement call. Sometimes one of the worst things that you can do when confronted by a prospective PR crisis is to merely communicate a denial and offer a statement for publication. This is likely to cause delight at the newspaper or broadcaster where the editorial lawyer will effectively treat this as your consent to the adverse story being published, just so long as your denial is summarized in a couple of lines at the end. This is of precious little use to you, your company or your client.

    ii) That means that if, after having made good use of your 'Golden Hour', you have crafted a detailed and robust response that you think will persuade the newspaper and/or broadcaster to abandon the story, then you should *not* offer up a statement.

    iii) One device that you can do is to put the newspaper or broadcaster in a position where they really have to come back to you before running the story. This gives you an opportunity to make a decision about offering up a statement at a point where you have a clearer idea of whether or not the story is going to run.

    iv) If despite your best efforts you think that the story is going to run, you should nonetheless rebut it to the fullest extent that you can on the expectation that what will be published or broadcast will be considerably less damaging than would otherwise

be the case; and you should then add a carefully
worded and succinct statement, which if well
enough judged should get into the article.

26. Should we simply send a rebuttal, but have a statement
ready just in case we are not able to kill off the story?

i)   There are some occasions where with
determination, diligence and skill a rebuttal of
such force (including deterrent regulatory and
legal elements) can be sent over with the effect
that the strong likelihood is that the story will be
abandoned.

ii) By way of an abundance of caution, it is worth
preparing a short statement to accompany what
should at least be a cut-down story or softened
broadcast piece. There is an art to drafting these
statements, which I deal with on pages 224–26. It
is also something which may draw in more cooks
to the kitchen than is ideal. It is generally best for
this work to be done by a PR professional with the
minimum possible interference from those who
lack the requisite expertise.

27. Should we be preparing a response to go on our website
and/or to our social media contacts?

i)   You are only going to persuade a newspaper
or broadcaster to include in the story a brief,
moderate and factual statement along with
(where appropriate) some acceptance of fault
and contrition.

ii) The same is not the case where you have a website
which you have managed to make attractive to
your customers. One of the reasons that your
website and social media reach should be a
priority is that it is one means whereby you can

mitigate the damage which the mass media can inflict on you.

iii) So, you should be preparing a more detailed response to the allegations, which can also be more robust and outspoken than anything a newspaper or broadcaster would accept. Ideally this should go up just before the programme or article sees the light of day, or very shortly thereafter.

iv) So, it should be with all your Twitter followers or other stakeholders that you can reach via social media. A carefully worded campaign by this means can sometimes antidote to a degree a story run by a newspaper or broadcaster.

28. Should we notify stakeholders of the possibility of the story emerging?

i) Make preparations to communicate this risk to stakeholders who will want to learn bad news from you rather than from the pages of a national newspaper.

ii) If you think that you have a real chance of killing the story off, then while all preparations should be made to do this, the 'send' button should not be pressed until it is as clear as it can be that the story will run despite your efforts to the contrary.

iii) Any such communication can be robust in its terms and, if appropriate, critical of the journalist and/or newspaper. There is no real defamation risk here – not that it is likely that a journalist or newspaper would sue; the reason being that this is what defamation lawyers call a 'privilege', i.e. the law will free it of libel risk as long as the communication is moderate in its terms and properly provides a reasoned rebuttal to allegations that are going to be made against you in the press or by a broadcaster.

The *Guardian* gets joshed by the *Spectator*

Sometimes a successful piece of crisis PR is not only satisfying, but also fun. Here is an example which I can write about because, with the client's permission, it is the subject of an article in the *Spectator*.

My client (DMS Plastics) makes PPE (personal protection equipment) for frontline workers such as medical staff and police officers. It received emails from both Sky and the *Guardian* with a link to a video of a US police officer using his DMS-made shield to barge a cameraman, though it was evident that no injury was caused. Both Sky and the *Guardian* put this to my client: 'We would also put to you that some may consider the behaviour of these law enforcement agencies may be tantamount to internal repression. How do you respond?'

The *Spectator* piece includes this paragraph from my reply to the Sky and *Guardian*: 'The suggestion in the Emails that my Clients are in some way responsible for the misuse of the PPE that they supply has as much merit as the suggestion that if a police officer kicks a protester then the manufacturer of the boot that he/she is wearing is in some way at fault; i.e. it is absurd.'

To the *Guardian* and Sky's credit, neither subsequently attributed blame to my client in their articles, which were mild and harmless – though also somewhat absurd.

Drafting statements

If you have concluded this is a story which you are going to have to attenuate rather than kill off, then a carefully worded statement should be prepared to be sent out into the ether to mitigate as far as possible the damage which the media crisis will inevitably cause. There is a real art to drafting statements designed for publication. I have seen some really dreadful examples and there is no 'one-size-fits-all' template. Here are some cardinal rules:

1. Neither a newspaper nor a broadcaster is obliged to publish a statement verbatim. You must therefore exhibit some guile if you wish to achieve this, or at least

get the majority of the messages out that you want to communicate via the statement.

2. You must use the smallest number of words that you can squeeze the key messages into. I have seen statements covering more than half a page which have been prepared to send to a broadcaster for inclusion in a programme which may be less than or as short as 26 minutes and where the section featuring the company may be two to three minutes. It would have taken most of that time to read the statement out.

3. My practice is to draft the statement with as few words as possible, have a cup of tea and then come back to it; at which point I always find I can reduce the number of words by at least 20 per cent, and often more.

4. The wording and the tone of the statement must be carefully thought out and be appropriate to your customer base. It must not contain PR or legal speak.

5. Do not use your statement to attack the newspaper, broadcaster or journalist involved. That part will simply be struck out and engender unhelpful ill-will.

6. If, as is often appropriate, it expresses contrition and admits to some degree at least responsibility, then it needs to be carefully checked by a lawyer and, if insurers may be involved, the insurers' consent obtained. This may be something of a struggle and I have had more than one dialogue with an insurer to try and persuade them that any such thing which is carefully worded will not increase the likelihood of successful claims being made, but is nonetheless essential for the good reputational health of the company.

7. In some circumstances it may be appropriate to thank the newspaper or broadcaster for bringing the issues to your attention thereby allowing you the opportunity to rectify them.

8. Where the publication of a statement may serve the publisher's purposes by reducing a perceived risk of a possible libel claim, it is more likely that the statement

will be published so that risk needs to be established in the communication in which the statement is put forward.

DEVELOPING AN EFFECTIVE MEDIUM-TERM MEDIA STRATEGY

Despite what I have said about the importance of making sure that you are in a position to win libel proceedings before commencing, ironically, so far as discouraging future attacks on your reputational brand, an unsuccessful libel action can be just as effective. That is because editorial decisions are made by assessment of risk. Where you are perceived as being prepared to issue libel proceedings even when you are more likely to lose than win, this will be a significant factor in the editorial decisions around the next story/broadcast which attacks you.

Tesla's eco-shot across the BBC's bows

In 2011, Tesla sued the BBC over a *Top Gear* review of its first Roadster. The claim never looked viable and was struck out. An appeal was thrown out in 2013.

The part of the programme subject to proceedings was when Jeremy Clarkson, after complimenting the car's speed, acceleration and cost of charging, then said: 'Although Tesla said it would do 200 miles, on our track it would run out after just 50 miles and it is not a quick job to charge it up again.' There followed a shot of people pushing one of the Roadsters into the hanger while Clarkson observed: 'What we have here, then, is an astonishing technical achievement. The first electric car that you might actually want to buy. It's just a shame that in the real world it doesn't seem to work.'

Despite the BBC having prevailed in those proceedings as was inevitable given the facts, I have no doubt that in considering what it might say about any future Tesla models, this spat was taken into account.

LESSONS FROM THE DUCHESS OF SUSSEX CASE

This has been confirmed by no less of an authority than the *Press Gazette*, which is essential reading for PR professionals and will report failings within its own industry. In an article written by its editor, Dominic Ponsford, he sets out some lessons that the media should draw from the brutal condemnation of Associated Newspapers and its lawyers in Warby J's judgment for the media from the Duchess of Sussex case.

This is Ponsford's key point for media professionals: 'With privacy [and defamation], a big factor remains the likelihood of those involved to sue. Harry and Meghan have succeeded in ensuring that an alarm will go off in the brain of every Fleet Street lawyer when their names appear in copy as they have shown themselves to be highly litigious.'

This is what I have been teaching for over 25 years in my crisis PR seminar. Editorial decisions are made by way of a risk assessment.

Another lesson in that case for the print press might be: if your behaviour is as despicable as that of the *Mail on Sunday*, which (as I presume) bribed a woman's father to let it publish an intimate letter from her and then deployed him to defend the indefensible, any decent judge (who also knows the kind of people you are) is going to throw the book at you.

DON'T BECOME A FREE HIT FOR THE MEDIA

At the other end of the scale, if you are repeatedly the subject of attacks in the media and consistently seen to take no effective action in your defence, you will increasingly be perceived as a 'free hit'. Negative stories about you will abound, which in turn will increase the perception that whatever is said about you, you will take no steps in your defence.

There is no effective way of dispelling this impression except by confronting a newspaper or broadcaster through (at least) a regulatory complaint in a way of saying, 'Thus far ... and no further'. Positive adjudications by IPSO or Ofcom are searchable, as are mediated outcomes for IPSO. A couple of those would certainly help.

Better still issue a Statement in Open Court which is read against a major publisher or broadcaster, which you also ensure gets some media coverage – as did the one read for the Duke of Sussex over false allegations made in the *Mail on Sunday* that he had turned his back on the army.

In the absence of any such evidence that you are in earnest about investing in the protection of your brand and/or reputation, then it is going to be difficult to persuade a newspaper or broadcaster when (prior to publication or transmission) you warn them that if the false and damaging allegations at issue are published you will take robust steps to correct them.

When I used to legal out *South Park* I had to deal with the fact that virtually every episode was potentially defamatory of someone or something, though I knew the court would take a generous attitude towards a satirical cartoon. Where this risk arose I would then do an internet search about the allegations to discover whether any action had been taken about them. On each occasion, I found that none had, which is why I passed every single *South Park* episode that I legalled. Mercifully, none of them generated libel proceedings.

TAKE A LESSON FROM DISNEY

By contrast, let me borrow an illustration from the law of copyright to make the point of how gaining a 'zero tolerance' policy concerning intellectual property (of which in one sense reputation is a part) pays dividends.

When I was asked to advise on the cover of a 'lads' mag' (I only briefly did some work for one such publication which had been bought by an existing client), I was sent over a picture of a topless young woman whose breasts were covered by two gloved hands, which anyone would have recognized as belonging to Mickey Mouse. As every copyright lawyer knows – or *should* know – Disney has a zero-tolerance policy when it comes to its intellectual property.

I did not bother with any detailed analysis of whether this was an actionable infringement of a Disney copyright. I simply told the publisher that Disney would undoubtedly sue and that, whereas Disney could afford a fight, they could not. For that reason, they had to change the magazine cover – which they duly did.

It is of course possible to take a 'zero tolerance' policy too far. A good PR lawyer will advise you to let certain moderate blows to your reputational brand pass rather than write a letter on every occasion. But there is a law of entropy when it comes to your reputation. If you do not tend it, then it will go to seed, like an unloved garden. It will be to your enormous cost if you let that happen.

8

Dealing with a Media Crisis if It Breaks

So long as you chose your words carefully in the UK you can say sorry without admitting liability. The situation is different in America where civil actions are still largely tried by juries. There, a public statement of contrition could be flourished by a claimant lawyer as an admission of liability.

There is no such risk here. No High Court judge is going to take the slightest notice of a PR statement put out (say) to commiserate with those injured in an explosion, in determining whether or not the company on whose site the incident occurred bore legal responsibility for it.

CONCENTRATE ON THE BIG MEDIA

Despite the fact that trust in the traditional media is limited – though broadcasters fare better than newspapers – I have no doubt, based on much reading on the subject since the advent of social media (I have been practising since before that phenomenon first struck us), that on all issues that are of real importance people with the power of reason are going to be far more influenced by what they read on, say, the *Mail Online*, than what emerges from their WhatsApp group.

Inevitably it will be to the media that the customers will be looking for their information. The capacity of a national newspaper or broadcaster to inflict damage on your brand or reputation is incomparably greater than even a large posse of customers or detractors via social media.

A national broadcaster or newspaper will have one or two individuals with whom you need to *parlez* as part of the process of attenuating a PR crisis. Dealing with two or three people by responding to them via social media has only a fraction of the equivalent benefit.

No PR crisis can effectively be tackled unless there is a robust dialogue underway with the media in which errors are corrected with reference to the relevant regulatory or legal principles. If the media is pumping out misinformation, I do not know what even the most powerful of companies can reasonably expect to do to correct it and also why would people necessarily believe a big corporation as against, say, the BBC. I certainly would not.

THE SOCIAL MEDIA

The distinction between the media and social media is breaking down. The major newspapers have a massive following on Facebook, Twitter, etc. The *Sun*, for example, has around 2 million Twitter followers, many of whom doubtless routinely re-tweet any news alerts to their own followers. All high-profile journalists use Twitter and other forms of social media. The BBC's political editor Laura Kuenssberg currently has around 1.4 million followers and BBC News has over 20 million followers on Instagram. Nothing other than the most enormous international companies can compete with this kind of figure in the social media realm.

There can come a point where a Twitter user reaches the stage where they are doing enough damage to warrant attention from a media lawyer. Sally Bercow (wife of the ex-Speaker of the House of Lords, John Bercow) and opinionated journalist Katie Hopkins' defamatory tweets constituted actionable libels. Sally Bercow's defamatory tweet cost her a great deal of money – and rightly so. In the case of Katie Hopkins, rather than apologize she lost a libel action which she should never have defended and which caused her the loss of her home.

Instructed by a corporate client, I sued a Twitter-user who made persistent serious and false allegations against the company's top management. After writing repeatedly to him asking him to desist, and then offering a virtually cost-free libel settlement if he retracted the allegations, after a series of amateurish attempts on his part to avoid being served with proceedings, a substantial award of damages and costs was made against him by the UK courts in his absence and the proceeds from the sale of the large French property which was part of his portfolio are in the process of being transferred to my client via a French legal process.

Strategies to minimize the negative impact of adverse media coverage

Some of my work has involved trying to rectify situations where before publication a client has not sought professional advice; and when even thereafter they are reluctant to invest in the expertise needed to minimize the damage which negative media coverage can cause. I believe this to be a false economy.

I go back to what Warren Buffett and Bill Gates have said about the importance of PR. For some, the term 'PR' has started to have negative connotations, becoming associated with the term 'spin' which is frequently used by the media to attack any apparent attempt by politicians to stem the flow of negative coverage. For the print press in particular, this is monstrous hypocrisy. The print press has no obligation to be fair or balanced in its coverage and according to its particular editorial bias, news will be 'spun' until it is giddy.

This 'spin' comprises presenting the facts in a hysterically negative fashion and then casting those which the newspaper holds responsible as pantomime villains – a corrosive societal pollutant. This in turn creates the necessity for there to be folk now termed 'spin doctors' working for political parties. Similarly, any company or individual which applies their trade in the public eye must invest in experts who will deter the media from unjustly placing them in the stocks and inviting the general public to hurl rotten fruit at them via social media.

When confronted by a newspaper or broadcaster which is going to publish material about you, your company or your client which cannot properly be denied, there is still much that you can do to mitigate the resulting damage.

Doing the obvious
I am going to take it as read that in a situation where the media is publishing material which is damaging to your reputation and/or brand and is essentially true, you will as a matter of course do the following:

1. Communicate in real time positively and reassuringly with your customers and all your stakeholders.
2. Use your website and every social media facility available to send out positive material to antidote as much as possible the negative material.
3. Engage courteously with all the elements of the media that contact you in advance of running a story, thanking them for having taken the trouble to do so and asking them to include your brief statement in their copy.
4. If you are contacted by an element of the media which threatens a new and false element to the story, immediately engage a PR lawyer to respond – which they can do with grace and moderation while still getting the job done.
5. Carefully monitor the flow both of the commercial and social media to ensure that no opportunity is missed to mitigate the damage being caused by the story.
6. Where the story highlights a failing of systems, attitude, respect, generosity, customer service, employee treatment, you should immediately set about tackling those issues; not only because it is the right thing to do, but also because it will reduce the risk of reputational damage of a similar nature occurring in the future – especially because

if the same situation re-occurs every lurid element of the previous story will be regurgitated at your expense.

7. If someone needs to be suspended or fired, that is done and announced as quickly as possible.

8. If the events give rise to a possible insurance claim, liaise with insurers to ensure that they are content with what you are saying and do not use any of your statements as an excuse to void the policy.

9. If it is likely that the events in question will generate litigation, then, despite the low risk of any adverse impact and legally to be on the safe side, all public statements which are going to be made should be considered by an individual who ideally is both a competent litigator and media lawyer.

Keeping the story to its proper bounds

Where a story is developing there is an ever-present risk that the coverage will stray off the straight and narrow and into the realms of lurid fiction given print press's proclivity for spin and awfulization.

You should be monitoring all the commercial media closely so that whenever that happens, there is an immediate missive sent to the entity in question via your PR lawyer. Early on in a media crisis, your PR professionals should be drawing up what are called Q&As, which is a way of preparing for what might be a flurry of questions coming in from the media, so that when they do arrive, carefully thought-out answers can be provided. Meticulous thought needs to be given to these answers, in particular:

1. You must be absolutely sure that they are correct. If you are perceived by a journalist to be lying to them (even if you are not), then serious consequences will follow.

2. Make sure that you do not disclose any information which you have which is confidential vis-à-vis third parties; especially clients, patients, etc.

3. You must be careful not to 'feed' the story. If you include more information than is necessary, you may add further

column inches to a story which you would much prefer to disappear. Generally in these situations, less is more.

4. Again, make sure that your insurer is on side.

5. Since legal issues may arise in this exercise, you should pass at least the final draft of your Q&As past your PR lawyer.

CORRECTING MEDIA INACCURACIES

I set out in Chapter 3 the various regulatory codes which apply to the media and the bespoke editorial values espoused by newspapers such as the *Financial Times*, the *Independent* and the *Guardian*. A key purpose of these provisions is to provide a means of correcting inaccuracies in the media, so they should be deployed accordingly.

It is essential that this remedial action be undertaken as rapidly as possible. This is a job for your PR lawyer, who should send a firm but courteous email to the journalist, managing editor and/or legal department; better still, the editorial lawyer if their identity is known, which will get you a faster response. The email should:

1. Say who the client is;
2. Identify the article and attach a link;
3. Identify any assertion in the article which is incorrect;
4. Cite the relevant regulatory provision;
5. If there is a legal infraction, this too should be cited;
6. A short deadline if there is a regulator to whom a complaint can be made and the newspaper told that if the correction is not made by then, a formal complaint will follow.

This will hopefully do the trick. If not, then by far the most likely regulator you will be dealing with is IPSO – IMPRESS deals with a much small number of publications – and because they have opted to be properly and independently regulated, it is likely they will have a more ethical set of editorial standards and will publish less inaccurate and misleading material.

MAKING A COMPLAINT TO IPSO

In theory the IPSO process should work well. Although the IMPRESS Code is better, the IPSO Code is generally a good document. The problem is that IPSO does not enforce it. If it did there would be a rapid and radical improvement in British press standards, as there would be if all the Fleet Street titles became part of the IMPRESS system. Sadly neither is going to happen.

The IPSO complaints system is reasonably straightforward. A quasi-legal process conducted entirely on paper, it carries no cost consequences (unlike litigation) and will reach an adjudication more rapidly than a legal case would ever get to a full trial – though it still takes much longer than it would if IPSO were a legitimate regulator.

As to the timing of a complaint, this is what the IPSO website says:

'It is always best to make your complaint to us as soon as possi-ble. Sometimes it is harder for publications or us to investigate complaints if too much time has passed. Normally, you will need to make a complaint within four months of the date an article was published, or of the date of the journalist's behav-iour. If you are complaining about an online article, we may be able to investigate your complaint up to 12 months after the article was published, but this depends on the circumstances.'

You start an IPSO complaint by writing to IPSO citing the offending newspaper, the errant article and the elements of the article which are inaccurate and/or misleading. IPSO will then invite you to try to negotiate a resolution with the newspaper. That is normally a waste of the two weeks given for that process, the newspaper having neces-sitated the IPSO complaint by not dealing reasonably with the issue from the outset. However, sometimes the prospect of IPSO's inter-vening will cause a change of mind. There is one major disadvantage in settling an IPSO complaint at this stage. Any resolution achieved with the paper will not be recorded on the IPSO website. I therefore always advise clients not to resolve a complaint at this point.

If that period has not brought resolution, IPSO begins what it calls its 'investigation'; a process whereby one of its case-workers will officiate over an exchange of correspondence directed to them in an attempt to establish whether the newspaper is in the right or wrong. Your chances of winning an IPSO adjudication very much depend on the skill and determination which you exhibit during the investigation procedure, since it is this material which will be considered as part of the adjudication process.

If the IPSO officer is doing their job properly, they will exert some pressure on the paper to justify the publication at issue. Sadly not all of them do. This is the key stage of the IPSO complaint, where the battle is won or lost. These are the key things which you need to know about this process:

1. The quality of the IPSO officers is variable. Some exhibit a degree of independence from their employers (effectively the newspaper industry – especially News UK and Associated Newspapers); some do not.
2. One of the many indicia of the incestuous relationship between IPSO and its predecessor the PCC, and the print press, is the number of IPSO employees who end up working for newspapers. One director of the PCC went on to become managing editor of a national newspaper. More than once I have encountered other ex-PCC staff working for newspapers. So you are sometimes going to have to press them hard to persuade them to do anything that might ruffle the feathers of a prospective employer.
3. Part of the goal-post-moving exercise undertaken when IPSO was set up to replace the PCC was a change in the *Editors' Codebook*. In the PCC version it was stated that in the PCC complaints process the burden of proof was on the newspaper. That provision has been excised from the IPSO equivalent, and I am guessing because I frequently quoted it in the complaints that I made during the life of the PCC and it therefore became a thorn in the side of newspaper lawyers and managing editors. It is therefore

not entirely clear where the burden of proof lies in the
IPSO system.

4. In my correspondence I proceed on the basis that it is for a
newspaper to make good any factual assertion that it makes
in its pages and my experience of dealing with IPSO since
its inception (I conducted its first complaint) is that, on the
whole, newspapers are expected to corroborate their factual
assertions in the face of an IPSO complaints process. That also
appears to be the premise of IPSO's *Editors' Code of Practice.*

5. Where a newspaper purports to rely on a document
or recording in defending a complaint, they should be
pressed hard to disclose that document or recording.
An IPSO complaint that I was conducting turned when
the newspaper in question (the *Sun*) claimed to have a
recording of this high-profile individual 'losing the plot'
during a flight. This was put forward by the newspaper
both prior to publication and during the course of the
IPSO complaint as proof of the false allegations against
my client, which were the subject of the IPSO complaint.

   After a great deal of arm-twisting on my part of the
IPSO officer, the paper was eventually required to provide
a copy of this recording. Only then did it emerge that it
was not a recording of the incident at all, but merely a
recording of a phone call made to the paper by someone
who claimed to have witnessed the incident. At that
point that newspaper's defence to the IPSO complaint
unravelled. The complaint was upheld and was followed
by adjudication; the IPSO officer apparently unperturbed
by the fact that they had been lied to by the newspaper.

6. On most occasions the newspaper will make some offer of
a correction during the course of this process. It is rare for
no concession to be offered. If you accept the offer of the
newspaper, the IPSO practice is to record the successful
mediation of the complaint on its website.

7. If no offer is made, then an adjudication will follow
and where it feels able to do so, IPSO will side with the

newspaper. I have seen both PCC and IPSO adjudications which are breath-taking in their intellectual dishonesty, yet still signed off by the 'independent' members of the complaints committee.

8. If the newspaper accepts that it has published something which is inaccurate but makes an offer of a remedy which you do not accept, as you will be tempted to do because it will be only a fraction of the prominence of the original, then the IPSO adjudication will determine whether the offer made by the newspaper is sufficient. Nine times out of 10, however inadequate the offer is, IPSO will deem it sufficient; thereby making a mockery of the term in its Code which states that corrections should be published with 'due prominence'. The IMPRESS Code, by contrast, specifies that corrections should be generally with equal prominence.

9. A situation can also arise where a newspaper makes an offer of a correction but does not accept that they have breached the code. In those circumstances the adjudication will be as to whether or not the code is breached and whether the remedy that newspaper has offered is adequate.

10. The sole sanction which IPSO will ever deploy in the case of a complaint is to require the newspaper to publish an adverse adjudication, which does inflict some pain on the newspaper. Getting an IPSO complaint from beginning to conclusion normally takes at least six months – despite the fact that its own code stresses the need for corrections to be published 'promptly'.

    However, if the paper spins it out – as alas IPSO will generally allow it to do – then it may take rather longer, in which you should always have in mind the 12-month limitation period for libel actions. A paper may be spinning out the IPSO process with the express intention of forcing you to miss the limitation period for a libel action, as has been the case in my work for clients.

11. In considering who should conduct an IPSO complaint, be aware that it will be dealt with at the other end by one of the

in-house lawyers or someone who is trained to do this work. IPSO complaints should not therefore be undertaken by those who are not fully familiar with its quirks, procedures, code and key provisions of the *Editors' Codebook*. Otherwise, you will be sending an amateur to take on a professional in a game where the referee is employed by the opponents who have also written the rule book.

IPSO's reporting of outcomes

The outcomes of complaints – adjudicated or resolved via mediation – are recorded on the relevant page of the IPSO website: https://www.ipso.co.uk/rulings-and-resolution-statements. This is a useful record both of the outcome of the complaint and a clear signal that you will not be supine when your reputation/brand is under attack.

Such is IPSO's confidence in its infallibility there is no appeal against its adjudications, with the useless exception that you can raise an issue over the process whereby the adjudication has been arrived at.

Making tactical use of an IPSO complaint – Part one

There have been two sets of circumstances when I have made good tactical use of a PCC/IPSO complaint. The first was when I was acting for a woman who had an affair with a high-profile politician which was discovered as a result of a *News of the World* phone hack. It became a massive media story, which the woman in question (who was not well at the time) was finding immensely distressing.

I explained to her when we met that there was little that I would be able to do to protect her; and for the sake of her physical and mental health I asked whether she had any relatives that lived abroad. It turned out her parents lived in America and I suggested that she took the first flight out of the UK to stay with them until the media furore died down, which she duly did.

Unfortunately, one of the Fleet Street titles tracked her down and the ailing, heavily pregnant woman, accompanied by her infant child in a pram, was chased down a street by a photographer. This was despite my having previously written to the entirety of the British press, telling them that my client's privacy should be respected and she did not wish to make any comments.

There was no need for this photograph to be taken, or published, as there were plenty of pictures available of my client for use in press coverage. This was an obvious case of harassment contrary to the relevant provision of the old PCC Code and I made a complaint accordingly. I did so despite the fact that I had little doubt that the PCC would turn it down because it was no more independent of the press than is IPSO. Sure enough, the complaint was rejected. However, for the six months that it took for the PCC to adjudicate the complaint, because I made it known in the press that the complaint was underway, my client was largely left alone until the scandal ceased to be of interest to the media.

MAKING TACTICAL USE OF AN IPSO COMPLAINT – PART TWO

The other tactical use that can be made of an IPSO complaint is as a dry run and information-gathering exercise in order to better be able to determine the viability of a libel claim.

This use of the IPSO process (and its PCC predecessor) irritates certain Fleet Street lawyers and I have more than once had to fend off claims under the old PCC system that no complaints should be permitted until the complainant has undertaken not to bring defamation proceedings. This was consistently turned down by the PCC and I am confident that IPSO would do likewise. The rule is that you cannot conduct an IPSO complaint in parallel with defamation proceedings. However, you are not obliged to abandon your right to bring a defamation claim as the price of making a complaint to IPSO.

It may well be that during the course of an IPSO complaint, even if unsuccessful, it is blindingly obvious that the newspaper has no justification or evidence for the offending story. That means that the door is probably open to a successful defamation claim if that is what the client wants.

Overturning a PCC adjudication

During the latter stages of the life of the PCC I made a complaint on behalf of Paul McKenna, about a series of articles which alleged he was claiming to have a legitimate doctorate from a US university, while knowing perfectly well it was a bogus qualification.

The PCC rejected the complaint with its customary intellectual dishonesty – describing the article as merely a 'comment piece'. This point was so manifestly bad it was not even advanced by the *Mirror*, either during the course of the PCC complaint or in the subsequent legal proceedings. However, during the course of the complaint it became clear that the *Mirror* had no way of standing the story up, which was effectively an allegation of dishonesty against Paul McKenna, should they be confronted in a libel action. By a combination of hubris and incompetence of its legal department, the case ran for many months and then ended in a trial, which the newspaper lost.

This was the case where the *Mirror*'s senior lawyer was described as indulging in 'armchair machismo' by the trial judge. I overturned other appalling PCC adjudications by using the legal process. I have not yet overturned an adverse IPSO adjudication, but look forward to having the opportunity to do so.

Complaints against broadcasters

If you wish to complain about the content of a BBC programme you must traverse the BBC complaints process before reaching Ofcom. There is a straightforward online procedure to follow to make such a complaint, although I suspect your prospects of success will increase if it is made by someone with the appropriate professional expertise.

For all other broadcasters there is again a fairly straightforward process to make a complaint via the Ofcom website. Again, I suspect you will do better if your complaint is handled by someone with the appropriate professional expertise. In my 30 years as a PR lawyer, I have only made a very small number of complaints about broadcast content because of the much higher ethical standards and better regulation of broadcasters.

KEY ISSUES TO CONSIDER BEFORE SUING FOR LIBEL

During the same 30 years of doing corporate reputation management work I have only had to issue libel proceedings twice. The first was against the trade magazine the *Insurance Insider* for two leading figures in the insurance industry, which we won at one of the last jury trials[1]. The second was for Ayman Asfari on his behalf and that of his company, Petrofac (*see* pages 95–6).

The only libel for an individual client against a Fleet Street title which I have had to take to trial was the one for Paul McKenna against the *Mirror*. That was only because of a combination of hubris and stupidity on the part of its ex-senior lawyer, whom I am reliably informed had been advised by counsel that he would lose the case – which I presume he never passed on to his editor or the board.

As to bringing libel proceedings against a publisher or broadcaster; as I have also explained, there is a world of difference between dealing with (say) a *Mirror* or Associated Newspapers title to a broadcaster or most other publishers. Associated Newspapers and the Mirror Group will generally fight litigation in an attritional manner and will hire lawyers who are entirely happy to assert that the world is flat if instructed to do so. You need deep pockets and a steely nerve to take them on, although this method of conducting litigation does not endear them to judges and can sometimes backfire. Mr Justice Warby made very clear his disdain of the arguments advanced by the Associated Newspapers' lawyers in the Duchess of Sussex privacy case.

I understand that Mr Justice Mann, to whom the phone-hacking cases were assigned, reached the point where he dismissed pretty well every submission that was made by the newspaper lawyers that

---

[1] https://swanturton.com/further-guidance-for-journalists-on-qualified-privilege-english-v-the-insurance-insider/

was before him. Doubtless it will have become clear to him that the paper's lawyers were engaged in an extended and unsavoury attempt to cover up their client's wrongdoing. The unprecedented level of damages awarded to phone-hacking victims against the Mirror Group – later upheld by the Supreme Court – was, I suspect, testimony to that fact.

One of the provisions in the Pre-Action Protocol for defamation in the Civil Procedure Rules (CPR) is to try to resolve your dispute with a publisher by means of what is called Alternative Dispute Resolution. Where a paper is regulated by IPSO, then that should be the forum where the ADR process should begin. As I have explained, not only is this the officially recommended way forward, it has distinct tactical advantages.

By the end of an IPSO (or Ofcom) complaint, a top-flight solicitor or barrister should be well placed to decide whether or not you will succeed in a defamation claim, so avoiding the fate suffered by Johnny Depp. I strongly advise clients against any legal proceedings unless they have a substantially better than 50/50 chance of winning, but an even more important consideration is whether these are proceedings you can afford to lose.

If you can afford to lose, you have a better-than-even chance of winning and a newspaper or broadcaster is still standing their ground, test their resolve by issuing proceedings. Most libel proceedings settle before trial and they are a considerable drain on not only the finances but the internal resources in terms of personnel and management time for any publisher or broadcaster. If you are prepared to be reasonable in your aspirations as to an outcome, there is a good chance that some form of settlement will be offered prior to a trial.

THE RIGHT TO BE FORGOTTEN

Where there is adverse material about an individual that is viewable online and which will appear on the results of a search via a search engine, there is a procedure whereby you can secure an order which has the effect of making that material 'disappear'. This is now called the right to 'erasure'.

In 1995, the European Union (EU) adopted the European Data Protection Directive to regulate the processing of personal data which is now considered a component of human rights law. The UK GDPR recognizes the importance of the right to freedom of expression and information and the Data Protection Act 2018 provides some protection regarding personal data processed for 'special purposes', including journalistic purposes. Google has tried unsuccessfully to rely on the journalistic exemption.

Judges in the EU ruled that in compiling its search results, Google is a collector and processor of data and should be classified as a 'data controller' under the meaning of the EU data protection directive. Under EU law, these 'data controllers' are essentially required to remove data that is 'inadequate, irrelevant, or no longer relevant'.

To request removal from a search engine you must complete a form through that search engine's website. Google's removal request process requires the applicant to identify their country of residence, personal information, a list of the precise URLs to be removed, along with a short description, and – in some cases – attachment of legal identification. The applicant receives an email from Google confirming the request but the request must be assessed before it is approved for removal. If the request is approved, searches in Europe using the individual's name will no longer result in the URLs appearing in search results.

After a request is filled, their removals team reviews the request, weighing 'the individual's right to privacy against the public's right to know', deciding if the website being linked to contains data which is 'inadequate, irrelevant or no longer relevant, or excessive in relation to the purposes for which they were processed'. Google says it has formed an Advisory Council of various professors, lawyers and government officials from around Europe to provide guidelines for these decisions. However, the review process is still a mystery to the general public.

The 'right to be forgotten' and 'right to erasure' are not absolute rights, which means that Google and other search engine operators can refuse to remove results. This will usually be where there is a 'preponderant public interest' that overrides an individual's data rights. For example, it is highly unlikely that an individual convicted of serious sexual offences will be able to satisfy a search engine operator that search results should be filtered. However, where they have committed a minor offence some time ago, there is a good argument that they should be able to move on with their life without the shackles of adverse search engine results against their name.

In cases where there is a disagreement over whether or not results should be removed, an individual may request that Google reviews its decision, complain to the Information Commissioner's Office (ICO) or seek a court order requiring Google to remove search engine results. The 'disabling' will however apply only to Europe and not to the world as a whole.

INTERNATIONAL MEDIA CRISES

My first piece of advice to any overseas reader of this book is that based on having dealt with international media crises throughout my career is that, if possible tackle it in the UK because this is the best place to do it. With the exception of New Zealand, Great Britain is the most claimant-friendly jurisdiction for the protection of reputation.

So far as I know you will find nothing like the array of remedies both to prevent the publication of and deal with the dissemination of fake news in other countries. Where possible you should secure some kind of remedy in the UK and then use PR to send the signal out worldwide that this particular allegation or set of allegations has been determined as false by a UK regulator or a UK court.

If you have instructed an experienced and competent PR lawyer they will have a good working understanding of the applicable law in most major territories since their work will have obliged them to find this out, either by research and/or dealing with practitioners from those countries. I was recently instructed by an offshore client for whom by using local experts I advised on PR remedies for the UK, America, New Zealand, United Arab Emirates, Malta and the EU generally.

America

I was fortunate to be invited by the New York Bar to speak at a conference about reputation management in the context of the Leveson Inquiry and how the means of undertaking that work differed between the US and the UK. I had assumed that deploying legal methodology in the US to protect reputation was more or less impossible because of the interpretation put upon the First Amendment of the US Constitution on the seminal case of *New York Times* v Sullivan[2].

It appears not however, and I have an excellent contact in a top New York law firm – a British barrister practising media law in the US who is my 'go to' when a problem arises in the States. A good PR lawyer with experience of dealing with overseas jurisdictions should be able to project manage for you a media crisis which has become international.

OVERSEAS PUBLICATIONS WHICH CAN BE ACTIONED IN THE UK

Even where a claimant resides in the UK and wishes to complain of damage to his reputation here, section 9 of the Defamation Act 2013 now provides that where the prospective defendant is not domiciled in the UK, a member state, or a Lugano Convention state: 'A court does not have jurisdiction to herein determine an action unless the court is satisfied that, of all the places in which the statement complained of has been published, England and Wales is clearly the most appropriate place in respect of the statement.'

---

[2] *New York Times* Company v Sullivan is a 1964 decision of the US Supreme Court ruling that the freedom of speech protections in the First Amendment to the US Constitution restrict the ability of American public officials to sue for defamation. It held that if a defamation plaintiff is a public official or running for public office they must prove that the statement was made with 'actual malice'; i.e. that the defendant either knew the statement was false or recklessly disregarded whether or not it was true.

9

Litigation PR

Litigation PR is managing the media in the context of legal disputes both to achieve the maximum PR and tactical benefit, and to mitigate to the fullest degree any reputational damage. My perspective comes from my commercial litigation practice, which because of the amount of high-profile litigation I have conducted has necessarily involved dealing frequently with the media. I used it as a weapon when, in my capacity as a commercial litigator, I was conducting Noel Edmonds' claim against Lloyds Bank (LBG), dealing regularly with a gaggle of about a dozen journos (print and TV) and working closely with PR legend Mark Borkowski.

In that case one of the reasons why they came back to me repeatedly for copy was that armed with my expertise as a litigator I could explain the complex factual and legal issues in a way they could understand and which in turn fed into their copy. That gave me the edge (as did the fact that they knew I wasn't lying to them) over the PR team at LBG, who did not appear fully to understand what the case was about.

THE DEARTH OF RELEVANT EXPERTISE

While researching this book I was astonished to discover the number of PR agencies offering litigation PR or litigation communications without apparently having anyone qualified to do the work. One major agency had a link to its head as the individual concerned, but when you looked at his CV there was no evidence that he had any expertise in the field. To do this work properly you must be expert both in crisis PR and litigation – as I had assumed would be obvious.

Do not leave it to Magic Circle or large corporate firms to do this work. They will not have the requisite media expertise. No Magic Circle firms and virtually no others in their sector have a media practice of substance because it does not generate sufficient income for their business model.

THE THINGS THAT AN EXPERT IN LITIGATION PR SHOULD BE ABLE TO DO FOR YOU

A litigation PR expert should be able to advise on media aspects from the moment a legal dispute arises (i.e. before legal proceedings have begun) right through to its conclusion by means of a trial or otherwise. You and your lawyers should meet with them at an early stage to advise on the likely PR consequences of their actions and those of their opponents.

A litigation PR expert should assess the likely media coverage at each stage of the action, as well as provide real-time updates during court hearings and inhibit wayward media comment. They will also engage with journalists covering the story to explain the legal process, promote positive coverage and discourage negative coverage.

THE UNIQUE CHALLENGES OF LITIGATION PR

Though related, litigation PR diverges from orthodox crisis PR because you deal with both the media and your litigation opponent, who will be doing their best to swing the media behind their client. It has the further challenge from the fact that the media has an almost unrestricted licence in reporting court proceedings, which is akin to reporting parliamentary proceedings. You also have to be sure that you do not irritate the judiciary. It is also different from mere crisis PR since, if expertly done, it can be used as both a shield and sword.

The combination of expertise required

Litigation PR is a specialist form of reputation management which requires this combination of expertise:

- A thorough knowledge of the legal process, ideally gained as a practitioner;
- A full understanding of the mindset of solicitors and barristers, both to facilitate communication and exert influence;
- A good knowledge of the mindset of judges – especially on media issues;
- Extensive experience of dealing with the media;
- A full understanding of the law and regulation governing the media's reporting of litigation.

A BRIEF GUIDE TO LITIGATION

Conducting litigation is like playing three-dimensional chess; though with the sobering knowledge that you do so not for your benefit, but that of your client. Trying to conduct litigation PR without fully understanding how litigation works is like trying to commentate on a chess match without knowing the rules.

So how does litigation work? This is an instance where a little knowledge is a dangerous thing when confronting the media, but where you also have a distinct advantage if you are better informed than the journos you are dealing with; though those in the nationals will all have access to an in-house lawyer who can guide them on litigation issues. So, if you are trying to do litigation PR without the requisite legal knowledge, then you are immediately on the back foot.

PRE-ACTION CORRESPONDENCE

Civil litigation comprises legal disputes where the parties are individuals or companies, as opposed to the criminal process where the state prosecutes an individual or company. The

CPR stipulate that all civil litigation should be preceded by correspondence between the parties in which the claimant sets out details of the claim and the defendant sets out in reply why the claim is rejected.

The most common exception is where an application is made for what is called an interim injunction, which is a court order usually preventing some unlawful activity – in the media realm usually a threatened breach of confidence. In that case there will sometimes not be time to set out the basis of a claim in a detailed letter; or if you are dealing with a blackmailer, as I have, where there may be legitimate grounds to give no prior notice.

Pre-action correspondence has become increasingly important in recent years and so needs to be finely judged, especially if some of it may end up in the public domain. Judges can also take against it – as did Mr Justice Eady against the *Mirror* correspondence in my libel action for Paul McKenna[1].

Some recipients such as *Private Eye* may publish it, as may some crazed social media warriors. All such correspondence concerning parties or issues which may interest the media should be drafted on the assumption that it may end up on a website.

The claim form

The next stage is the issue of the claim form, once called a writ. That is usually served on the other side with the first really important document in a claim: particulars of claim. This is nearly always prepared by a barrister and sets out in detail what the claimant wants from the action and why they believe they are entitled to it. It is however possible to apply for an order to seal a court file where issues of confidentiality are concerned, as has in my experience been done by Simon Cowell's lawyers when I have both opposed and worked with them on privacy issues. The same

[1] https://www.5rb.com/wp-content/uploads/2013/10/McKenna-v-MGN-QBD-28-July-2006.pdf

principle would apply where commercially sensitive information was at issue.

The defence

The next stage will usually be that the defendant serves a defence. But there are alternatives if – for example – you wish to strike out parts of the particulars of claim, as was done in the Duchess of Sussex privacy case, before serving the defence.

You may wish to do so because there are allegations made in the particulars of claim that you do not want to have to deal with and which a judge may strike out, as Warby J did in the Sussex case. You may also add a counterclaim to the defence, which is a good way of seeing a claim off – especially if it is for a larger sum.

The reply and costs budgeting

The defendant may then serve a 'reply' to the defence (and a defence to the counterclaim, if there is one), at which point there is what is called a Case Management Conference, where a judge sets out how the case will progress to trial and set limits on how much each side should spend on legal costs – known as 'costs budgeting'.

Disclosure

The next stage is what is called 'disclosure', which in the US is still known as 'discovery' (as it used to be called in the UK). At this stage both sides in the action are supposed to prepare lists of all the documents they hold, including electronic documents, which both support and undermine their cases.

This process requires both sides to act ethically in fulfilling their duties to the court – especially the lawyers who have professional obligations to ensure that this exercise is done properly. No one wants to disclose a document undermining their chances of success. Where the solicitors are acting for a client (such as a newspaper group or bank) which pays them millions of pounds in fees every year to win at all costs, the temptation not to comply with this obligation is strong. I have seen it done on a number of occasions in my practice. It has been routine conduct by those defending the phone-hacking claims.

Where you suspect that documents are being withheld, then you can apply to a judge for a disclosure order. But you can only apply for such an order where you can persuade a judge on the balance of possibilities that such a document exists. You must also know that there is such a document or class of document and be able to persuade a judge of that fact.

Witness statements
The next stage is usually to prepare statements for all the witnesses that you intend to call to give evidence at a trial. An immensely skilled job, it can make or break a case. Witness statements should comprise as much as possible the words of the witnesses, but the precision required for them necessitates the expert input of a lawyer.

Expert's reports

After witness statements of fact are exchanged, you prepare reports of the evidence that any experts would give at trial if such evidence is required. Preparing those statements is also a very skilled exercise and there is a strict set of rules by which you must abide to ensure that at least the appearance of independence is maintained. Sometimes it is possible to agree the instruction of a joint expert.

Trial

Then comes the trial, at which point not only the media has a very great degree of latitude to report events, but also the witnesses are – subject to any restraints imposed by the judge – free to make hugely defamatory allegations open court for which there is no legal recourse. Litigation PR should have kicked in at the beginning of the legal process, but if ever it is needed, then it is at trial.

A fainting witness

There is always the possibility of something completely unexpected happening at a trial. In the case of Paul McKenna's libel action against the *Mirror*, Victor Lewis Smith who wrote the article chickened out and sent in a sick note for the trial. His problem was that on the eve of the trial, he was spotted by one of Paul's friends at the Groucho Club – a smart arty club in Soho beloved of celebrities. This did not go down well with the judge.

His business partner with whom he had apparently written the short article was sent to obfuscate in his place. Such was the stress of this exercise that during his cross-examination the man collapsed in the witness box and had to be revived by paramedics.

BEING AHEAD OF THE GAME

To do litigation PR effectively you must stay ahead of the media – which you have every opportunity to do if you are geared up for the task. Where there is a high-profile trial or hearing I attend court with my laptop, which means that I am able to brief/advise on developments before the media get (say) a Press Association report. That means where either – for example – there is a key document handed in evidence or something dramatic emerges in the evidence, the client and their advisors get to learn in real time and are ready with statement/refutation, etc. If you are not at least a competent litigator, then you are not going to be able to fulfil this role effectively.

ERNST & YOUNG GETS IT WRONG

For most large corporations the general rule is that the sums of money at stake in litigation are substantially less than the commercial risk to its brand or reputation. This claim against Ernst & Young (E&Y) is a prime example, about which I know something because I advised a related party in the dispute.

The claimant, who characterized himself as a whistle-blower on malpractice at E&Y, was awarded around £9 million in damages and the combined costs will be no less than £6 million, given the complexity of the issues and the long journey of the dispute to the trial. It is always difficult to judge the negative impact of such reporting on a huge brand like E&Y but it must be a multiple of £15 million.

As far as I know, E&Y did not engage litigation PR, but if it did then they should be fired. This is yet another example of a completely misleading *Mail* headline: 'WHISTLEBLOWER WHOSE CAREER WAS "RUINED" AFTER HE EXPOSED BRITISH ACCOUNTANCY FIRM ERNST & YOUNG FOR "USING BLACK MARKET GOLD TO LAUNDER DIRTY MONEY" IS AWARDED £8 MILLION.' The truth is that it was not E&Y that was allegedly trading in black market gold, but its client Kaloti (a Dubai-based bullion company). E&Y's media professionals should have secured an immediate correction of that headline via the available regulatory and legal means. But even with an accurate headline this is a very damaging story for the E&Y brand. Incredibly E&Y has allowed that headline to remain online right up to the completion of this book – an extraordinary failure of litigation PR.

THE MEDIA RISK MAY WELL BE HIGHER THAN THAT OF THE LITIGATION

While the PR tail should generally not wag the litigation dog, for major corporations – especially those with a public profile – the PR stakes will often be higher than those which are the subject of the litigation. This will be particularly the case when a claimant is using the litigation primarily as a means of inflicting reputational damage on the defendant, or as a way putting pressure on the defendant to compromise the litigation rather than suffer brand damage – even more so if the claimant has limitless funds.

Trouble with a Ferrari

That was the situation when I was doing the litigation PR for a leading international auction house, which was sued by an American billionaire who bought a classic Ferrari during the course of an auction, which turned out to be not as he had expected. For him the purpose of litigation was not primarily to recover money, but to wreak vengeance against the auction house which he held responsible by the procuring of the worst possible media coverage of the case to inflict the maximum damage. The billionaire presumably had been advised that the media has considerable licence when reporting litigation – which meant that it was the platform whereby he could publicize his allegations against the auction house. This meant that the primary battle between the two parties was fought in the media.

I was brought in by the PR outfit that did the work of the auctioneers because they recognized that this was specialist work. I then liaised closely with the major corporate firm of solicitors conducting the action who briefed me thoroughly. Armed with my knowledge of the litigation process from being a commercial litigator I was able to engage with the media and parry the black propaganda from the billionaire's side.

A key element was to be on top of the detail of the case – what were genuinely factual issues in the litigation and what were not – the latter falling outside the ambit of litigation privilege. This enabled me to ensure that the client's robust and detailed defence was fully understood by the media. I was also able to feed in background which cast the claimant as the villain of the piece. To do so requires access to the key documents and the ability fully to understand them. You are then able to deliver their content to a non-lawyer journo in a comprehensible and persuasive manner, which in turn secures the most favourable coverage.

The journalists I dealt with also knew that I had the means of delivering regulatory and/or legal sanctions if they ignored me. The result was only a modest dent in the client's historic brand.

Trouble cooking at the Fat Duck[2]

Sometimes litigation and PR must be in tandem, with the PR element being done on the hoof. I was acting for the culinary genius Heston Blumenthal, whose Fat Duck restaurant had – through no fault of his own, but one of his suppliers – been afflicted by norovirus, which had caused unpleasant symptoms in some of his guests.

As we learned about those customers who had suffered after having ingested the guilty oysters, we settled with them all on generous terms – except one. Veteran sports commentator Jim Rosenthal issued a county court claim for a refund in addition to the generous compensation that he had received.

Such small claims trials are usually dealt with in a meeting room in a court complex, so to save Heston money I elected to do the advocacy rather than instruct a barrister. However, when I arrived at Oxford County Court, my first surprise was that I found a phalanx of reporters at the court building. Thank goodness I advised Heston not to come.

My second surprise was when I discovered that our hearing had been moved into the main courtroom, which was the size of a small theatre complete with a gallery full of the media. Plainly, Mr Rosenthal and/or his coterie had rung every journalist they knew to report his public revenge against Heston. It was far too late to call in a barrister so I had to conduct the trial myself. Given the modest sum of money at stake the most important element in the court was not the judge but the press gallery so it was primarily to them that I addressed my opening remarks.

Mercifully, I was able to persuade the judge that since Mr Rosenthal had already been paid the maximum sum which he could recover in any legal action, his claim should be

[2] https://www.dailymail.co.uk/news/article-1321182/TV-sports-presenter-Jim-Rosenthal-loses-claim-Heston-Blumenthals-Fat-Duck-restaurant.html

dismissed. Both he and his legal team (which included a barrister) were somewhat forlorn figures as they exited the courtroom
because, as it turned out, they had gathered the media only to
report on their defeat.

OPEN JUSTICE

One of the reasons why litigation PR is so essential is the extent
to which the justice process is open to public scrutiny via the
media. The courts are increasingly determined to ensure that they
undertake the business of justice openly. This is however a historic
legal principle. In 1924, Lord Chief Justice Hewart stated, '[It] is of
fundamental importance that justice should not only be done, but
should manifestly undoubtedly be seen to be done.'

Nearly 100 years later the Supreme Court declared that the
principle of open justice has two main purposes: first, 'to enable
public scrutiny' in order to hold the Court to account and second,
'to enable the public to understand how the justice system works
and why decisions are taken'. The way that the public is going to
understand this is via media reporting.

The courts have an inherent power to facilitate access to their
proceedings. It is open to a court in all proceedings to permit access
to court documents and order that a party to the proceedings
provides the documents to a non-party. There is a strong
presumption that access requests from journalists will be granted.
As the great judge Lord Reed said, '[the media are] the conduit
through which most members of the public receive information
about Court proceedings.'

In practical terms, documents which form the 'records of the
Court' can be secured, which include skeleton arguments, witness
statements and generally 'documents that have formed part of the
decision-making process in a public hearing'. Even affidavits (sworn
documents) and expert's statements, even if they have not been
read in open court, can be obtained where there are 'strong grounds
for thinking that it was necessary in the interests of justice'.

Generally speaking those applications will be granted because of the necessity of applying the fundamental open justice principle: 'The default position is that the public should be allowed access, not only to the parties' written submissions and arguments, but also to the documents which have been placed before the Court and referred to during the hearing.' Furthermore, 'where access is sought for a proper journalistic purpose the case for allowing it will be particularly strong'.

For practical reasons the media may not be aware of court proceedings, or may not be able to attend each hearing. It cannot realistically be expected to have reporters present at all times and in all cases in which there is a public interest. The ability to access documents relating to previous hearings in ongoing litigation is therefore important to ensure journalists' ability to properly understand the case and may make fair and accurate reports on the proceedings.

These principles apply even in circumstances where, as is the modern trend, judges make determinations on issues merely on the basis of written submissions. As Mr Justice Nicklin recently observed,[3] 'decision by a Court to deal with an application without a hearing is in substance a decision to depart from the principle of open justice.' He duly ordered, 'at the hand-down [of the judgment], together with copies of the judgment, the Court will make available all written submissions that were considered by the Court before making the determination.'

The open justice principle can even require a court to permit access to evidence that was not admitted in a trial, or referred to in open court. The rationale being that scrutinizing the justice system could plainly require that the media be permitted to ask whether there was evidence that should have been admitted or relied on in open court and assessing the significance of any such evidence. Such an order can be made even when the court no longer has itself copies of the relevant documents.

---

[3] Hanson v Associated Newspapers Ltd [2020] EWHC 1048 (QB)

A non-party seeking access to court documents should 'explain why he seeks it and how granting him access will advance the open justice principle'. These are the principles which a court will apply: 'Central to the Court's evaluation will be the purpose of the open justice principle, the potential value of the material in advancing that purpose and, conversely, any risk of harm which access to the documents may cause to the legitimate interests of others.'

Woe betide you if you make an ill-founded or ill-judged application to a judge for a hearing to be held *in camera* (i.e. in secret) or for press coverage to be limited. Under relatively recent rules, the same principles apply to court documents, which are generally accessible by the public and media. It is possible to apply to a master (a junior judge) to 'seal' the file, but you must advance good reasons if you are going to succeed in so doing.

The principle of open justice also requires the media to report legal proceedings accurately. Alas, it is my experience that the press in particular considers that it has no obligation to do so, especially when its own interests are engaged. By far the best place to read faithful reports about media law cases is the BBC News website.

LITIGATION PRIVILEGE CREATES INJUSTICE

Inevitably this can cause injustice because of the almost complete privilege which the media has in reporting litigation. This means that they are free to report allegations made during the course of legal proceedings which may not only be entirely false, but the author of those allegations may know perfectly well they are false – as may the lawyers who advance them to their shame.

But the law, rightly or wrongly, has decided that the principle of open justice and the consequential ability of the media to freely report on our behalf what the courts are doing has been determined to be more important than the potential damage which reputations and confidentiality often suffer as a consequence. That is why litigation PR is both immensely important and exceedingly difficult to do well.

Litigation PR for Paul McKenna

My client Paul McKenna was being sued in the US by his ex-fiancée, Clare Staples. The legal battle had spread to the UK, where I was acting for him. Paul had a high profile, both in the UK and the US, and Clare's attorneys were deploying this against him. When both pieces of the litigation were resolved in Paul's favour, it was important that the world knew this.

My solution was to write up the litigation in a piece that I wrote for my then client the *Huffington Post*, which I titled: 'VICTORY FOR GOOD GUY PAUL MCKENNA IN HIS LEGAL BATTLE WITH CLARE STAPLES.'[4]

Here is an extract from the piece illustrating the problem:

'The document which sets out a claim in the US is called a
Verified Complaint. In Britain we call it the Particulars of
Claim, but the purpose of both documents is to set out what
the claimant wants from the legal actions, and the evidence
on which they are going to rely. In both countries those
documents are open to the public and so can be a rich source
copy for journalists. Legal privilege means that they can be
both made and reported with no risk of a libel action. It is
therefore an opportunity to abuse the legal system and put an
opponent under enormous pressure to settle a legal claim or
suffer reputational damage.

Clare Staple's Verified Complaint was laced with poisonous
allegations against Paul McKenna which she ensured were
picked up by several British newspapers with the inevitable
damage to his reputation.'

As I explain in the piece I was able to disprove Clare Staples evidence by digging out the witness statement she had signed in Paul's libel claim against the *Mirror*. So she and her lawyers eventually had

---

[4] https://www.huffingtonpost.co.uk/jonathan-coad/paul-mckenna-and-clare-staples_b
_11659648.html

to throw in the towel, which they effectively did in a judicial mediation in LA.

I wrote the *Huffington Post* article as a way of undoing – to the greatest degree possible – the reputational damage which Clare Staples and her unprincipled US lawyers had done to my client by leaking the US legal documents to journalists.

KEY PRINCIPLES FOR LITIGATION PR

1. Assess the likely PR consequences (both positive and negative) of litigation *before* you commence proceedings, or before proceedings are commenced against you. If you do so later it may be too late.
2. Some apparently more minor types of litigation process can cause immense damage – in particular, employment tribunals and inquests. Particular care needs to be taken around them.
3. Do not let litigation PR be done by lawyers who are not expert in doing media work, or by PR people who have no expertise in litigation.
4. There should be a close working relationship between those conducting the litigation and those responsible for PR, which should involve to the greatest degree possible the sharing of information and documentation.
5. You need to have a PR expert present at any hearing or trial which is likely to attract media attention.
6. However important litigation PR is, it must not be conducted in a way which would irritate a judge.
7. You may get some resistance from senior barristers in particular when eliding PR issues with those which are strictly legal. This must gently be resisted and it is more likely that a reluctant QC will be talked around by a fellow lawyer than someone they perceive to be only competent in PR.

8. You need to step back and undertake a candid review, to which a good PR lawyer should be central, around the question: 'if we bring this claim, or try and defend a claim, are we going to come across as monsters even if we are in the right?'

9. Another factor differentiating litigation PR from its other forms is that whereas a journalist will nearly always contact you before writing an adverse story in ordinary circumstances, where they are reporting the legal process they may not. This is because of the sense of invulnerability which they, and their employer, feel because of the legal privilege which reports of legal proceedings enjoy. That means that you may need to go on the front foot and contact in particular any legal journalists, or journalists who include legal coverage in their work.

10. You should seek out any journalist actually attending a trial or hearing. This will normally be an agency journalist or a freelancer. Either way you need to get alongside them, hand them your card, chat through your/your client's perspective of the case and (if at all possible) get them on side – and always buy them a coffee. This can make a world of difference to their coverage, especially if you help them in writing their copy by explaining how the legal process is playing out in front of them.

11. Quite often when hearings or trials are of major significance, the two sides will have agreed to engage an official shorthand writer who will produce transcripts of the day's hearing within an hour or so of its conclusion. Those are invaluable and unlikely to be available to any journalist. Your litigation PR expert should be provided with them at the same time as they are received by the rest of the legal team, at which point they will provide invaluable material for their work on any coverage of

the hearing which appears the following day. In an argument between which is right – a journalist's note or the official transcript – there is only going to be one outcome.

This will also provide an incontrovertible means of getting briefings out to the key journalists, who will know that if you are citing elements of the official transcript they are on the safest possible ground in their reporting – which hopefully will favour you rather than the opponent.

12. A major crisis may emerge (say) at 11 a.m. during a hearing, where either a judge makes a damning observation, or one of your witnesses or an opposing witness says something you know is going to look dreadful in print. That is why it is essential that you have a PR expert in the courtroom (virtual or otherwise).

He or she is not allowed to record the hearings, but if they are a good typist they can immediately send in an email the gist of what has been said so that the process can begin of deciding how to minimize any consequential damage. Equally, if the judge's comment or the witness says something which is very much in your favour, again you want to be first off the blocks in making best use of it.

13. The only way that you will be in a position to recognize when such an event has occurred is if you are fully embedded in the legal team and are familiar with the relevant law and facts on which the litigation is based. It is not reasonable to expect a busy legal team to pick these points up on top of all their other responsibilities. It is also unreasonable to expect busy lawyers to take time to explain legal principles with which the individual undertaking the litigation PR should already be familiar.

THE DANGERS POSED BY INQUESTS

I have three times represented a client during the course of an inquest which had the potential to do immense reputational damage. One was a blue-chip school where tragically a teenager died during an overseas trip. The second was another school where, equally tragically, a teenager committed suicide. The third was a top fashion brand whose most famous designer took their own life.

Inquests are run entirely by the coroner, who has a great deal of latitude as to how things are done. Very few inquests now have a jury and so the coroner makes all the key findings. There are two primary dangers during the course of an inquest: one is the evidence which can be freely reported, and the other is the 'judgment' as delivered by the coroner, which in my experience may or may not faithfully reflect the evidence. In both cases the practice of the print media especially is to awfulize in its coverage.

If your company or institution has a genuine interest in the issues to be determined by the inquest, then they can make an application to be represented at it, which should be done by a barrister who is expert in the field. I did this in one of the cases I undertook for a school and it was an important factor in ensuring that the minimum damage was done by the process. Also, if you are represented, you will have a better chance of seeing the evidence in advance, so you can be forearmed by being forewarned.

10

Looking to the Future

There are practical steps which you can take to make your own brand, reputation, confidentiality and/or privacy less at risk of damage from the media. These all require a degree of resolve because a lion stalking gazelles is not targeting the strong but the weak. So it is with our predatory commercial media. A major investigatory piece in which aims searing criticism at online retailers is (as advised by the editorial lawyer) going to be much more wary of a brand which has shown resolution in protecting itself against predations by the media than one that allows its brand to suffer death by a thousand journalistic cuts.

You/your company should be looking for an opportunity to send that signal. When I am engaged by a company which has had a period of adverse coverage, I ask for links to all examples from the last 12 months to establish whether any is susceptible to effective challenge; though more likely will be press incursions by IPSO titles within the last four months – the limitation period for an IPSO complaint. If there is not one susceptible to challenge then I will invite the client's PR team (internal or external) to monitor Fleet Street's output about my client, which is likely to reprise a false allegation which is time-barred, which will give me the opportunity to challenge it.

PRACTICAL STEPS THAT WILL MAKE A DIFFERENCE

Here are some practical things that you could do which would not only improve the quality of our British press – itself a highly worthwhile aspiration – but also make it less likely that you will be the victim of press abuse of one sort or another; even if it is only being misled by the press; something of which we are all victims:

1. Lobby your MP to raise the manifold failings of IPSO in Parliament, or via the Culture, Media and Sport Committee, or in some other way which will put pressure on that fatally compromised regulator to do a better job.
2. Next time there is a General Election tell canvassers that improved press regulation is an important issue for you.
3. If you make an IPSO complaint and the outcome (either as to adjudication or prominence) is not as it should be, make as much noise about it as you can. Write to its chairman, to your MP, to the Home Secretary or the Culture Secretary. See if you can persuade the *Media Guardian* or *Byline Investigates* to pick the story up. You could also use your website and/or social media contacts to rubbish any defective adjudication and highlight its failings – which will generally not be difficult and with which I would be delighted to help.
4. Write to the editor of your favourite newspaper and demand an explanation as to why it is not part of the Leveson-compliant IMPRESS scheme[1]. You are sure to receive a disingenuous response, but if enough people write, then some change in mindset will be achieved.
5. Though I do not entirely share its political outlook and think it should be IMPRESS-regulated, you might support the *Guardian* financially to ensure that it can continue its good work (unique in Fleet Street) in holding its less ethical peers to account.

[1] When Lord Leveson's report included a series of recommendations for a regulator to replace the PCC, the press industry ignored them in setting up IPSO. IMPRESS complies with them.

6. Subscribe to *The Week*, which has no editorial axe to grind and provides excellent coverage both of the news and how it is reported.
7. Become a Hacked Off supporter.
8. Read the *Press Gazette*, which courageously reports press failings.
9. Discover Bylineinvestigates.com, which focuses on press reform and Fleet Street's abuse of us all. Though originally connected, it is now separate from *Byline Times* (which on the basis of my recent dealings should be avoided) and Byline.com. *Byline Investigates* is IMPRESS-regulated. It only employs trained and experienced journalists like its editor Graham Johnson, who was investigations editor at the *Sunday Mirror* for many years and specialized in probing organized crime. Unlike Fleet Street, it only publishes stories with a high standard of corroboration – i.e. emails, documents, payment records, High Court records/ police information, etc. Send links to its stories via every social media device you can.
10. You should also follow the *Press Gang* (https://press -gang.org/), which has 'exposing rogue journalism' as its mission. I particularly recommend its Piers Morgan page.
11. Read *Private Eye*'s 'Street of Shame' page and use social media to tell as many people about it as you can. Why not make a collage of those pages and put it up in your loo?
12. Read Nick Davies' *Flat Earth News* (https://www. flatearthnews.net/), which is an excellent expose of press malpractice.
13. If you have a heart to improve our press, and a good measure of moral courage, apply to become a lay member either of IPSO's Complaints or Code committee.
14. If you are already a lay representative at IPSO, please either resign or grow a backbone.

15. Write to the chairman of IPSO and ask how they and the Committee explain how a story which was so important that it warranted appearing on the front page then ceases to be that important when it comes to a correction which never appears on the front page.
16. In the same letter you could ask why IPSO does not apply the same prominence measure as do the rate cards used by the papers for advertising.
17. Go to the IMPRESS website and choose one of the titles that it regulates to subscribe to.
18. If you are ever for a moment tempted to sell a story to a tabloid either about you or someone else, please think better of it.
19. For the best news portal, for all its imperfections, place more confidence in the BBC than any other news source, and be grateful for the unique way by which it is funded.
20. Be suspicious of any 'news' that comes to you via social media and tell your friends and family likewise. It is likely to be both poisonous and false.
21. Fleet Street would have you believe that no politician is to be trusted. Don't believe it. There are good men and women in politics. I know because I have dealt with them.

Plus ça change

Some things have not really changed over the 30 years that I have been a media lawyer. When I started out, there was good news and bad news. There is still good news and bad news (in the sense of its quality). All that has really changed is that there is now more of both – save that unfortunately the growth of bad news has outstripped the growth of good news. However, where there are journalists who are intent on fulfilling their public service obligation to tell us the truth, it makes no difference whether they are on a big screen, a small screen, communicating via Twitter,

Facebook, TikTok, Instagram or with printed words on paper. There has always been, and will continue to be, good and bad journalism, whatever the various mediums that now exist through which journalists can ply their trade. The work of good journalists should be lauded. The work of bad ones needs to be exposed – best of all by good journalists.

The trend for the instant news will inevitably continue and accelerate with the inevitable result that quality will suffer. A news cycle used to be 24 hours with the printing of newspapers in the evening when I started out as a PR professional. Now events can be reported literally as they occur. Journalists are even permitted (by judicial edict) to tweet during the course of trials – as they should be. The effect of this however is that the essential process of checking (to ensure good quality) will become ever rarer. The main reason why the BBC is sometimes later to a story than other news outlets is because they apply higher editorial standards and will generally not run a story until it has been properly checked. The BBC is sometimes (wrongly) criticized for not being first to break a story.

CAMERAS IN COURTS?

Surely the day will come when the UK public will routinely gain access to the courtroom not by having necessarily to turn up, but by there being cameras placed there. We have seen that work in the Supreme Court and I imagine that it will gradually filter down to the lower courts and we will thereby follow the American precedent – COVID-19 has inevitably speeded that process up.

This will of course provide opportunities for abuse by both lawyers and witnesses, but that really only increases an opportunity already there. In my practice I have encountered corrupt individuals who have abused the privileges which they have as participants in legal proceedings to make wholly false and defamatory allegations against third parties, and lawyers who have facilitated this.

It will be the job of judges to take a firmer hand in these circumstances if cameras are allowed in to a greater degree. One expedient which could be tried is for there to be a delay in transmission so that such abuse can be edited out. If, however, we have cameras in Parliament, surely we should have them at least in the senior courts where in some cases events of a similar level of importance to those of the Palace of Westminster occur.

11

Conclusion

As I have explained, there is an immense discrepancy between the method and effectiveness of the regulation of the broadcast media and the print media. In an age when both communicate via words and images on screens, this is anomalous; as is the fact that at present news websites such as Sky and the BBC are regulated neither by Ofcom or either of the print regulators – a lacuna which needs to be addressed.

One of the things which powerful companies and individuals could do is to add their weight to organizations such as Hacked Off which is a courageous advocate for much-needed improved regulation of the press. Fleet Street has been permitted to foist IPSO on us because of a lack of protest by the nation as a whole against this fourth incarnation of press self-regulation, which ill-serves the nation in ways and to an extent which most of it will never appreciate. One of the key drivers for me in writing this book has been to try to rectify that.

THE DESPERATE NEED FOR PROPER REGULATION OF THE PRESS

We have a press which is substantially free to mislead, to judge unfairly, to stir conflict, wrongly to undermine trust and confidence and thereby infect society with its grinding and poisonous cynicism. Some think this is a good thing. I do not.

In March 2021, Eleanor Mills resigned from the Society of Editors board, condemning 'structural racism' in the UK media. This was prompted by the body's executive director Ian Murray provoking a storm of outrage on 8 March when he issued a statement saying 'the UK media is not bigoted' in response to criticism levelled against the tabloid press in particular by Prince Harry and Meghan Markle. Although this is not solely the product of a lack of effective regulation, it is symptomatic of how far the press in particular diverges from the ethical standards to which society aspires.

To its immense credit the *Press Gazette* both undertook and published a survey on this issue. Some 1,002 *Press Gazette* newsletter subscribers responded to its survey, 72 per cent of whom described themselves as journalists. Some 66 per cent of journalist respondents said the UK media is bigoted or racist in some way and 79 per cent of those said it was a problem across all media, not just tabloids. Some 50 per cent of journalist respondents said at least some coverage of Prince Harry's wife Meghan Markle had been racist in tone or presentation and 38 per cent said they had personally experienced or witnessed racism while working in the UK media. Unsurprisingly, this went unreported in Fleet Street[1].

The UK is greatly enriched by the work of its best investigative journalists, including some excellent and courageous individuals that write for newspapers, and it has been my privilege to support their work in my capacity as an editorial lawyer. But the malign and mendacious output of many print journalists has not only injected poison into our society, it has also wrecked many lives; and with very few honourable exceptions, our politicians have not lifted a finger to protect us from such activity. This will remain the case until we can collectively persuade them that there are votes to be won by protecting the public from the daily predations of the big newspaper groups. While this situation continues, borrowing from

[1] https://www.pressgazette.co.uk/survey-funds-media-coverage-of-meghan-markle-racist/

the great Winston Churchill, 'the price of freedom [from media abuse] is eternal vigilance'.

As a devout Christian for whom truth holds a higher value than free speech, I am convinced that we do not need more information, we need *better-quality* information. The question is, how can that be achieved? Ultimately, this will only come about when two things happen. The first is when the reliable sources of information and those which are not are clearly delineated so that people can know where to find a trustworthy source of news. The second is that the regulation of these news media outlets is truly independent and effective.

STARSUCKERS

A 2009 film called *Starsuckers*[2] showed vividly how the press goes about lying to our politicians – who appear to be willing dupes – about the regulation of its industry. It included footage of four of the most powerful editors in Fleet Street giving evidence to the Culture, Media and Sport Committee which was looking into press regulation. I was also a witness to this inquiry when I spoke about Peaches Geldof and her treatment by the press and the PCC.

Colin Myler (previously editor at both the *Sunday Mirror* and the *News of the World*) said that he took judgments of the PCC (as was then the regulator) 'very seriously'. Rebekah Brooks (previously Wade) tells the Committee solemnly that a PCC complaint being upheld is 'what terrifies editors'. Andy Coulson speaks of the 'humiliation that comes with a PCC adjudication' and adds that it 'carries an enormous amount of weight and carries far more significance than a fine'. Paul Dacre tells the Committee members how well self-regulation works and there is a 'deep shame when you have to carry an adjudication'.

Cut into that sanctimonious and mendacious claptrap was a secretly filmed interview with an unnamed journalist who says

---

[2] https://www.filmsforaction.org/watch/starsuckers-2009/

this: 'Getting a PCC isn't great, but a lot of papers push it aside. All it is, is a little apology somewhere in the paper. You get a slap on the wrist but there is no money and the PCC is run by newspaper editors.' For the PCC, read IPSO. Ten years after these individuals were exposed as presiding over serial criminality, as was the PCC, and the publication of the Leveson Report, the situation is no different.

THE SERIAL AND DISMAL FAILURE OF SELF-REGULATION

It was at a later meeting of the Culture, Media and Sports Committee that that the senior figures from the tabloid press, including Andy Coulson and Rebekah Brooks, were telling MPs that self-regulation works well – as it plainly was for them because they saw it as no hindrance to their serial breaking of the law. The PCC was already the third failed incarnation of press self-regulation and apparently turned a blind eye to such activity.

As we now also know, the *Mirror* was also heavily engaged in phone hacking at that time – the common thread being Piers Morgan, who at different times edited both the *Mirror* and *News of the World* while that activity was underway. Incredibly, neither the PCC Code of the time nor its IPSO successor places any obligation on newspapers to abide by the law.

Such was the abject lack of independence on the part of the PCC that, in 2011, it was revealed (despite having tried to cover it up via a confidentiality agreement) that it had had to pay a claimant lawyer £20,000 in libel damages because its then chairman, Baroness Buscombe, had libelled him. Leading phone-hacking lawyer Mark Lewis had sued the PCC over remarks that she had made at the Society of Editors conference in 2009; doubtless with the intention on her part to convince them that the PCC would continue to accommodate their every whim.

The new IPSO regime which took over seamlessly from the PCC has been more sure-footed; doubtless learning from the mistakes of its predecessors. It has however presided over a press which primarily serves its own interests rather than those of the society which it should serve. This could not be more clearly proved than the grudging, belated and covert way in which it corrects its mistakes – if it does so at all.

THE CONSISTENT FAILURE OF SELF-REGULATION FOR THE PRESS

Self-regulation has been tried and has failed four times now over a period of nearly 70 years so it is time to accept that it does not work.

In 1949 the first Royal Commission on the Press recommended that a General Council of the Press be formed to govern the conduct of the print media. In response to a threat of statutory regulation, the General Council of the Press was formed in 1953, membership being restricted to newspaper editors, funded by newspaper proprietors.

By the time of the Second Royal Commission on the Press in 1962, the General Council had suffered robust criticism. The Commission's report demanded improvement, particularly the inclusion of members not employed by print media. The General Council was reformed as the Press Council in 1962, with 20 per cent lay members.

The Press Council was heavily criticized in 1973 by the Younger Committee Report on Privacy and in the report of the Third Royal Commission on the Press in 1977, which recommended the adoption of a code of practice. But the Press Council rejected this recommendation and, in 1980, the NUJ withdrew from membership because it was incapable of reform. It had also lost the confidence of many in the media and indeed the 1980s saw some of the worst excesses of unethical journalism and intrusions into privacy by the tabloid press.

In response to two Private Members' bills promoting privacy laws, the UK government set up a committee chaired by David Calcutt QC to investigate in 1989. At the same time, work was begun on the development of a Code of Practice.

The 1990 Calcutt Report recommended the setting up of a new press regulator to replace the Press Council, which would be given 18 months to prove non-statutory self-regulation could work effectively and if it failed to do so, then a statutory system would be introduced. In response to this, in 1991 the Press Council was replaced by the PCC – which closed in 2014, having proved beyond a shadow of a doubt that non-statutory regulation of the UK press will not work. However, rather than being replaced with a body which had any democratic legitimacy, it was replaced by IPSO – which is no better than any of its forebears.

THE CHAOTIC STATE OF MEDIA REGULATION

The current situation is a mess:

1. Most of the print press is regulated by a hopelessly compromised and ineffectual body (IPSO).
2. The three national titles outside the IPSO system are 'regulated' by an even less credible process.
3. Increasingly the 'press' is 'broadcasting' footage and so competing with the broadcasters – but under a completely different regime.
4. Ofcom has much more to commend it than IPSO, but does not regulate important news websites such as the BBC and Sky, which are unregulated.
5. So-called 'premium' news providers such as Bloomberg appear not to allow any form of independent scrutiny and will ignore proof that they have misled their readers.

Surely there has never been an era where public access to accurate information has been more important. The current IPSO chairman Lord Faulks appears to agree and says this in his introduction to the *Editors' Code of Practice*: 'Now, more than ever, there is a desire and need for content that can be identified as accurate and accountable. Trusted, regulated news has never been more important …'

Lord Faulks is right about the importance of news that is 'trusted' and 'regulated'. He cannot surely believe what he then goes on to claim, 'We at IPSO will continue rigorously and fairly to enforce the Code which reinforces that reliability and accountability.' It manifestly does nothing of the sort.

Would that that were true of the titles 'regulated' by IPSO. As Lord Faulks must know, the entity that he chairs owes its very existence to the fact that its creators and funders have preferred hubris to accountability – and the liberty to mislead rather than truly serve the public interest.

ONE MURDOCH GETS IT

Even James Murdoch has spoken about the damage that the media can cause if it does not fulfil its responsibilities to tell us the truth – in this case commenting on the role played by the US media, including his father's Fox News – in the storming of the US Capitol: 'Spreading disinformation – whether about the election, public health or climate change – has real world consequences. Many media property owners have as much responsibility as the elected officials who know the truth but instead choose to propagate lies.'

Amen to that, young James. Let's hope your father has read these wise words.

It is difficult to suggest an answer when time and time again our politicians have wilted in the face of pressure from the self-righteous and hubristic empire of Fleet Street and done nothing to secure for us a press which we can trust and truly serves the community rather than just mendaciously claiming to do so. Things will only change if we, the voters, become vocal about these issues and thereby create a situation where it is in the interests of our politicians to bring about changes in press regulation, which a whole series of reports, most recently by Lord Leveson, have determined are desperately needed. If this book in any way facilitates that, then for that reason alone it will have been well worth the investment in writing it.

Appendices

The risks of sending over a statement of publication in the face of a media crisis

The temptation for many internal and external PRs when confronted with the threat of a damaging article or broadcast is to reach for their metaphorical pen and draft up a statement to offer in response. It is sometimes entirely the wrong thing to do.

For a number of regulatory and legal reasons a newspaper or broadcaster will provide a summary of any forthcoming publication or broadcast to enable you to respond to the allegations which are the intended subject of an article or programme. As much as anything else, this is done to protect the position of the newspaper/ broadcaster, should there be any legal or regulatory complaint post-publication/broadcast. You assist the tick-box process if you deliver up what might be the last element necessary for the publication/ broadcast to take place.

If you are approached by a newspaper, most of which are regulated by the Independent Press Standards Organisation, then the regulatory provision the newspaper is accommodating is Section 1 (i) of the IPSO Code, which provides thus: 'The Press must take care not to publish inaccurate, misleading or distorted information or images, including headlines not supported by the text.' Here, the key words are 'take care'.

Journalists have been trained by their lawyers to provide the subject of forthcoming articles with a key points summary because they know if that is done, and at least half a statement is then published, if there is subsequently a complaint to IPSO that the article is inaccurate then the newspaper will be able to defend it by saying it had done all reasonably expected – which is to publish both sides of the story even if the exoneration is token.

For a broadcaster the obligation to give notice comes from Paragraph 7.11 of the Ofcom Code, which requires broadcasters to notify the subject of any programme where allegations of wrongdoing are being made so that they have the opportunity to respond. The legal reasons for this exercise overlap.

Paragraph 4 of the Defamation Act 2013 created a statutory version of a public interest defence first by the House of Lords in 1999 by a case called Reynolds v *Times* Newspapers[1]. In that case, the House of Lords set out 10 criteria by which it would judge whether or not the publication was responsible and one of those was whether it has been sought by the subject and the 'gist' of the response published in the article.

You can therefore ignore the suggestion by the journalist that the approach is just so that they can publish both sides of the story. An editorial decision has been made, evidenced by the damaging article or programme with which you are confronted. The aim will be to leave the reader/viewer in no doubt about the 'true' case affairs; and your statements will be deployed in a way (especially by the press) which ensures the minimum impact on the reader.

Where the allegations and issues are either wholly or partly inaccurate, then the right response is to challenge those allegations robustly and demand that, in compliance with the relevant provisions of the IPSO and Ofcom codes, they not be published because they are inaccurate.

By contrast, a statement will be taken by the newspaper/broadcaster as effectively your consent for false allegations to be published to your detriment on condition that some of what you say is published afterwards – usually in a short concluding paragraph which many readers will not even reach, having formed their view long before getting halfway through the article.

[1] https://publications.parliament.uk/pa/ld199899/ldjudgmt/jd991028/rey03.htm

If the story is wrong, the publisher/broadcaster should be told that and then it should not be published or broadcast, because if it is, the Ofcom/IPSO Code will be breached. This should be communicated in such a way that the publisher/broadcaster perceives that there is a genuine risk that they will be held to account.

How best to deploy a statement

If a statement is appropriate, then the second key principle is that it must be kept short, whether it is for publication or broadcast. If it is too long it will either be brutally cut and the parts that were most important omitted, or it will be summarized briefly in a way that will have the same effect. There is no obligation on a newspaper or broadcaster to carry any statement in full. But if you keep it short, moderate and factual, you have a fair chance of getting it set out/ read in its entirety.

You have a better chance of your statement being faithfully reproduced if you raise the risk level as perceived by the publisher/ broadcaster of it being held to account after publication or broadcast. That will be achieved if the statement is sent under the letterhead of a known-quantity media lawyer, who the newspaper/ broadcaster knows equips the subject of the broadcast/article with an equality of arms, should the article/programme be challenged and the use of a media lawyer will make it clear that there is a real risk of that to the editorial decision makers.

How do I know this? I have participated with media clients in editorial decisions about contentious programmes/articles for over 25 years. Please don't let anyone (especially a journalist or ex-journalist) spin the nonsense that by making a proper stipulation that your legal and regulatory rights should be respected you are going to give the impression that you are guilty as charged. This is just self-serving propaganda. Even if you were dealing with a journo so shrivelled by cynicism to think that, then they are still going to be more careful before writing copy about you that they cannot stand up. In the end, in Fleet Street at least, editorial decisions are taken primarily based on an assessment of risk rather than a bona fide assessment as to whether the article is or is not true and accurate. If you present your client or company as being a high-risk target for poor journalism, then you will less often be the victim of it. If you are passive in the face of such journalism, you will attract more of it.

Index